BRAVE NEW CANADA

Brave New Canada

Meeting the Challenge of a Changing World

DEREK H. BURNEY AND FEN OSLER HAMPSON

McGill-Queen's University Press
Montreal & Kingston · London · Ithaca

ISBN 978-0-7735-4398-0 (cloth)
ISBN 978-0-7735-9621-4 (ePDF)
ISBN 978-0-7735-9622-1 (ePUB)

Legal deposit third quarter 2014
Bibliothèque nationale du Québec

Printed in Canada on acid-free paper that is 100% ancient forest free
(100% post-consumer recycled), processed chlorine free

McGill-Queen's University Press acknowledges the support of the
Canada Council for the Arts for our publishing program. We also
acknowledge the financial support of the Government of Canada
through the Canada Book Fund for our publishing activities.

Library and Archives Canada Cataloguing in Publication

Burney, Derek H. (Derek Hudson), 1939–, author
   Brave new Canada : meeting the challenge of a changing world /
Derek H. Burney and Fen Osler Hampson.

Includes bibliographical references and index.
Issued in print and electronic formats.
ISBN 978-0-7735-4398-0 (bound). – ISBN 978-0-7735-9621-4 (ePDF). –
ISBN 978-0-7735-9622-1 (ePUB)

   1. Canada – Foreign economic relations – Forecasting. 2. Canada –
Foreign relations – 21st century – Forecasting. 3. Canada – Economic
policy – 21st century – Forecasting. 4. Canada – Social policy –
Forecasting. I. Hampson, Fen Osler, author II. Title.

FC242.B869 2014   327.71009'05   C2014-901850-9
                                           C2014-901851-7

Typeset by Jay Tee Graphics Ltd. in 10.5/13 Sabon

Contents

Abbreviations and Acronyms

ADIZ	Air Defence Identification Zone
ADMM-Plus	ASEAN Defence Ministerial Meeting-Plus
ASEAN	Association of Southeast Asian Nations
ASPI	Australian Strategic Policy Institute
BMD	Ballistic Missile Defence
CETA	Comprehensive Economic and Trade Agreement
CIDA	Canadian International Development Agency
CIGI	Centre for International Governance Innovation
CNOOC	China National Offshore Oil Company
CTBT	Comprehensive Test Ban Treaty
DFAIT	Department of Foreign Affairs and International Trade
DFATD	Department of Foreign Affairs, Trade and Development
EDC	Export Development Corporation
EEC	European Economic Community
EFTA	European Free Trade Association
EU	European Union
FDI	foreign direct investment
FIRA	Foreign Investment Review Agency
FSB	Financial Stability Board
FTA	Free Trade Agreement
G7	Group of Seven
G8	Group of Eight
G20	Group of Twenty
GATT	General Agreement on Trade and Tariffs
GM	General Motors
GPP	Global Partnership Program
GW	Gardaworld
IAEA	International Atomic Energy Agency

ICANN	Internet Corporation for Assigned Names and Numbers
ICISS	International Commission on Intervention and State Sovereignty
ICT	information and communications technology
IJC	International Joint Commission
IMF	International Monetary Fund
ISAF	International Security Assistance Force
ITU	International Telecommunication Union
LICS	low-income countries
LMICS	lower-middle-income countries
LNG	liquified natural gas
MICS	middle-income countries
MTCP	Military Training Cooperation Programme
NAFTA	North American Free Trade Agreement
NATO	North Atlantic Treaty Organization
NEP	National Energy Program
NFZ	no-fly zone
NGOS	Non-governmental organizations
NORAD	North American Aerospace Defense Command
NPSIA	Norman Paterson School of International Affairs
NPT	Non-Proliferation Treaty
NSA	National Security Agency
NTBS	non-tariff barriers
ODA	official development assistance
OECD	Organisation for Economic Co-operation and Development
OPEC	Organization of the Petroleum Exporting Countries
P5	Permanent Five
R2P	Responsibility to Protect
R&D	research and development
RCMP	Royal Canadian Mounted Police
SDI	Strategic Defensive Initiative
SDRS	Special Drawing Rights
SMES	small- and medium-sized enterprises
SOES	state-owned enterprises
SWFS	sovereign wealth funds
TPP	Trans-Pacific Partnership
UN	United Nations
WCIT	World Conference on International Telecommunications
WTO	World Trade Organization

Foreword

THE HONOURABLE BRAD WALL, PREMIER OF SASKATCHEWAN

I get the feeling that if policymakers feel like they have been grabbed by the lapels and shaken by this book and its compelling, even urgent, message, the authors will be pleased but not satisfied until we start doing something about it.

Mark them well. Their message is quite simply that Canada must not only aggressively engage with the emerging markets of the Asia-Pacific and the developing world, but that we also need a wholesale reorientation of our foreign policy and national mindset to secure Canada's future in a rapidly changing world.

Unparalleled levels of cooperation between the federal government, the provinces, and the private sector, along with persistent leadership to secure Canada's future, are the key messages of this timely book.

In the fall of 2013, I had just returned from a trade mission to Asia when I learned that Canada and the European Union (EU) had announced an agreement-in-principle on the Comprehensive Economic and Trade Agreement (CETA). This is a vitally important deal for Saskatchewan's uranium industry. It would lift ownership restrictions for EU-based companies, which could mean $2.5 billion in investment and the creation of another 1,200 jobs. It is also a good deal for our beef, bison, and pork producers, and agriculture in general. And the consensus seems to be it's a pretty good deal for Canada generally.

Closer trade relations with the EU will make Canada stronger and more prosperous. But the opportunities to be gained from freer trade with Asia are greater by a significant degree.

Here are some facts to consider. From 2013 through 2018, EU GDP is expected to rise from $17.3 trillion to $21.5 trillion – a 24 per cent increase, according to the International Monetary Fund. In the same period, the GDP of Asia – excluding the Middle East – is forecast to rise from $20.3 trillion to $28.8 trillion – a 42 per cent increase.

Asia is expected to grow nearly twice as fast as the EU in the medium term. And in five years the combined Asian economies will be a third larger than the EU economy.

Demographics and urbanization in the emerging economies of the developing world are at the root of their future growth. Between 2010 and 2025, Asia's population is expected to grow by about 550 million people. Europe's population is projected to actually decline slightly and North America is expected to increase by about 50 million people.

These statistics illustrate what the National Intelligence Council in the United States describes as a dramatic diffusion of power in our world. The Council says that by 2030, "Asia will have surpassed North America and Europe combined in terms of global power, based on GDP, population size, military power and technological investment." And it is no wonder that Larry Summers, the former economic advisor to President Obama, calls the modernization of the Asian economies one of the most important developments in world history – ranking right alongside the Renaissance and the Industrial Revolution.

All of this may seem like hyperbole, until you visit Beijing or New Delhi or Manila and see the growth first-hand.

But I wonder sometimes whether Canadians are acting like this is hyperbole. Sometimes it seems as if we don't really believe this change is really happening. Unfortunately, our zone of comfort does not extend very far beyond the shores of the North American continent.

Outside that comfort zone are the undeniably fastest growing regions of the world. The good news for Canada is that they need the foundational precursors to sustainable growth: security of food and energy. Trade in durable goods and technology is the logical entresol to a foundation of trade in resource staples. Other than Australia, is there a country better situated geographically or by the fact of its resources and current sector strength than Canada to build a promising future and robust economy on this fact? Of course, we will have to do something about it. And that is the central point of the book.

As Derek Burney and Fen Hampson persuasively argue, Canadians have to move beyond their customary complacency and risk averse approach to new challenges if Canada is to take advantage of the fundamental shift in global power and influence that is underway. We will also need to reorient some of our geostrategic priorities away from the Atlantic to the Pacific as we develop stronger economic and political ties with countries in the Asia-Pacific. In a world where liberal pluralist values have not only lost their allure but are under direct assault, Canada will also have to work much more closely with other liberal democracies to promote and secure its values and a more peaceful world. (I must point out parenthetically to prospective readers that chapter 6 on the matter of international democratization is most provocative. The philosophical rivalry of Mills versus Locke and modern-day geopolitics is very much worth considering given the slowing and, in some instances, the reversal of international democratization. Lockean principles would portend success. That is why this section is a particular joy to those many of us political nerds who delight in the application of old debates in such a modern context.)

The authors also canvass opportunities outside Asia, including a helpful refresh of NAFTA, our old and currently faded relationship with the US, and the opportunities of a Canada-Mexico dynamic more vital in the future than today.

The US will continue to be our top economic priority, but the global economy's centre of gravity is very clearly moving to the Asia Pacific region and the world's emerging markets. The better able we are at seizing this potential the stronger we will also be in managing relations with our southern neighbour.

We can do better. We must do better. *Brave New Canada* offers provocative analyses and prescriptions that should command widespread attention. This book does not offer tired platitudes about the "need for more Canada in the world," but rather a confident game plan for the Government of Canada, the provinces, and our business community to endorse. It is a wake-up call for our country that is as welcome as it is compelling.

We Canadians like to quote Gretzky's famous secret of success; that he always tried to anticipate where the puck was going to be rather than focus on where it was at a moment in time. While we like to quote him, applying his example is too often another matter entirely.

We should know it already but Burney and Hampson helpfully and cogently point to where the puck is going to be for the next while and how exactly we might use this information to win.

Preface

The idea for this book germinated in the seeds of our 2012 report, *Winning in a Changing World*, co-authored with Thomas d'Aquino and Len Edwards, which was presented to the prime minister of Canada, each of Canada's premiers, and senior officials in the Government of Canada in June and August of that year. That report argued that Canada has to make a more serious and concerted effort to engage with the world's fast-growing emerging market economies to secure Canada's future. Our recommendations were based on a series of extensive consultations we had with business leaders and other experts across the country.

We have developed and expanded those ideas in our analysis for this book. We have also developed a much larger canvas that addresses the broader foreign policy, security, and diplomatic challenges Canada confronts as the geopolitical tectonic plates of international relations shift with the rise of China and other regional and global centres of power and influence. Institutions that ensured stability and prosperity for much of the last half of the twentieth century are losing traction as well as relevance. They cry out for reform. Values that we assumed had world-wide resonance are being questioned. We explore the implications of these changes and of the "great awakening" taking place as peoples around the world become politically mobilized and struggle to define a new social and political order for themselves.

Although we recognize that the United States will continue to be vitally important to Canada's future, we see the US increasingly turning inwards, weary of inconclusive yet costly military interventions and giving priority to its own internal economic and political challenges. Canada will face an uphill battle getting its voice heard and its concerns addressed. We cannot count as heavily on US demand to sustain our own growth and prosperity as we have in the past. That is because our trade with the US is in secular decline as we lose market share to other global competitors and US demand for some of our key exports softens. Managing relations with the United States will remain our top foreign policy priority but we contend fundamentally that, by shrewdly cultivating relations elsewhere, we can also improve our leverage in this otherwise lopsided relationship.

The problem with many recent discussions of Canada's role in the world is that they tend to ignore or discount the degree to which the world and Canada's place in the world are changing. Neither conventional tactics nor customary assumptions will resonate. For a country that depends on what it sells to the world for roughly a third of its GDP, ignoring the importance of economics is not an acceptable proposition. Trade does not follow the flag, it accompanies it. That is why we argue that foreign policy has to be anchored in a much deeper understanding of the relationship between economics and politics.

Foreign policy in a globalized world where transnational forces and influences cut across porous state boundaries also involves domestic policy. A concerted and coherent effort by the provinces and the private sector is absolutely essential to developing a coherent international strategy. But if the provinces and others are to follow, Ottawa must still lead to ensure that the national interest is enhanced globally.

Our primary purpose in writing this book is to provoke debate and discussion and to push Canadians out of their comfort zone in terms of how they think about the world. We believe that we have become much too complacent as a nation, too reliant on the North American cocoon. As we diversify and strengthen our economic and political ties with emerging market countries our influence with Washington may actually increase. The paradox of influence is that the less dependent we are on the US for our growth and prosperity, the more they will see us as a valued ally and partner in their own dealings with the rest of the world. We offer prescriptions intended to move beyond what may have worked in the past and to serve as a wake-up call for governments and citizens alike.

In the course of writing this book we have benefited greatly by working together on our weekly column for *iPolitics*, Canada's leading online source for politics and business, and the support we have received from its publisher, James Baxter, as well as our readers. We have drawn on our weekly columns to shape and sharpen many of the ideas in this book. We would also like to thank our friends and colleagues who have reviewed and commented on different sections of the book, including the two anonymous reviewers of the manuscript after it was submitted to McGill-Queen's University Press. They include Thomas d'Aquino, James Baxter, Len Edwards, Philip Hampson, and Fred Kuntz. We are also indebted to Simon Palamar, who provided superb research assistance during the course of writing and revising this book. He also helped draft the country and business case studies, which appear in chapters 3 and 8 respectively. Cara O'Blenis provided invaluable administrative support in helping assemble the manuscript as it went through endless rounds of writing and revision and we extend a special word of thanks to her as well. We salute Joan Burney for her intellectual rigour and steadfast encouragement for our collaborative effort. We are particularly grateful to Premier Brad Wall for writing a foreword for our book and commend others to emulate the example he is setting in Saskatchewan on policy and vision for the future.

BRAVE NEW CANADA

I

Five New Challenges in a Turbulent World

Aldous Huxley's *Brave New World* was intended as satire but there is nothing satirical about the need for Canada to be brave in meeting the challenges of a dramatically changing world. The purpose of this book is to explain those changes and present ideas on how Canada should respond.

With the collapse of the Berlin Wall and then the Soviet Union more than twenty years ago, then-US president George H.W. Bush predicted that the world was on the cusp of a "New World Order." To other pundits, in the memorable phrase of the American political scientist Francis Fukuyama, we had also reached "the end of history" with the collapse of the Soviet Union and communist regimes in Eastern Europe."[1] At the time, there appeared to be no attractive alternative to western-style democracy and market economies and the values that go with both. Yet, in what is surely a relatively brief passage of time when measured by the broader sweep of history, much has changed in our world. We are neither at the end of history nor has a new world "order" emerged. In fact, there seems to be more chaos and turbulence than ever before.

China, which had quite self-consciously eschewed the Soviet model of glasnost and perestroika, but nonetheless embraced western-style capitalism under one-party rule, has risen to become the second largest economy in the world. The United States, which like a young and vigorous David stood over the fallen Soviet Goliath when the Berlin Wall came crashing down, has suddenly become the world's "weary titan." It is showing many of the symptoms of imperial decline and "overstretch" that Great Britain displayed at the end of the nineteenth century.[2]

Europe, which picked itself up after the ravages of the Second World War and embarked upon one of the most ambitious strategic enterprises in history – political and economic consolidation leading to the formation of the European Union so that Europeans would never fight one another again – is faltering under the weight of massive public debt and the ravages of a serious financial meltdown that shows few signs of abating because the political will to drive needed policy solutions is simply not there.

In the triumphalism that accompanied the end of the Cold War little thought was given, save by a few Cassandras, to the threat posed to global stability by the unrelenting assaults from extremist Islamic factions, most evident in the 9/11 incidents but spreading ever since beyond Afghanistan through to the always volatile Middle East and North Africa. Although many left-wing critics at the time derided the great conservative American thinker, Samuel P. Huntington, his prediction in the mid-1990s that we were about to witness a "clash of civilizations" between the dark forces of Islamic extremism and the West proved to be singularly prophetic as Osama bin Laden and his al-Qaeda acolytes launched a day of devastating terrorist attacks on American soil on the key symbols of American prosperity and power.[3]

These climactic events, and especially the financial meltdown and prolonged recession that began in the last decade, have had a deleterious effect on America's capacity and inclination to lead on global challenges. They have shaken confidence, too, in the values of pluralism, liberty, and tolerance that underpin western-style democracies. Equally, they have diluted the tone and many of the sinews of US relations with key allies, including Canada. Personal relations at the top and the informal cooperative spirit among senior officials have suffered in the process as well. Relations may be correct, but they are no longer warm. The US approach to allies is now less magnanimous. In the absence of a single threatening power like the Soviet Union, the US feels that it no longer needs close allies and has begun to return to its pre-Wilsonian default of isolationism, or narrow self-interest. No country is more affected by this change than Canada.

While there is little evidence of a new order or that we have reached the "end of history," what is palpable is that the tectonic geopolitical and economic plates of the world are shifting, setting in motion powerful forces that are shaking the postwar world to its very foundations.

Alas, there has been precious little analysis of what these changes mean for Canada, our place in the world, and our strategies for global engagement. Many pundits are caught in a time warp of the 1960s and 1970s. To some degree, Canadians can be forgiven for their lack of interest in international affairs because they have been fed a steady diet of bromides that suggest that Canada's future is pinned to the fate of the United Nations, a liberal international order, and a benign and mostly satisfactory relationship with the United States. In the words of a well-known tourist commercial of the mid-1990s, Canadians have bathed themselves in the belief that "the world needs more Canada."[4] We seem to have convinced ourselves that we are a "land of tranquility, safety and whales coming up for air in slow motion" and "a place to go for global spiritual renewal."[5] In truth, that was always fiction, not reality.

Others have become smug because we weathered the severe economic depression better than most, albeit primarily on the back of strong demand for our commodities.

The rest of the world, including many of our close allies, views us, if anything, as cosseted and complacent. Yes, we are a place of comparative tranquillity, but that has more to do with geography and happenstance than the way we choose to protect our interests and influence.

Unlike many other countries, Canada faces few threats, existential or otherwise. We remain comfortable and protected within a North American cocoon. But even that may be less certain in our future than it was in our past.

During the Cold War, the Americans had no choice but to look after our security interests because we were their front door to a potential Soviet bomber and missile attack across the North Pole. In the Trudeau era, we could avoid paying our full dues in NATO (North Atlantic Treaty Organization) to defend western Europe because we knew that others would fill the gap. However, that didn't always stop some of our leaders from lecturing our allies, including the Americans. Pretensions of moral superiority rang hollow in the absence of tangible commitments.

FIVE KEY TRENDS THAT ARE RESHAPING OUR WORLD

Any serious analysis of Canada's international relations and role in the world must first grapple with the ways the world is changing before offering foreign policy prescriptions or a new vision of Canada's interests. As we argue below, successful foreign policy cannot be based on a one-dimensional view of the world. The problem with some of the recent studies on Canada's foreign policy and our place in the world is that they look backwards to the Cold War and the halcyon days of Pearsonian internationalism, rather than looking forwards.[6] A successful foreign policy cannot be crafted by looking at the world from a rear-view mirror. We must grapple with the world as it is today, and how we suspect it will change in the coming years, not chart our future according to the past.

However, one of the difficulties in describing our contemporary changing world is that we confront the dilemma humorously identified in John Godfrey Saxe's poem "Six Blind Men and the Elephant," based on an Indian legend. Some feel the trunk and say the elephant is a snake, some feel a leg and say it is a tree, others feel a tusk and say it is a spear. As Saxe concluded his poem, "And so these men of Indostan / Disputed loud and long, / Each in his own opinion, / Exceeding stiff and strong, / Though each was partly in the right, / And all were in the wrong!"[7] Unlike Saxe's elephant, which may have been hard to see but was nonetheless an elephant, the contours of our current world are not only hard to see, they are also mutable, and there may well be more than more than one elephant in the room.

In our assessment, there are five key trends that are reshaping the global landscape, with profound implications for Canada's future prosperity and security.

I The US Is More Focused on Itself Today

Any reset of Canadian foreign policy must begin with a careful examination of relations with the United States, which is still the biggest elephant in the room. The US has huge domestic challenges of its own. Sluggish economic growth and political gridlock in Washington on necessary fiscal reforms are sapping much of Americans' confidence and optimism. The inconclusive outcome of western intervention in Afghanistan haunts any future outlook as does the debacle of a different sort in Iraq, one with similar civil war fallout. Both exemplify flaws in leadership, primarily, but not exclusively, by an unusually inept US administration (the utterly dysfunctional House of Representatives deserves some blame as well). Afghanistan is unravelling because the US has been unwilling to confront the real source of instability in the region – Pakistan. Having successfully ejected the Taliban from Kabul in 2002, the US and its allies then played an inconsistent game of containment and counter-insurgency but one that stopped short of eradicating the threat from within Pakistan, presumably for broader strategic reasons. The US hesitated, too, on a broadly gauged diplomatic solution, relying instead almost exclusively and somewhat erratically on military means to restore stability. Military engagement was hampered by alliance caveats of one form or another, and ultimately by withdrawal timetables determined in advance because of US electoral campaign demands. An increasingly corrupt Karzai regime only aggravated matters.

But as events in Syria dramatically illustrate, the result is that there is now little appetite in the US and elsewhere for military intervention of any kind. Long and costly, the lost wars in Iraq and Afghanistan will likely have a debilitating effect on US global leadership for decades.

As the provocative title of Richard Haass's (president of the Council on Foreign Relations) recent book, *Foreign Policy Begins at Home*, suggests,[8] the US must reduce not just runaway fiscal deficits, but also its mounting piles of public debt. As demonstrated by mandatory sequestration cuts, most of which remain in place, the ability of the US to fund its formidable military machine will be diminished. The resources that are available will almost surely be directed at strengthening the Pacific "pivot" against China. There is little support in the US on all sides of the partisan divide post-Afghanistan and Iraq for nation-building exercises and democracy promotion in other parts of the world. The Middle East has become a muddle, with potentially explosive tendencies from Egypt to Syria, Iraq, and Iran. Meanwhile, the nuclear aspirations of rogue states like North Korea and Iran continue unabated and unconstrained by any real threat from the US or the international community.

The more opaque the Obama administration's foreign policy has become, the more difficult it is for allies and foes alike to take Washington seriously, a point underscored in spades when foreign policy announcements are made by the president on late-night talk shows![9]

Canada is not immune from the implications of the lone superpower functioning on global issues with diminished credibility. The value of being an ally and neighbour of the US loses its currency when domestic political priorities and constraints overwhelm other considerations. Geography is the inescapable reality of our destiny and relations with the US will persist as a priority without equal. Our partnership has enormous advantages for Canada, notably in the economic sector and in terms of our security. But these ties also give us a comfort zone that breeds complacency. Besides, when North America is looked at by others, except possibly for resources, Canada is inevitably a distant second, an afterthought. This imbalance of power and attention is not likely to change any time soon. Any reset of Canadian foreign policy must begin with a careful examination of the elephant we know, the one right next door. After years of essentially running in idle, our relationship with the US merits recalibration. In chapter 2, we elaborate on what this means for Canada.

2 The Global Economy Is Undergoing a Major Transformation

The global economy is experiencing dramatic shifts in economic power with the rise of so-called emerging economies, notably China, but also countries like India, Brazil, Mexico, Vietnam, Turkey, and Indonesia, and the prominent role of state-owned enterprises in the economic policies and strategies of these countries. Many of these economies experienced double-digit-level growth during the past decade while western economies were sluggish and generally stuck in the doldrums.

This trend is not absolute, however.[10] The US economy is now performing better than many of its Organisation for Economic Co-operation and Development (OECD) counterparts. But job numbers remain weak after several years of monetary pump-priming through the quantitative-easing policies of the Federal Reserve, which are only now beginning to taper off. If most of the 2013 sequestration cuts remain in place – reducing fiscal spending by more than $1 trillion over the next ten years – the total US deficit will be reduced to $3.4 trillion, just $600 billion short of the $4 trillion in reductions (the amount often referred to as a "grand bargain" figure) that many argue is necessary for fiscal stability over the next decade.[*]

Even the most generous recovery assessments predict that US growth and that of other industrialized nations will be modest in the years to come. Some analysts, such as Paul Krugman and Joseph Stiglitz, believe that reduced federal spending will harm growth and productivity in the US[11] because of continuing weak demand in the private sector and a lack of real investment. In the absence of continued

---

[*] Note: All figures are in Canadian currency unless otherwise indicated.

government support in the form of deficit spending, especially on education, technology, and infrastructure, there is a risk of continued stagnation, i.e., weak growth and high levels of unemployment.

Economic fundamentals, however, are ultimately stacked against the West. Growth in any country is a function of population increases, productivity, technological innovation, and other factors, such as demand for exports, as in the case of resource-rich countries like Canada. The reality is that the world's industrialized economies are already heavily urbanized and mature and their populations are aging. The prospect for a return to the high growth rates that indus-trialized economies experienced in earlier decades is therefore lim-ited because factor productivity is already high relative to emerging economies. The latter have younger populations and lower levels of urbanization. By definition, they will grow faster because demand in those countries will be higher.

The US will unquestionably remain a dominant economic player in the global economy because of its size, diversity, and capacity for innovation, but its relative power and influence in global markets will diminish as the economies of the developing world grow. The global consequences of this transformation and its impact on Can-ada are the subject of chapter 3.

3 International Institutions Are Declining in Effectiveness and Relevance

Although dedicated "revival internationalists" will rankle at the sug-gestion, the painful reality is that the international institutions that guided and stabilized global events in the post-Second World War era, specifically the UN, the Bretton Woods institutions (IMF [Inter-national Monetary Fund)], World Bank, and GATT/WTO [General Agreement on Tariff and Trade/World Trade Organization]), and even our main security alliance, NATO, are losing their lustre, their relevance, and their utility. Uncertainty rather than stability is the order of the day. The declining effectiveness of these multilateral institutions has profound implications for middle powers like Can-ada as they search for traction in a rapidly changing world.

In responding to global flashpoints, military interventions by "coalitions of the willing" have tried spasmodically to fill the vac-uum, e.g., in Iraq, Afghanistan, and Libya, only to prove that mil-itary muscle in itself is not an adequate response. The inconclusive yet costly consequences from these interventions have sapped the desire for more of the same, e.g., in Syria. Meanwhile, the UN

Security Council and the less formal Group of Eight (G8) have been stalemated. In responding to these conflagrations, major powers like Russia and China are, for their own reasons, increasingly determined to thwart collective action.

NATO has tried to find new purpose in a post-Cold War world, but its collective will to respond to global crises is seen more in rhetoric than in commitment. The Responsibility to Protect (R2P) principle, supported fervently by the UN in 2005, is simply no longer in vogue. Consensus – when it can be found at the UN – is either too feeble or too late, often both.

Meanwhile, Russia and China are showing more signs of cooperation with one another, whether on Syria, where they successfully stalemated action by the UN Security Council, or on cyberspace attacks, where they both target primarily American companies, or on naval exercises ostensibly intended to flex their combined muscles against the US. As Leslie Gelb and Dimitri Simes observed in *The New York Times*, 6 July 2013, "in world affairs, there's no better way to flex one's muscles than to visibly diminish the strongest power."[12] Both Russia and China sense America's decline and decadence and realize, too, that unquestioned US military superiority isn't worth much in achieving global policy objectives. We can expect Russia and China to collaborate selectively and warily, more or less the way porcupines make love – very carefully!

At the depth of the economic recession in 2008–09, the newly-minted Group of Twenty (G20) rose to the most serious threat with a spirit of collective resolve that staved off panic in the markets. However, the hopes of a more persistent consensus on substance quickly disappeared as different paces of recovery inspired different priorities among the participants. Common resolve dissipated and, in the absence of credible US leadership on macroeconomic policy, the annual sessions have become little more than expensive photo ops.

The G8 has fared little better. The inclusion of Russia has frequently frustrated consensus on political flashpoints, consensus that usually helped mask unsettled squabbles on economic issues. Indeed, a case could be made that, since Russia shares neither the political nor the economic values of the other G8 countries, it should no longer participate. The diminished leadership role of the US in the G8 is all too evident.

The Doha Round of multilateral trade negotiations, launched in December 2001, has, to date, found little consensus on major adjustments to trade barriers. Born in the political wake of 9/11, Doha had been intended to bring the developing world more into the disciplines of the WTO. But an intransigent India and an equally unrelenting Brazil proved more than a match for the US and developed-nation negotiators with the result that the focus of global trade has now shifted dramatically to a flurry of bilateral and regional initiatives (see chapter 4).

4 The Post-Cold-War Order Is Breaking Down and New Geostrategic Rivalries and Threats Are Emerging

Analysts have not settled on a common label to describe the world in the second decade of the twenty-first century. They tend to agree that the unipolar moment following the end of the Cold War when the US was only remaining superpower is over. Some refer to our new world as a G-zero world, because no single country dominates the global agenda.[13] Others argue that we are living in an era of failed states because of chronic instability in many regions of the world, especially in the Middle East, Central Asia, and sub-Saharan Africa. Still others refer to the coming era with China and India's rise, as the Pacific (or Indo-Pacific) century. As a recent study notes,

> None of these labels adequately describes the world we live in. Yet, they point to a common denominator – the global order is breaking apart, conceptions of national sovereignty are changing, boundary lines are becoming more fluid, new norms are forming, old norms are withering away. There is, in short, a systemic transformation occurring in which we see some regions on the rise, some in decline, and some in open revolt. A new order has not yet materialized. In fact, there seems to be a diffusion of agency, authority, and action that will make a new global order unlikely to materialize soon. There are new actors who operate under new authorities, using new approaches and methodologies.[14]

New security threats are also emerging from cyberspace, while old threats, such as the danger stemming from nuclear proliferation, have grown as a result of Iran and North Korea's efforts to acquire the bomb, and containment measures for either don't seem to be working.

Quite apart from the jockeying among major powers to try to exploit perceptions of US weakness, there are regional tensions, particularly in Asia, fueled by long-standing territorial disputes and negative sentiments deeply rooted in history. According to Ian Bremmer, of the Eurasia Group, "China–Japan is the most significant geopolitical tension on the map, in terms of direct bilateral conflict in coming years."[15]

Prime Minister Shinzo Abe has persistently promised to improve "the quantity and the quality" of Japan's military.[16] He also advocates changing Japan's constitution in order to broaden its military capability beyond "self-defence" strictures.[17] Neither development sits well with China, Japan's most obvious regional antagonist, nor with putative allies like South Korea. For both of them, and others in the region, memories of Japan's brutal occupation in the Second World War have deep roots.

The US may indeed welcome efforts by Japan to shoulder a larger piece of the defence burden but the US is equally concerned about actions that could exacerbate tensions in the region. Nonetheless, in his recent book *Restless Empire*, Odd Westad contends that when it comes to the historical rivalry between China and Japan, "the only power to benefit in a strategic sense is the United States, which can use Chinese and Japanese fear of each other to its own advantage."[18] One way or another, some rebalancing is under way. (The Stockholm International Peace Research Institute ranks Japan as the world's fifth largest military by annual spending after the US, China, Russia, and the UK.)[19]

Along with the Strait of Hormuz in the Persian Gulf near Iran and Oman, the Strait of Malacca off Malaysia, only 2.7 km wide at its narrowest point, is the world's most important, hence most sensitive, shipping choke-point. Fifty thousand merchant ships carrying 40 per cent of world trade pass through the 900-km strait each year.[20] More than 15 million barrels of oil, or one-third of all seaborne oil, transited the Strait in 2011.[21] For Northeast Asia, the route is a vital link to energy supply. Japan relies on the Malaccan Strait for 90 per cent of its oil imports, China, 80 per cent.[22]

Over and above what these two countries' navies are doing to safeguard the channel, the US Navy is regularly on alert. So, too, are the littoral states – Singapore, Indonesia, and Malaysia – which are upgrading their submarine fleets as a "fleet-in-being" deterrent capacity against any potential foe. As the submarine capacity of various players expands, so does the potential for a major global flashpoint, accidental or otherwise.

As we discuss in chapter 5, the new and changing geostrategic realities of the global order have real implications for Canada's traditional defence posture, which is currently oriented toward NATO and the transatlantic. We will need our own pivot toward the Asia-Pacific region, but we will also have to recalibrate our diplomacy and security policies to contend with a whole range of new threats and challenges in the global security environment.

5 Pluralistic Democratic Values Are under Siege in Many Parts of the World

Ironically, notwithstanding what former US National Security Adviser Zbigniew Brzezinski called "the global political awakening," which has seen the overthrow of unpopular authoritarian rulers in many parts of the world, there has not been a corresponding rush to embrace western democratic values and the promotion of human rights by those who have taken control.[23] Western democracies have lost of much of their allure, especially in the Islamic world, as a result of the military interventions in Iraq and Afghanistan and, ironically, a failure to intervene and assist rebel forces in Syria. Similarly, events in Egypt are a sober reminder that stability tends to command stronger support than concepts of freedom or pluralism.

The values cherished by western democracies are now in a minority in global assemblies, a real low point being the 2014 election of Cuba, Saudi Arabia, China, and Russia to the UN Human Rights Council. Religious zealotry and nationalism are in the ascendant. More often than not, the powerful track record of authoritarian China has more political and economic appeal to many developing countries than the sputtering economic performance and fractious, if not dysfunctional, political discourse of western democracies, notably the US. Nations that cannot put their own fiscal house in order have few lessons of policy or governance to offer as models to the world no matter how progressive their values seem to be.

The dramatic surge of China's economy under monopolistic state capitalism, warts and all, is shaking many conventional theories of governance. Even the maxim that democracy is the worst "except for all the others" is being questioned given the inability of so many western democracies to revive economic growth and restore some level of sanity to public finances.[24] Orwellian revelations of cyberspace monitoring of phone calls and Internet exchanges add to disillusionment if not mistrust about those in power. The essential balance between liberty and security is being tested in western democracies as never before. What is certain is that China's capacity to influence global events, good or bad, will increase commensurate with its burgeoning economic strength.

IMPLICATIONS

One way of dialing down escalating tensions is to engage substantively in bilateral and regional trade negotiations and encourage others to do the same on the theory that the more nations trade with one another the less likely they are to wage war with one another. As a non-regional player, but one with Asia-Pacific aspirations, Canada cannot ignore either the potential risks or the potential opportunities in this dynamic region.

The Middle East is in turmoil. At best, the US and like-minded allies could, nonetheless, help encourage moves to greater pluralism and adherence to the most basic principles of democracy in the region, while being realistic about the time required for them to take root and the difficulties to overcome. What events in Egypt and elsewhere suggest is that, without the temper of genuine pluralism, unvarnished majority rule can quickly succumb to "might is right" authoritarian exclusionary diktat.

Some, like Ian Bremmer, call it a G-zero world in which national interest – every nation for itself – is the order of the day.[25] Others, more on the basis of hope than analysis, look to a G2 world, one in which a rising China and an established but somewhat hesitant US will shape some degree of consensus on major challenges and provide an anchor of both economic and political stability.

It is no secret that the key foreign policy question for the world in the foreseeable future will be how China, under its new leadership, and the US, choose to manage their significant, complex, and sensitive relationship. Canada has an interest in ensuring that this relationship evolves in a manner that puts a premium on stability. Yet both China and the US have huge, albeit very different, domestic problems that will undoubtedly preoccupy decision-making, and may distract attention from global issues as well as from prudent management of their bilateral ties.

China faces enormous challenges, changing its model of economic development more to domestic consumption and managing the societal impact of its dynamic growth – the internal imbalances between urban and rural communities and the growing gap between rich and poor. Corruption is epidemic, affecting even public education, and is clearly a top priority for the new leadership. And there are growing ecological challenges in major urban communities flowing from vast economic production. China will inevitably move beyond its benign "non-intervention" role and take an approach on global affairs more proportionate to its growing economic strength. But we do not really know how that will develop, especially in relation to the US and to China's regional neighbours.

The Asia-Pacific region has a veritable alphabet soup of organizations and associations meeting annually which seems to have primarily produced annual photo ops and agreements to meet again. Something more concrete is needed. Associations without obligations easily become a substitute for tangible engagement. Canada is no stranger at such gatherings and used to be known as the consummate joiner, ready to participate in any international organization that would invite us. But Canada needs to make choices based on strategy, not attendance.

The dynamics of the world are changing dramatically, with many uncertain consequences. Continued stability should not be taken for granted. Wherever you look – on trade or security issues – power politics and nationalism are on the rise. Multilateralism and the notion of global consensus, once the hallmark of foreign policy for many middle powers like Canada, are waning.

With "the intensifying turbulence caused by the phenomenon of the global awakening," many regions, even the Asia-Pacific, which has been one of the most stable and peaceful during the last thirty years, may experience social unrest and political instability that will project onto their external relations.[26] Historically, leaders facing unusual domestic dissent have sometimes tried to divert attention by manufacturing foreign policy crises with neighbours, especially on territorial disputes, where emotions of nationalism are most easily aroused. There are already several signs of this in China's relations with its smaller neighbours. On top of all that, we have the persistent peril of an unpredictable, irrational North Korea and the uncertain or unknown nuclear ambitions of countries like Iran.

And yet, the resolve to act in order to ensure stability or curtail aggressive behaviour is by no means assured. This may be the objective of the US pivot to Asia and that may be something several in the region would welcome. But uncertainty about motives can also be a catalyst for tension.

That is why there is such a need for fresh thinking and more strategic engagement by Canada in our shared Asia-Pacific region, for imaginative diplomacy, and for regional confidence-building measures of the kind that helped contain tensions between East and West during the Cold War, enabling a peaceful transition for the former Soviet Empire. We need to make a similar effort to ensure that cooperative institutional undertakings are implemented to manage the transformation already underway and to ensure a more stable security environment.

At a minimum, there is scope for more substantive dialogue by and in Canada on geopolitical and security issues. That is what a foreign policy of substance entails. As our engagement in Korea in the 1950s attests, Canada is no stranger to security issues in Asia and is certainly capable of an expanded role, especially now that we have a reinvigorated and battle-hardened military.

We will have to resist our customary inclination to try to be all things to all people. Our emphasis should be determined by how our interests can best be safeguarded and enhanced. We may have to make hard choices about where we engage and why and what we want to achieve. What is certain is that the more we do to enhance trade and economic partnerships – and that should be the driving force – the more committed we will need to be on issues of security and stability.

What is also increasingly apparent is that there is a need for new multilateral approaches both to strategy and to effective effort in the face of global uncertainty. The choice is between attempting to reform global institutions like the UN that have been sidelined from effective action or giving life to new approaches to global stability. The challenges of the twenty-first century call for both and Canada should recalibrate its foreign policy objectives and commitment accordingly to help fill the power vacuum. Some (e.g., former State Department advisor Ash Jain) suggest developing an initiative first proposed by the US State Department in 2008.[27] This called for a concerted dialogue and coordinated actions to deal with global challenges involving a "D10" (Democracy 10) group of countries – the

US and its closest allies, such as the UK, France, Germany, Italy, Canada, Japan, and Australia. A group of like-minded nations that would uphold essential democratic values and jointly commit the requisite economic, military, and diplomatic resources to address certain global threats.

Among other things, the D10 group could strengthen cooperation on preventing nuclear proliferation, provide a coherent response to outbursts of state violence, and promote basic democratic principles, with an emphasis on freedom of expression and freedom of assembly in support of pluralism. D10 discussions would be informal and intended to complement, not displace, existing institutional networks. Nor would the D10 be precluded from working constructively where possible with China, Russia, and other world powers. But it would serve as a catalyst for fresh strategic collaboration involving the US and its closest allies. Canada could play a prominent advocacy role, giving impetus to the concept.

Canada, along with most other western countries, has been slow to react and adapt to the changes underway. Our foreign policy has featured spasmodic points of principle, e.g., on Israel, Iran, Sri Lanka, and Crimea, but constitutes essentially reflex reactions to global events rarely designed to serve or enhance Canadian interests. We are hidebound in a sense by the nostalgia of "virtuous multilateralism" and reluctant to move too far from the comfort of our North American economic and security blankets to seek advantage from opportunities elsewhere. Our trade policy has been ambitious in rhetoric but, apart from agreements with the EU and South Korea, short on achievement, especially in areas of significant economic growth. On the security front, our substantial engagement in Afghanistan and our lead role in Libya were overwhelmed, if not undermined, by the absence of clear strategic leadership on both fronts.

A "might is right" law-of-the-jungle world may leave little room for middle powers like Canada on major issues of the day. It means that we have to strive more strategically and selectively to advance our interests and collaborate with others of similar weight who share similar values to influence global action where we can. A modest but realistic role, commensurate with our interests, our values, and our capacity for influence – a far cry from attempting to be "all things to all people." We should also recalibrate our support and contributions to international agencies on the basis of assessments that measure effectiveness as opposed to intent.

We need more than a one-dimensional foreign policy. Europe offers the immediate prospect of broader economic links but the Asia-Pacific region and our own Southern Hemisphere give even more scope to adjust our focus. In pursuing broader global prospects we would not only safeguard and serve our own interests but also scratch the itch for diversification and inject a healthier balance into managing our relations with the US. There are substantive reasons and welcome signs that Canadians now are more confident about their distinct identity in North America. Our foreign policy should adapt accordingly.

Our outlook and our global approach need to be tailored more to what interests and values we need to safeguard and what influence we can bring to bear in the company of others on the global challenges of the day. It is not that the "world needs more Canada." Rather, Canada needs to define shrewdly what it expects to achieve in a rapidly changing world.

2

Canada-US: A Time to Reset

Canadians have conflicting sentiments about their southern neighbour, covering a gamut of emotions ranging from admiration and envy to suspicion and moral superiority. The latter prompted US Secretary of State Dean Acheson on one occasion to chide Canada for acting "like the stern daughter of the voice of God."[1] The lopsided power imbalance has a lot do with Canadian anxieties. The fact that it often prompts more neglect (usually benign) than attention for Canada from Washington only compounds the challenge for those managing the relationship – a relationship that over the years has seen many ups and downs, but that now needs a new trajectory.

A CHEQUERED HISTORY

In the last century, periods of close cooperation between Canada and the US in Korea, and in later crises such as the Sinai in 1956 and the Balkans in the 1990s, and more generally in NATO and North American Aerospace Defense Command (NORAD), were also marked by instances when Canada and the US were not in complete agreement. During the Kennedy-Diefenbaker era, for example, relations between the two countries were decidedly cool, notwithstanding the fact that President Kennedy, during his spring 1961 visit to Ottawa shortly after his inauguration remarked, "Nothing is more vital than the unity of the United States and Canada," and, "Geography has made us neighbors. History has made us friends."[2]

Notably in the 1962 Cuban missile crisis, Canada was clearly not on the same page as the Americans, a pattern that would later repeat itself when Lester Pearson took Lyndon Johnson to task over his handling of the Vietnam War and when Jean Chrétien refused to join the United States in the 2003 invasion of Iraq to unseat Saddam Hussein.

Canada's prime minister in 1962, John Diefenbaker, was the "Doubting Thomas" among America's allies about the severity of the threat and how to deal with the Russian missiles in Cuba. When informed by Kennedy, just hours before Kennedy took his case to the world, Diefenbaker expressed skepticism about Soviet intentions while demanding further, irrefutable evidence about the Soviet installations. He urged Kennedy to send a team of UN inspectors to Cuba to find out what the Soviets were up to before taking any further action.

Diefenbaker also refused to put Canadian forces on a state of high alert, over the objections of his own military advisors. Fearing the worst, Canada's military nonetheless took informal steps to ready Canadian forces.

Diefenbaker's judgment was undoubtedly clouded by his personal loathing of the young attractive American leader. And as we now know from secretly audiotaped conversations with Kennedy's wife Jackie, the negative feeling was entirely mutual. Diefenbaker continued to believe until his death that Kennedy had played a high-stakes game that needlessly risked the fate of the world.

But it was Diefenbaker's antagonism to the idea that American nuclear weapons should be stationed on Canadian soil that sealed his own political fate. In the 1950s, the US army began to deploy Nike surface-to-air missiles to be used to attack Soviet bombers at its northern bases. The US air force's competitor to the Nike was the Bomarc surface-to-air missile built by Boeing. In addition to the fourteen Bomarc sites in the US, there were two in Canada – one at North Bay, Ontario, and the other at La Macaza, Quebec – with fifty-six missiles in total.

In a major political crisis, which precipitated a federal election, Diefenbaker balked at the prospect that the Bomarc would be tipped with nuclear warheads. However, Lester Pearson, who won the 1963 election – with, some suggest, US support – reversed Diefenbaker's decision, thus allowing the nuclear-armed Bomarcs to be deployed on Canadian soil in accordance with a NATO decision. They stayed there until 1971 when Prime Minister Trudeau (who, before entering politics, had quoted Pierre Vadeboncoeur to mock Pearson for this decision as the "defrocked prince of peace")[3] quietly phased them out.[4]

Relations with the US deteriorated yet again in the Trudeau years when the Canadian government flexed some nationalist muscle with legislation to control both foreign investment (which established the Foreign Investment Review Agency [FIRA]) and the development of energy (the National Energy Program [NEP]). Both measures clashed sharply with free-booting American capitalist inclinations and with the ideology of the Reagan government.

Also, at a time when President Reagan was increasing the US military and raising tensions generally with the Soviet Union – "Mr Gorbachev, tear down this wall"[5] – Pierre Trudeau's quixotic attempt at being a global peacemaker and appearing to see the US and the USSR as moral equivalents did not sit well in any allied capital. An unnamed American official branded Trudeau as "a pot-smoking pipsqueak."[6] Margaret Thatcher more derisively dismissed him as a candidate for "the Lenin Peace Prize."[7]

The election of Brian Mulroney in 1984 ushered in an entirely different and more positive atmosphere in bilateral relations. Mulroney declared Canada to be "open for business" and quickly nullified both FIRA and the NEP. He also declared a willingness to give the US "the benefit of the doubt" on global issues. Differences did not disappear but the tone was markedly different and the relationship was epitomized by the close personal rapport between Prime Minister Mulroney and both Presidents Reagan and George H.W. Bush. The Canada-US Free Trade Agreement (FTA) in 1987 was followed by the North American Free Trade Agreement (NAFTA) in 1994, greatly energizing economic relations between the two countries. The Acid Rain Accord (1991), which was negotiated by President Bush and Prime Minister Mulroney, put to rest what had been a chronic festering irritant in bilateral relations. Canada's staunch support in the first Gulf War, and on global issues, such as the unification of Germany, underscored the best of shared values being nurtured skillfully by the leaders at that time. Canada was a significant player on the global stage primarily because it became an influential ally in Washington. Access – the lifeblood of diplomacy – was consistently open and influential, especially at the very top, setting a spirit of mutually constructive dialogue that cascaded down and across the span of both governments. Leaders can and do make a difference.

Relations continued on an even keel with President Clinton and Prime Minister Chrétien, but slipped back following the 9/11 attacks when security threats became the almost exclusive focus of the

George W. Bush administration. Canada's decision to stand down on Iraq exacerbated a host of bilateral issues, despite Canada's firm support for and close cooperation with the US in Afghanistan.

Emotions run hot or cold or lukewarm, depending on the circumstances of the moment. The multifaceted nature of the relationship means that its usual state is a mix of emotions. Finding the right balance between substance and emotions is one challenge. Charting a course that safeguards and enhances Canadian interests vis-à-vis the US is another.

CANADA-US RELATIONS DURING THE OBAMA ERA

Convening at the downtown Conference Centre in Ottawa in December 2008, one month after the election of Barack Obama as the 44th president of the US, a group of more than 200 experienced officials (past and present), scholars, and pundits agreed on a "Blueprint" for Canada-US engagement. The Blueprint was sponsored primarily by the Norman Paterson School of International Affairs (NPSIA) at Carleton University and was intended as advice to the Canadian government for the February visit to Ottawa of the newly elected president.

Consistent with what was becoming a custom, Barack Obama's first foreign visit would be to the capital of his northern neighbour. Hopes were high. The new president was much more popular in Canada than in his own country, just as his predecessor George W. Bush had become more toxic in Canada than in the US. Obama's call for a new internationalism was compelling to many Canadians anxious to see the bilateral relationship move to a more productive footing. There was a sense that the common crisis stemming from the meltdown of financial markets could be a catalyst for a convergence of mutual interests that would spur economic recovery.

Polls suggested strongly that, particularly with an Obama administration, Canadians would be receptive to a bilateral agenda that would involve closer economic and security relations. In the wake of 9/11, the border had become dysfunctional. Time and again security trumped trade, impairing economic benefits for both countries. It was also recognized that the bilateral relationship needed to be more strategic, with Canada ready to tangibly engage on global issues of primary concern to the US – from the turbulence in the global economy to climate change, the dramatic rise of China, and the challenges from terrorism.

Three former US ambassadors to Canada who attended the December session – David Wilkins, Gordon Giffin, and James Blanchard – each emphasized that mutual respect, global engagement, and personal relations at the top were the major ingredients for a positive, productive relationship. Because of that, the NPSIA report underscored the importance of regular meetings of the two leaders to shape the direction of and give impetus to the relationship.

The prescriptions proposed included:

I On Security
Revamping the Canadian military and redefining the interoperability of Canadian and US forces would enable Canada to support US global objectives when needed and to provide constructive criticism where necessary.

II On Economic Relations
(a) Energy security and environmental stability were seen as the "two hottest political buttons" in both countries.[8] Both should be priorities in a broader economic agenda. In fact, no two files offered greater need or scope for closer collaboration. Canada is essential to greater energy security for the US and, given the integrated nature of the two economies, a joint approach to the control of carbon emissions was essential.

(b) Modernizing the border in a manner that serves both security and trade agendas rather than favouring one over the other would make enormous economic sense for both countries.

(c) Similarly, a more integrated approach to regulations would reduce duplicated effort, overlap, and impractical differences.

III On the Arctic
Finally, the Blueprint advocated commitments to more responsible stewardship of the fragile Arctic waters and Archipelago.

Throughout the full report, which was presented personally by its co-chairs to the prime minister in January 2009 and copied to all ten premiers of Canada, the theme stressed was that "vision and commitment at the very top will be key to unblocking lethargy and kindling imagination."[9]

President Obama spent nine hours in Ottawa in February 2009. He has only been back to Canada once since, to attend the G8 and Group of Twenty (G20) summits in Toronto in June of 2010. Prime

Minister Harper has had three working visits to Washington in the last five years. He also attended the G20 summit in Pittsburgh in September of 2009 and the G8 and NATO summits in Camp David and Chicago, respectively, in May 2012. So much for commitment from the top.

Attempts were made to move forward on the energy/environment nexus but they quickly languished as the president's own cap-and-trade initiative was blocked by the US Congress. Efforts were also made to rejuvenate border management under the "Beyond the Border" accord – the main reason for Harper's 2011 visit to Washington – but the results have been spasmodic at best.

The title of the NPSIA report is *From Correct to Inspired*. In the years since, even "correct" has been a reach. Inspiration for a more productive relationship became an early casualty. Relations with Canada regressed quickly as Washington became preoccupied with the domestic challenges of the prolonged recession and serious global challenges that inevitably captured centre stage. Whether because of differences in priorities, ideologies, or personalities, there seemed to be little chemistry between the two leaders. A true sense of partnership and clear direction from the top seemed as elusive as direct communication.

Perhaps the authors of the Blueprint mistakenly thought that the positive chemistry at the top so evident in the Mulroney era could be reignited, whereas the period from the mid-eighties to 2000 was more likely proving to be the exception to the rule.

In any event, sentiment and ad hoc personal relationships do not compensate for the institutional deficiencies in our relationship. Those that do exist – like NORAD and the IJC (International Joint Commission) – remain useful but with their effect and relevance somewhat diminished. We have shared infrastructure – from power grids to bridges, railways, and pipelines that operate essentially on the basis of informal undertakings about mutual interests. But we lack the governance mechanisms to ensure more efficient border management and to address shared security and environmental concerns. Provided there is the necessary political will, there is scope for more formal links on each of these twenty-first-century challenges. Otherwise, we will be left to respond to crises after they occur.

Trilateralism continues as the avenue of preference for Washington and Canada has gone along, more or less, partly by design but more because it had little choice, even though its bilateral issues of concern with the US are markedly different from those of Mexico. The veneer of equivalent treatment has done little for any of the three North American countries other than provide a reason for colourful, more or less annual, summits of the "Three Amigos" straining to produce wordy, but essentially empty, press communiqués. More courtesy and show than substance but also the route of least pressure for a US administration preoccupied with domestic political problems and the perennial costly American election cycle.

Unlike Mexico, Canada has close security ties with the US. On energy, trade, and investment, the relationship is also different, namely more open. Even border management issues have little in common other than shared geography. The drug trade and immigration concerns are top of mind for Mexico and the US. Neither resonates significantly with Canada.

The unfortunate by-product of trilateralism has been reduced engagement by all three leaders on bilateral issues that are important, neglect that ultimately favours the interests of the US over and above those of its two neighbours.

A WAKE-UP CALL

President Obama's procrastination over the Keystone XL pipeline has been a major ongoing irritant in the relationship. The project would have seen the shipment of more than 800,000 barrels a day of Albertan oil to refineries in the US Gulf Coast and generated tens of thousands of jobs for American and Canadian workers, indeed, by the State Department's own estimate, some 42,000 jobs in all.[10] Because it would cross the US border, the pipeline requires a presidential permit declaring it to be in the national interest. Since it was intended to bring Canadian heavy oil to Gulf refineries in Texas, thereby replacing imports of heavy crude from Venezuela, it was seen initially by many, including Prime Minister Harper, as a "no brainer," complying fully with a fundamental principle of NAFTA guaranteeing the US security of supply in exchange for security of access to the US market for Canadian energy.

However, after more than five years and voluminous pages of scrutiny there is no sign yet that the president has been convinced. He has had stern words for Canada, vowing that the permit will only be granted "if this project does not significantly exacerbate the problem of carbon pollution."[11] By using the pejorative term "tar sands" the president unwittingly signalled a personal bias. If the tar sands were in Montana or Texas, there would be little debate in Washington. But Canada is an easy foil for the president's crusade, which resonates favourably with major campaign donors and Hollywood backers.

Some have suggested that the president wants to lever his permit to gain tighter regulation of carbon emissions from Canada but his moral high ground is a bit shaky given the continuing heavy dependence of the US on coal, whose carbon emissions are far greater than any other fuel. As it is, Canada has fully aligned its environmental policies with those of the US and has similar approaches to transparency and oversight. We share a goal of 17 per cent in reductions by 2020 and have adopted identical fuel standards for vehicles.[12] Per-barrel emissions from the oil sands have been curtailed by 26 per cent since 1990 and, with new technology, there will be scope for more.[13] However, given the highly integrated nature of our two economies it would be suicidal for Canada to act unilaterally in a manner not replicated by the US. It is always important to judge the US by what it does rather than what its political leaders say. We can and should match action step by step because it would serve our own interests as well.

At the time of writing no one really knows how or whether this tug of war will be resolved. What is certain is that a negative verdict will have consequences for the broader relationship. The unwarranted delay already threatens to sandbag an initiative of major economic interest to Canada. It also jeopardizes American self-interest. The president's vacillation on an issue of major importance to Canada's economy is, by most accounts, a triumph of campaign posturing over pragmatic considerations and sensible diplomacy.

If nothing else, President Obama's procrastination about or rejection of this project should provide a clear wake-up call about the risk of relying on either history or sentiment as a guide for Canada's relations with the US. Most certainly, we should no longer rely on the US as our exclusive market for energy exports.

On Keystone, domestic politics in the form of election fundraising and the siren song of zealous environmentalist supporters seem to be trumping any consideration of mutual economic benefit or the need to support a priority project of the US's neighbour, ally, and still #1 trading partner. The significance of the partnership ultimately carried little weight, nor did a rational assessment of US national interest.

American procrastination on Canada's attempts to join the Trans-Pacific Partnership (TPP) only added to a climate of aggravation. Washington's customary benign neglect has become more malign. There is in fact no better sign of ineffectual US global diplomacy than the desultory manner in which relations with Canada have been managed in recent years. "Buy America" sentiments in the US Congress were used by the White House to extract further trade concessions from Canada in 2010. When in 2009 the Softwood Lumber Agreement, negotiated by Prime Minister Harper in an attempt to reset the relationship, came under predictable attack from segments of the industry, the administration ducked. Significantly more than 40 per cent of Canada's lumber exports now go to Asia.

Even though US labelling practices for beef imports were declared illegal by the WTO in 2013, the US blithely ignored the ruling. The restrictions are costing Canadian producers more than $1 billion annually.

When Canada ran for a non-permanent seat on the United Nations Security Council in 2010, US "support" was noticeable by its absence. Portugal was, for whatever reason, a more compelling choice.

The only positive initiative to emerge in recent years has been the "Beyond the Border" declaration intended to alleviate much of the sludge that has thickened the Canada-US border in the name of security since 9/11. Many of these impediments served more blatantly to undermine the efficiency of what we make and trade with one another. Despite the initial fanfare, the border initiative has yet to deliver much of substance and there is little to suggest that the president remains engaged.

Before the financial meltdown, more than 80 per cent of Canadian exports went to the US. The percentage is now closer to 70 per cent. Some sectors will continue to thrive – such as lumber and other construction-product sales geared to growth in the US housing market, which is expected to grow at a 10 per cent annual clip for the next few years. The question is whether the mills that shut down during the prolonged recession and the workers who moved on will come back in response to increased demand. Durable household goods is another sector expecting rising demand but this is a sector in which Canada has lost significant ground (from 20 per cent in 2002 to 7 per cent in 2012) – to China, among others.

Most worrying is the auto sector which, since the time of the Auto Pact, has ranked first or second in Canadian exports to the US.

Those heady days are long gone and there is little prospect that they will return. An elevated Canadian dollar, tougher competition from abroad, and the skewed terms of the bailout of General Motors (GM) and Chrysler in 2008 have combined to sharply weaken Canada's share of the US market. (Only 24 per cent of US auto imports came from Canada in 2012 versus 32 per cent a decade earlier.) Even as demand has picked up in the US, GM, Chrysler, and Ford have all reduced the range of models being manufactured in Canada (e.g., the GM truck plant closed in Oshawa just before record sales of pickups in the US were announced). In other words, as North American automakers shutter plants in Ontario they are expanding production in US plants.[14]

The $1.1 billion stock sale by the government fell well short of the $13.78 billion "investment" bailout. Production is booming in the US and Mexico but eroding in Canada. Canada's GM plants produced 11.5 per cent fewer cars in the first half of 2013; Chrysler was down 6 per cent. Little of what Canada has invested and continues to invest in the "Big Three" – GM, Chrysler, and Ford Canada – has much influence on the Big Three. Of the $12.2 billion invested by the industry in recent years, only 3 per cent was allocated to plants in Canada. Few, if any, of the engineering, software, and innovation design jobs are coming to Canada. Instead, the "Baby Three" are becoming, in effect, wards of the state.[15]

To add insult to injury, other trade partners, like the EU, Korea, and Japan, reject the notion that the North American auto sector is integrated and are reluctant to grant trade terms to Canada similar to those offered to the US. The branch-plant model of our major manufacturing sector is steadily putting us in double jeopardy.

There are other reasons, of course, for the decline – from exchange rate fluctuations to lower productivity levels and a shortage of skilled workers – but the biggest challenge of all for Canada will be to move beyond our almost exclusive reliance on the US for growth and spread our market focus and our comparative advantages to other prospects.

NAFTA ON THE WANE

The substance and spirit of NAFTA are on the wane. Intended to spark broader trade expansion by all three partners, NAFTA languished on the shelf while each country negotiated a spaghetti bowl of separate trade agreements in the Western Hemisphere and beyond. In fact, building strong relationships with other world leaders does not seem to be a priority for a US president whose foreign policy is essentially delivered in speeches.

Canada learned abruptly from Keystone the risk of being dependent on one customer for energy exports. But scrambling to find other markets and countries that actually need and want our commodities may be the best outcome of all, as long as we can overcome our own domestic political and regulatory obstacles that inhibit necessary infrastructure. Canada needs to decide whether and how it wants to forge closer, more substantial links with the US on, for example, security and environmental issues. At the same time, by cultivating closer economic partnerships with the EU and major Asian and Latin-American countries, Canada would reduce its vulnerability to excessive reliance on the US economy and the whim of any given US administration.

It is often said that Canada's greatest advantage is living alongside the world's largest economy. The two-way trade of goods and services exceeded $600 billion in 2012 versus $75 billion with China, Canada's second-largest trade partner. Canada is the leading export market for thirty-six of the fifty US states, receives 19 per cent of total US exports, and supports more than 8 million US jobs. While true in many ways, our extensive linkages to the US can also be a distinct handicap, particularly on trade and economic issues. The Free Trade Agreement and NAFTA were high points in the Canada-US relationship. They significantly increased economic growth and improved the competiveness of many Canadian economic sectors at a time of intensifying global competition.

But Canada had to fight hard to be included in NAFTA, against the best efforts of many Americans and Mexicans. Our reasons were primarily defensive. We did not want to see the benefits of our own FTA with the US diluted by a separate bilateral preferential agreement with Mexico. We were determined then to thwart US desires to establish a "hub-and-spoke" pattern of trade agreements going forward. It was only because of the generally positive tenor of the bilateral relationship at that time and the very close personal relations between Canada's prime minister (Brian Mulroney) and the US president (George H.W. Bush), that Canada was eventually accepted as a full partner in NAFTA. Once concluded, the agreement was intended to serve as a template for additional negotiations. Regrettably, this is not what happened. Self-interest trumped mutual interest as, first the US, and then its NAFTA partners, embarked unilaterally on further trade negotiations. That has been the pattern ever since.

The US embarked on its own, negotiating free trade unilaterally with Chile. Canada and Mexico followed suit with similar but not identical agreements. Trade initiatives beyond our hemisphere followed in the same manner, including, most notably, the TPP, which is currently the top trade priority for the US, designed to serve both geopolitical (the Asian pivot) and economic objectives. The TPP is actually unfolding as a series of bilateral negotiations with the US at the centre – a hub-and-spoke approach to trade consistently favoured by the US – and with US interests as the determining factor, with an umbrella of broad principles as the common factor.

After 9/11, security trumped trade even more emphatically and, increasingly, self-interest alone governed bilateral trade. The terrorist attacks triggered new oversight procedures at the border, additional inspections, passport requirements, etc., all of which have resulted in restricting the efficient flow of people, goods, and services. What had been an instinctive and informal relationship based on personal links has become more formal and formula-driven, chilling the tone and limiting progress on most bilateral issues. An America perceived to be in decline is not given to magnanimity toward others, including its immediate northern neighbour. Notions of a "special relationship" are now a thing of history with little contemporary currency.

A DOUBLE DILEMMA

What has become increasingly apparent on trade issues is that the US would prefer to use its economic weight exclusively to its own advantage and not in a manner in which countries like Canada might be seen to benefit at America's expense. Not surprisingly perhaps, the theme song for Barack Obama's re-election campaign in 2012 was Bruce Springsteen's patriotic "We Take Care of Our Own." A triumphant assertion of self-interest above all else!

This poses a double dilemma for Canada in large part because so much of our economy – notably the auto sector – is integrally linked with the US. And yet, the EU and countries like Japan and Korea are not prepared to give Canada the same terms on bilateral trade agreements as they give to the US, on auto trade in particular, because for them, the US is not just a huge market but also a guarantor of their security. As a result, Canada is left playing second fiddle with them or no fiddle at all.

Negotiations with Korea are a clear illustration of the double dilemma. The Canadian subsidiaries of the Big Three auto companies initially lobbied to thwart progress in these negotiations while their parent companies went along with the terms of a FTA between Korea and the US. Having secured access to the larger US market, Korea lost interest in the negotiations with Canada for two years and was most reluctant to agree to similar terms for trade in autos despite the integrated nature of the North American market.

When it comes to international security matters, a similar problem exists. NORAD is a shell of what it once was. What was once the bulwark of bilateral security cooperation has faded along with the threat of raids by Soviet bombers. NORAD was summoned as a result of the 9/11 attacks, and the Canadian Deputy was in charge at the time, but NORAD was unable to respond effectively. The US Northern Command now shoulders much of the burden for the US and the emphasis has shifted more to anti-missile defence against the threat from rogue states like North Korea and Iran (which one day could develop missiles capable of reaching North America). Canada, for a variety of domestic and political reasons, has, at least thus far, chosen to stand on the sidelines, bringing back memories of the Bomarc missile crisis of the early 1960s.

Missile development has come a long way since the days of the Bomarc but Canadian attitudes have not adapted. Some suggest, incredulously, that we should not become involved lest we stoke the global arms race. Others suggest that Canada knows it can, in any event, rely on the US to do the job, acting in its own interest, and has no qualms about being a free rider. Neither view says much for Canada's contribution to its own security, nor does it bolster our credentials or capacity for influence in Washington.

Ever since 9/11, security has become a dominant topic for America and a litmus test of sorts for America's allies. There is no perfect defence against rogue missiles or terrorist attacks but some defence is better than none, and if Canada wants to be treated as a serious player in the security of our continent, empty statements about global arms control offer little practical defence against real, tangible threats. We may be a target whether we like it or not but we can hardly complain to Washington about being sidelined if that is where we choose to sit.

In a world of rising self-interest, one in which alliances of the past are less likely to be reliable anchors for the future, Canada must pursue its own destiny, assert its own interests, and cultivate relationships and agreements that will safeguard and enhance those interests. But we need to be more assertive in bolstering our first line of defence – our security links with the US. This means negotiating participation in American ballistic missile defence schemes such as the Ground-Based Midcourse Defense program and attempting to revitalize the role of NORAD. It also means giving a higher priority to defence against attacks from cyberspace. Geography will be a constant factor but sentiment and nostalgia are not prescriptions for future success, especially when dealing with a superpower whose preoccupation is increasingly domestic.

The lopsided power imbalance is an omnipresent fact of life – a source of frustration, fear, and easily bruised sensitivities in Canada – but a reality that affects all facets of the relationship. We are obliged to work with it pragmatically, and take the initiative, more often than not, in order to safeguard our own interests.

THE NEW REALITY: A SELF-PREOCCUPIED AMERICA

The halcyon days of warm chemistry at the top from the mid-1980s to about 2000 are not likely to return. America is preoccupied now with domestic challenges – fiscal and economic – concerned about its broadening rivalry with China, and weary of its role as global sheriff. Self-interest is paramount. Isolationist strands are on the rise along with concerns about excessive surveillance in the name of security. "Special relationships" with any ally are more a matter of rhetoric than substance.

As William Galston observes, "The years since 9/11 have taken a toll on the American dream ... In many ways, today's mood reminds me of the immediate post-Vietnam years. Controversies about new economic challenges and America's role in the world produced fundamental divisions in both political parties, which persisted until Ronald Reagan routed his intraparty rivals and then his Democratic adversaries. We can expect a similar period of volatility until the emergence of leaders who are able not just to articulate a vision of a better future, but also to offer a credible strategy for reaching it in this era of polarized politics."[16]

For decades, governments of different stripes in Canada have tried to assert varying degrees of "independence" versus the overweaning pull of all things American, notably the popularity of what is loosely described as American "culture" – everything from movies, television, and books to sports – especially for English-speaking Canadians. Some presidents, like Barack Obama, are more popular in Canada than at home. Others, like Reagan and George W. Bush, are much less so. To many Americans, Canadians seem "soft," or, in Margaret Thatcher's definition, "wet."

What has changed in recent years is that, as America's sense of self has declined to some extent in the face of prolonged fiscal and economic doldrums, Canadians' sense of self has risen, in large part because we have coped more positively with the ravages of a deep recession. A superior economic performance is a more tangible tonic for the psyche than any perceptions about moral virtue! The confidence of being distinctly Canadian in North America can be a solid building block for an approach to foreign policy that moves beyond an almost exclusive fixation on relations with the US. By reaching out selectively to serve Canadian interests with other partners such as Japan, China, Mexico, and the EU, among others, we will also inject a healthy dose of realism into our bilateral relationship with the US. The latter will always be a top priority of vital interest to Canada but it need not be either exclusive or the cause of knee-jerk differentiation simply for the sake of wanting to be different.

Above all, we should rise above both a yearning for a "special" relationship and the appeal of differentiation. Neither offers a mature sense of how we should conduct our affairs. A reset of the bilateral relationship is in order, one that focuses more on substance than sentiment and reinforces the rule of law and the values that underpin this complex relationship. By injecting more balance into our foreign policy generally we will also better ensure that we get attention from Washington where we need it.

Canada's best recourse is to safeguard its economic interests with the US as a matter of consistent priority and vigilance. The obvious corollary to an America adapting to a diminishing role in global affairs is a recalibration of Canada's own focus, building on a more confident identity and establishing links that will complement and balance the persistent priority for relations with the US. Geography may always oblige us to give primary attention to the extensive,

intricate nature of relations with the US but it should not obscure
our ability to do more, much more, with others. We also need to use
our comparative advantages more selectively and more aggressively
in order to gain improved market access elsewhere, especially in the
more dynamic emerging markets. We may have to rely on uncon-
ventional tactics to get attention, but so be it. We can never win in a
"might is right" contest nor should we be patsies to those, including
the US, who seek unfettered access to our market.

A "Third Option with Legs" strategy – as outlined in chapter
9 – would inject more balance into Canada's economic profile and
would, at the same time, contribute to a healthier, more mature relationship with the US. Following on the success of our CETA (Comprehensive and Economic Trade Agreement) negotiations with the
EU, and a FTA with Korea, an economic partnership agreement with
Japan would offer similar substance and balance. The fact is that
Canada and Japan should both rise above their respective obsessions
with the US and forge agreements that will not only enhance bilateral ties but also facilitate their respective relations with Washington. A bold trade and economic initiative with China should also be
part of the overall game plan. Traction with China will serve more
than bilateral Canadian interests. It will draw attention to Canada
from others in the region and the US. Scratching the perennial Canadian itch to be seen doing something constructive in the world distinct from what the US may be doing would be a bonus.

3

The Global Economic Transformation

The global economy is changing dramatically, but Canada has not kept pace. The Chinese, Indian, Brazilian, Korean, Mexican, Indonesian, and Turkish economies have been expanding at more than twice the rate of Canada's more traditional markets.[1] Although growth rates are now slowing in some (but clearly not all) emerging markets, the reality is that by the middle of this decade emerging economies will account for more than half of the world's production and consumption of goods and services.

Although Prime Minister Stephen Harper and his ministers have made significant strides in boosting Canada's ties with emerging economies with a steady round of ministerial and prime ministerial visits to the Asia-Pacific region, both business and government efforts to harness these new economic opportunities are still largely unfocused and episodic. Canadian firms have made little progress in penetrating the new markets of emerging economies while losing market share in traditional ones.[2] Unless Canada dramatically ups its game and changes the way it does business, it will assuredly not be a significant player in these markets and will become increasingly marginalized.

The rise of emerging economies signals a profound shift in the global economy. They have become integral to the success of new production strategies focused on global value chains, as well as important markets in their own right. The postwar Bretton Woods trade and investment architecture is inadequate to meet these new challenges. We will see more volatility going forward as fast-developing countries exercise their new-found power. The quasi-market nature of these newer global players poses unique challenges and requires

innovative approaches and different negotiating, trade, and investment strategies from those that Canada has traditionally pursued.

The simple reality is this:

- Canada's economy is stuck in the slow lane and will probably only
  grow around 2 to 3 per cent in 2013 and 2014.[3] Canadian consumers who carry heavy debt loads are spending less. Federal and
  provincial governments are reining in spending to balance their
  books and businesses have curbed their capital spending plans.
- Canada's export performance has to improve dramatically to
  secure higher levels of economic growth and compensate for
  reduced domestic demand.
- Canada is far too reliant on the US market, which accounts for
  more than 70 per cent of our total trade.[4] US economic recovery is
  steady but slow.
- Since 2000 we have lost more than a quarter of our market share
  to foreign competitors in US markets.[5]
- We have failed to diversify and capture market share in the faster-
  growing emerging-market economies of the Asia-Pacific and Latin
  America.
- Less than 8 per cent of Canadian exports and 4 per cent of out-
  ward investment go to these emerging markets.[6]
- Canadian participation in non-North American value chains
  remains low.[7]
- Global trade volumes will quadruple by 2030.[8]
- In the next decade, China's GDP may be bigger than the US's.[9]
- By 2030, the individual GDPs of Turkey, Indonesia, and Mexico
  may surpass Canada's GDP.[10]
- By 2050, emerging markets will be home to 60 per cent of the
  world's wealth and 70 per cent of global trade.[11]
- By 2050, less than 8 per cent of global trade will take place in
  North America, compared with 15 per cent today.[12]

RISKS AND OPPORTUNITIES

The group of fast-developing dynamic economies led by China,
India, and Brazil, but which now includes Colombia, Mexico,
South Korea, Turkey, Poland, Indonesia, Vietnam, and South Africa,
achieved more than double the growth rates of advanced economies
during the past decade. Notwithstanding the difficulties that some

of these economies – such as China, India, and Brazil, in particular – are now experiencing as their growth slows down, they are all in a very different position today from where they were at the beginning of the twenty-first century. All of these countries now enjoy rapidly growing middle classes, high savings rates, and generally more stable regulatory regimes – three solid pillars for continued growth.

Another important fact that Canadians must grapple with is that aging populations do not make for fast-growing economies. While some of the world's new economic powerhouses are growing due to abundant natural resources and strong commodity prices (e.g., Russia) or because they are catching up by unleashing their potential after years of mismanagement (e.g., Poland), one of the principal factors driving across-the-globe growth is having a young population. Older people are less likely to participate in the labour force. They are also less likely to form new families and households, and as people age they are less likely to buy new homes and cars, and make other large purchases. In short, consumption declines with age. So in sum, *ceteris paribus*, having a large proportion of senior citizens in a country's population tends to mean lower growth rates.

Figure 1 compares the average old age ratio (the number of people over age 64 per 100 people aged 15–64) and the average annual GDP growth rate for selected economies from 2003 to 2012. While the relationship between age and growth is not perfect (no correlation is!) the message is clear: countries with older populations grow more slowly. Getting to know and doing business with the world's young economies must be a priority for Canada's government and business.

Canada's Export Development Corporation notes, "Collectively, emerging markets are forecast to grow by 5.5 per cent in 2013, and to build up further to 5.9 per cent next year. China's path is the most convincing, turning around last year's deceleration into 8.2 per cent growth this year, and an even more comforting 8.5 per cent in 2014. India is less certain, plodding more slowly to higher growth than was realized in 2012. Brazil's disastrous 1.0 per cent showing will not be repeated this year, looking more like a 3.4 per cent growth clip, and 4.0 per cent in 2014. Russia and Mexico appear to be the stalwarts in the large-market club, posting stable and impressive growth in the next two years."[13]

Alas, as noted earlier, Canadians are minor players in these emerging markets: less than 10 per cent of our exports and less than

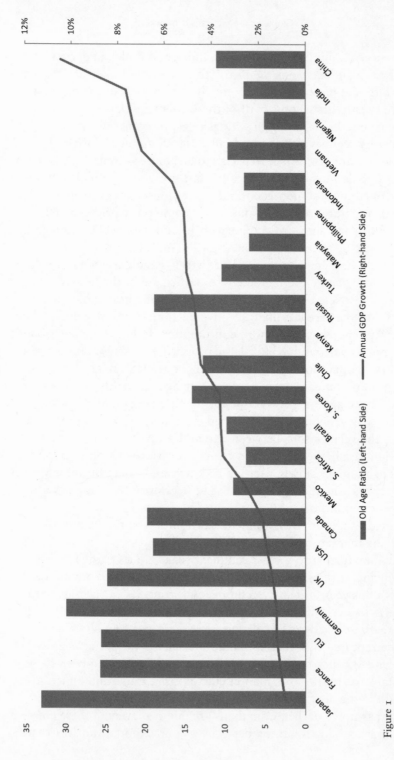

Figure 1
Average old age ratio and average annual GDP growth rates, 2003–2012

Source: World Bank and World Development Indicators.

Old Age Ratio (Left-hand Side)

Annual GDP Growth (Right-hand Side)

4 per cent of outward investment go to them. Worse still, the lion's share of our exports are headed to slow-growing economies, as figure 2 shows.

In the aftermath of the disastrous economic and financial crisis of 2008–09, global trade rebounded, thanks largely to new trade opportunities in developing economies. Canada's own trade performance, however, continued to underperform, largely reflecting continuing generally anemic demand in Canada's traditional markets, the US and Europe in particular. As a result, trade has not played its historic role as an engine of growth in Canada, leading to the weakest post-recession recovery since the Second World War. Exports of goods and services as a share of GDP have steadily declined since they hit a high of 45 per cent in 2000, falling to 29 per cent in 2010. On the import side, there has been less of a decline, to 31 per cent, from 40 per cent of GDP.[14]

As the former deputy governor of the Bank of Canada, Tiff Macklem, explained in a speech he delivered at Queen's University in January 2013, "The underperformance of our exports is due in part to weakness in foreign demand. With the United States – our major trading partner – experiencing its worst recession and weakest recovery since the Great Depression, our exports fell sharply in 2008 and have recovered only slowly ... In the last decade, Canada's share of the world export market has slipped from about 4.5 per cent to about 2.5 per cent and our share of the export market for manufactured goods has been cut in half. Even more revealing, our export performance has been the second worst in the G20."[15] As figure 3 shows, Canada's share of the world's exports has slipped considerably since 2000.

As Macklem further pointed out, "A comparison of the evolution of unit labour costs in Canada and the United States is telling. Between 2000 and 2011, the labour cost of producing a unit of output in Canada compared with the United States, adjusted for the exchange rate, increased 75 per cent. The majority of this loss of competitiveness reflects the appreciation of the Canadian dollar, but weak productivity growth in Canada relative to the United States played a significant role. Business sector labour productivity in Canada has grown at an average annual rate of just 0.8 per cent since the start of 2000, compared with 2.3 per cent in the United States. This accounts for about one-third of our lost competitiveness."[16]

Figure 2

Canada's exports are directed at slow growing economies

* Country is not one of Canada's top fifteen trading partners.

Sources: IMF *World Economic Outlook*, Industry Canada, and Bank of Canada calculations.

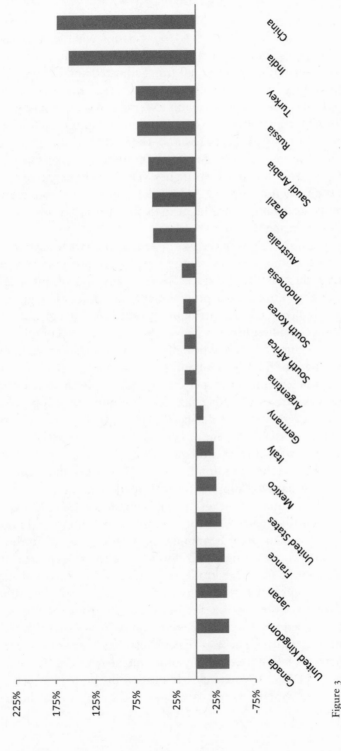

Figure 3
Per cent change in share of world exports, 2000–2011

Source: IMF and Direction of Trade Statistics.

How different the situation is today from what it was some twenty-five years ago. In anticipation of the 1989 Canada-US Free Trade Agreement, many Canadian firms adjusted and became more competitive to better serve the more integrated cross-border market. Today, they need to retool again to serve a more dynamic global economy. The transformation of Canadian trade, production, and investment patterns in the 1980s and 1990s flowed not only from more liberal terms of access to the US market, but also from new technologies and corporate strategies. The development of more dispersed production through value chains and other cooperative, inter-corporate arrangements helps to explain the rapid rise in cross-border trade during the 1990s.

The structural changes in the North American market have spread to other parts of the world, bringing more players into global production. The right approach to trade, services, investment, intellectual property rights, government procurement, and domestic regulatory regimes have become key contributors to success in the global economy. Many Canadian firms, however, were lulled into complacency because the United States had become such a reliable market. In fact, Canada's share of the US merchandise import market fell to around 14 per cent in 2010 from 19 per cent in 2000.[17] In the other direction, the US share of Canada's merchandise imports dropped from 64 per cent to 50 per cent during the same period,[18] representing 23 per cent versus 19 per cent of US merchandise exports.[19] On the basis of conventional trade statistics, China has overtaken Canada as the leading merchandise supplier to the US market and is now the second largest national supplier to the Canadian market.

The Bank of Canada believes that US demand for Canadian goods and services will remain weak for the foreseeable future as do other economic projections. TD Economics projects that by 2020 the US market will account for only two-thirds of Canadian exports.[20]

The decline in Canada's trade performance has involved more than a decline in bilateral trade with the United States. The robust export growth of the 1990s ended in the 2000s. From 2000 to 2010, Canada dropped from sixth place to eleventh in our share of global merchandise trade.[21] The IMF calculates that Canada's share of world markets fell more than any other member of the G20 except for that of the UK.[22] We are clearly headed in the wrong direction and are going to have to radically change the way we do business with the world.

Global trade volumes could nearly quadruple by 2030,[23] but competition will be fierce as developing-country firms fight for market share – at home and abroad – against suppliers from more advanced economies. By mid-century, it is expected that emerging markets will be home to 70 per cent of the world's wealth and 60 per cent of global trade. According to the Asian Development Bank, by 2050 Asian economies will account for 50 per cent of global GDP and have 50 per cent of the world's population.[24] The opportunities are enormous for Canada, but then again so are the challenges.

THE AUSTRALIAN EXPERIENCE

Canada's overall economic performance in this century contrasts sharply with that of fellow Commonwealth member Australia. Australia is the only G20 developed country that experienced growth in its trade during the first decade of the twenty-first century, increasing its share of global exports from 1 per cent to 1.4 per cent, and its share of global imports from 1.1 per cent to 1.3 per cent from 2000 to 2010. Over that same period, Canada's share of global exports slipped from 4.3 per cent to 2.5 per cent, and its share of imports fell from 3.7 per cent to 2.6.[25] Much of Australia's growth came from exports to rapidly growing emerging economies, as Australian firms increased their presence in these markets from a base that was already stronger than that of Canadian firms.

While Canadian proponents of free trade with the US had to overcome deep, entrenched opposition to the idea, Australians in contrast have enthusiastically accepted their geographic destiny next door to the rapidly growing markets of Southeast and Northeast Asia. They pursued a program of unilateral reforms, symbolized by the transformation of the inwardly focused Industries Assistance Commission to the outwardly oriented Productivity Commission.

For twenty-one consecutive years, from 1991 to 2012, Australia was enviably recession-free and enjoyed unprecedented levels of economic growth. Australia's per capita GDP is also higher than Canada's and its unemployment rate is lower (5.2 per cent versus 7.2 per cent in Canada).[26]

Australian resource and service firms responded by aggressively pursuing markets in emerging Asia. Nowhere is the difference between Canada and Australia clearer than in agricultural policy, where, in the 1990s, Australia's dairy industry convinced the government to work with it and phase out supply management.[27] Today, while Canada fights to keep supply management away from the TPP trade talks, Australia's meat and dairy industries have become leading suppliers of protein to Asian markets.[28] Australia also developed an aggressive comprehensive program to attract Asian students to Australian universities, building relationships that are now paying dividends.[29]

More recently, Australian firms, backed by government policy, have been using the base built in Asian economies during the 1980s and 1990s more strategically to better secure Australia's economic future. Australia's trade with Asia is now over 50 per cent of its total trade with the world, and over one-third of Australia's Asian trade is with China.[30]

But Australia is not resting on its laurels. Worried about falling prices for its coal and iron ore as China's demand slackens, forcing its resource extraction sector to cut back on its ambitious plans for further expansion, and by a buoyant Australian dollar that has crimped its manufacturing sector, Australia's government has come up with a bold new plan to ensure that the country stays globally competitive.

That plan is contained in a white paper, *Australia in the Asian Century*, which was unveiled by the Australian government in late 2012 and received all-party support.[31]

Drafted by Australia's former treasury secretary Ken Henry, Australia's white paper is not short on ideas or details. It runs a staggering 312 pages and covers every topic from trade to investment, to education, to immigration, to defence, and even to the requirements for effective corporate governance if business is to succeed in the new markets of Asia.

Australia's white paper also sets ambitious targets. It seeks to increase Australia's trade with Asia by a further one-third by 2025.[32] It recognizes that deepened ties require shaking up a culture of complacency in education and business. To that end, the government will offer 12,000 scholarships to allow Asian students, researchers, and professionals to study in Australia while ensuring that every student who graduates from high school will have a working knowledge of Mandarin, Hindi, Bahasa Indonesian, and/or Japanese.[33] The plan will also allow visitors from Asia to stay longer, by extending visa periods and allowing for multiple entry.[34]

The white paper also calls on business to ensure that at least one-third of those who sit around the boardroom table have a "deep experience in and knowledge of Asia."[35]

Australia's focus is commendable but implementation is, in some respects, being buffeted by nervousness that Australia is becoming too open, e.g., on foreign investment and on immigration. Latent undercurrents, bordering on xenophobia, are generating political problems, notably with Indonesia and China, that will require sensitive management if Australia expects to derive maximum benefit from the white paper's recommendations.

In any event, Canada should not try to emulate the Australian model. While we share many views on global issues, we are also vigorous competitors in many Asian markets. There are areas for greater cooperation, including security, but our own economic interests dictate an enhanced yet genuinely Canadian approach to the region. The growing demand for food, energy, minerals, education, and tourism should be as compelling for Canada as it is proving to be for Australia.

If Canada is going to make inroads in Asia it will need its own action plan with clear targets to attract investment and promote trade. Such a plan should aim to double Canada's trade with Asia by 2020, establish clear priority markets for negotiations to meet that goal, set investment targets in line with the objective of developing our natural resources and relevant infrastructure, roughly triple the number of Asian university students in Canada from approximately 80,000 now to 240,000 by the same date,[36] and redirect a healthy share of federal research funding to target deeper high-tech and applied science training at select universities.

Debates in Australia, which are similar to our own about foreign direct investment by state-owned enterprises (SOEs), as discussed in chapter 7, also suggest that there is broad scope for the two countries to work together to define a common approach on principles regarding SOEs that reflects both our need for foreign capital, especially from those who have it, and our political desire to control our destiny.

Canada will only secure its own place in the Asian century if, like Australia, it has a real game plan. And closer cooperation with our Commonwealth cousin from down under should be a key element of our engagement. While circumstances may not be exactly the same, there is much Canada can learn from the Australian experience.

CANADA'S FOREIGN INVESTMENT PERFORMANCE

Unlike trade, Canada's investment has been both more active and more imaginative during the past decade. Canadian direct investment abroad and foreign investment in Canada grew steadily in the 2000s.[37] Growth was most evident in bilateral investment flows between Canada and the Asia-Pacific. While absolute numbers remain modest, the rate of growth is encouraging.

There has also been a significant increase in two-way investment with Europe, but with an important difference.[38] Most of the two-way investment flows across the Pacific are trade-creating, either involving value-chain production in Asia or investment in resource exploitation in Canada. Transatlantic investment, on the other hand, tends to be a substitute for trade, with Canadian and European firms locating in each other's markets to serve those markets.

Citigroup projects that by 2020 China will be the world's largest economy.[39] Canada is falling off the list of top ten traders and is the twelfth-ranking exporter and tenth-ranking importer.[40] Many emerging markets are expected to exceed Canada's GDP by 2030 (e.g., Turkey, Indonesia, and Mexico).[41] Some of these countries, while growing quickly, face serious challenges – observance of the rule of law, poor governance, corruption, and cronyism. However, many are finally building economies that offer their populations decent standards of living and hope for the future. They will become both formidable competitors and markets of opportunity.

The above evidence of changing Canadian and global trade and investment patterns points to the inescapable conclusion: it's time for major efforts that strengthen Canada's relationships with emerging markets, especially in Asia. While not without risks, these relationships will prove much more rewarding going forward than those with our traditional trade and investment partners.

THE NEW REALITY: QUASI-MARKET ECONOMIES

However, there is a major challenge facing Canadian firms and that is that governments and firms in major emerging markets (China, India, and Brazil) do not play by conventional, market-based rules. Of particular concern are SOEs, which may receive preferential treatment – such as cheap financing or favour when bidding for government contracts – over privately owned firms. SOEs are big players in the global economy. For example, the OECD reports that "of the 2000 largest companies, 204 have been identified as majority SOEs in the business year 2010–11 with ownership spread across thirty-seven different countries. The numbers vary significantly by country, with China leading the list (seventy SOEs), followed by India (thirty), Russia (nine), the United Arab Emirates (nine) and Malaysia (eight)."[42] It also notes that "the combined sales of the 204 SOEs amounted to USD$3.6 trillion in the business year 2010–11, representing more than 10 per cent of the aggregate sales of the 2,000 largest companies and exceeding the 2010 Gross National Incomes of countries like the United Kingdom, France or Germany."[43] The ten countries with the largest share of the world's SOEs – China, the United Arab Emirates, Russia, Indonesia, Malaysia, Saudi Arabia, India, Brazil, Norway, and Thailand – also account for more than 20 per cent of the world's trade.[44] Many of the world's SOEs operate no differently than private firms. But others reap enormous advantages through their access to cheap capital and other benefits.

According to a major study reported in *The Economist*, "China spent over $300 billion, in nominal terms, on the biggest SOEs between 1985 and 2005. This help often came in the form of cheap capital and underpriced inputs unavailable to international rivals. The glass industry got soda ash for a song, for example. The auto-parts business got subsidies worth $28 billion from 2001 to 2011 through cheap glass, steel and technology; the government has promised another $10.9 billion by 2020. The subsidies to the paper industry topped $33 billion from 2002 to 2009. All industrial SOEs benefited from energy subsidies … Rivals are forced to go up against national champions that enjoy subsidised inputs and seemingly free money in markets that are protected. Worse yet, the bosses of Chinese SOEs are not in business principally to make a profit: they are often encouraged by the government to pursue other goals, such as resource acquisition, foreign policies and technology transfer, regardless of cost."[45]

The reality is that, in some emerging economies, like China, the state also uses its power to direct its major companies to act in the national interest. The supercharged industrial policies of emerging economies thus pose a major challenge and barrier to private companies that want to do business there and when SOEs backed by sovereign wealth funds (SWFs) do business here. China and Brazil, for example, have become important new sources of foreign direct investment in Canada through entities that are subject to influence only by the policies and objectives of their home governments, i.e., by non-market considerations.

Existing regulatory frameworks are inadequate to level the playing field between SOEs and private firms. Traditional antitrust laws in most countries, including Canada, are designed to prevent anti-competitive behaviour and price gouging, but they cannot prevent subsidies or eliminate the competitive advantages that SOEs enjoy in the area of taxation or financing on highly preferential terms. Only the European Union and Australia have state-of-the-art competitive neutrality arrangements to lessen the competitive advantages of SOEs. Further, although "WTO rules impose obligations on Member governments as opposed to private entities ... WTO rules are generally ownership-neutral; the disciplines which they impose with respect to government regulations and actions do not distinguish between situations where the provider of the goods or services covered by the regulation or action is a public or a private entity."[46]

Canadian policy needs to better account for firms that benefit from access to low-cost capital through sovereign wealth funds and to seek ways to level the competitive playing field between state-backed and private enterprises.

Our trade negotiating agenda also has to reflect this reality. In markets where the rule of law is elastic or non-existent, conventional trade rules will not suffice. Firm arbitration and dispute settlement mechanisms will be needed to anchor any trade agreement with emerging economic powers, especially those where the role of government is predominant.

The terms of market access have to be balanced and mutually beneficial, and in negotiations the government should not be reluctant to safeguard and enhance the competitive position of the few global champions we have. It is not a question of picking winners or adopting an "industrial policy," as critics are tempted to complain. Rather, it would be smart policy, reflecting a realistic assessment of the competitive challenges our companies face. There is no need to coddle national champions, but equally no need to hobble their success in our own market.

A case in point has been articulated in compelling fashion by Serge Godin, the founder and executive chairman of CGI Group Inc., a leading-edge information technology service company. On negotiations with India in particular, he has, in a private communication, urged the government to adopt a strategy that would safeguard Canada's (and CGI's) capabilities in the information technology (IT) sector. The basic risk he sees is that Canada might lose many of the almost one million information technology jobs spread across the Canadian economy. Additionally, Godin proposes that regulated industries in Canada (banks, insurance companies) be encouraged to adopt "remote delivery" of information technology *from within Canada* rather than off-shoring. (This concern came under a spotlight when it was discovered that one of Canada's major banks had brought in a number of temporary foreign workers to staff their IT department.)

Godin also proposes that the government create IT centres of excellence across Canada, particularly in areas of high unemployment as a compelling alternative to offshoring such work.

Godin's fundamental argument is that information technology companies in Canada and India should be able to compete on a level playing field. He noted that, as a result of various incentive programs (or subsidies), Indian IT companies have an effective tax rate of 12 per cent (versus 26 per cent plus in Canada). This is precisely the kind of imbalance that Canadian trade negotiators are obliged to reconcile, and not just on information technology.

It is not known to what extent this advice has registered in Ottawa but what is evident from the example of CGI and others faced with the challenge of state-backed competition is that, if these concerns about playing fields tilted against Canada are not redressed through future trade and investment treaty negotiations, our companies will have to find outlets for employment and business elsewhere.

In all these negotiations, our officials should consult systematically with those in the private sector, whose interests will be affected by the result. They need to know what obstacles to market access need to be addressed, how access by Canadian exporters will be assured, and precisely what access Canada is ready to exchange in a mutually beneficial manner.

Making choices in a turbulent, highly competitive global economy is not easy. Emerging markets entail higher-risk judgments and Canadians are known to be risk averse. That is a habit we have to change. The government will have to decide whether it wants to "walk the talk" on diversification and whether it seriously intends to broaden economic ties beyond traditional but sagging markets like the US and the EU.

Canadian firms are also going to have adapt to the new reality of quasi-market economies and to leverage their strengths in an exacting manner to advance their interests. Governments – federal and provincial – need to work out rules and arrangements that account for this new reality and which will level the playing field so Canadian firms can succeed globally.

IT'S NOT ALL ABOUT CHINA

Although China is by far the biggest player in emerging markets and a behemoth that is also driving much of the current growth in the global economy, not to mention the growth of many of its smaller Asian neighbours, there are other countries that Canada needs to engage more deeply. Some, like Mexico, are close to home and present major targets of opportunity. Others, like Indonesia, are countries with which we have historically had extensive and important relations, but who we need to engage (or re-engage) because they are democracies and may be somewhat easier places to conduct business. The potential is enormous, as the HSBC and Oxford Economics detail in a 2013 report. Exports to China, India, and Vietnam could increase by 12 per cent annually in the next fifteen years or so, to be joined by Indonesia and Malaysia at similarly high levels of growth. And so-called "middle-income countries with high population growth, such as Egypt and Turkey" could also join "the ranks of fastest growing export destinations for Canada."[47]

MEXICO

On 28 November, 2012, President-elect Enrique Peña Nieto paid a visit to Ottawa just days shy of his formal inauguration. In recent years, such visits by the president-elect have become a regular feature of Canada-Mexico relations, though rarely have they generated the kind of buzz and excitement of Peña's visit, not only because of his relative youth and vigour, compared with his predecessors, but also because he revived the political fortunes of Mexico's historical governing party, the PRI (Partido Revolucionario Institucional), which had spent several decades in the political wilderness, at least when it came to occupying Los Pinos, Mexico's equivalent to the White House.

During his short visit to Ottawa, Peña made a point of getting together with Canada's top business leaders at a special session that was organized jointly by the Canadian Council of Chief Executives and the Canadian Chamber of Commerce. His message was a simple one – Mexico wants a lot more Canadian business in both trade and investment. And it was a message that was reciprocated by his hosts – Canada should do more business with Mexico. As a CIGI (Centre for International Governance Innovation) report that was delivered personally to the president after his meeting with Canada's corporate leaders makes abundantly clear, Canada and Mexico "must work harder to make their bilateral relationship work to their mutual benefit."[48] Although, in the words of the report, "Bilateral trade and investment have grown steadily from very low pre-North American Free Trade Agreement (NAFTA) levels ... there remains enormous, untapped potential, particularly in Mexico. Student, tourist, investor and temporary worker exchanges are enhancing familiarity with each other, but unhelpful stereotypes remain common. New investment and trade opportunities should flow from the new Mexican administration's commitment to open up the energy sector to foreign participation."[49] Consider the facts:[50]

- Canada (and the United States) is rich in skilled labour and value-added industries, whereas Mexico boasts a young and growing workforce. Our population is aging fast. Theirs is not.
- Since NAFTA, Canada's trade with Mexico has grown nearly six-fold. Today, Mexico is Canada's third-largest trading partner, with two-way trade reaching CAD$34.4 billion in 2011.
- Today, Canada's economy is larger than Mexico's, but within a few decades the relative position of the two countries will switch. PricewaterhouseCoopers projects that, on a purchasing power parity basis, Mexico's GDP will be USD$6.6 trillion by 2050 – the seventh-largest economy in the world – twice Canada's projected GDP of CAD$3.3 trillion. Additionally, by 2050, one in six Americans will be of Mexican ancestry. In short, the Mexican economy and the Mexican diaspora will provide new and compelling opportunities for trade and investment far too large for Canadians to ignore.
- Canada is also becoming an increasingly important source of capital for Mexico. Canadian FDI (foreign direct investment) in Mexico has doubled since NAFTA, and Canada is now Mexico's fourth-largest source of FDI. More than 2,600 Canadian companies have offices and operations in Mexico, including major firms

such as Bombardier, Goldcorp, and Linamar. Companies in industries ranging from finance to pharmaceuticals, such as Scotiabank
and Apotex, have used their Mexican operations as launch pads
to reach other markets in Central and South America. However,
this figure represents less than 1 per cent of Canada's overseas FDI
stocks, suggesting that there may be mutually profitable investment opportunities waiting to be pursued.

Mexico clearly represents one of the most important targets of
opportunity for Canada in key emerging markets. The fact that it is
a NAFTA partner and a country with which we have strong historical ties and are connected by geography means that we don't have
to start from the beginning, but we are still going to have to work
a lot harder to tap the enormous unrealized potential that exists in
this relationship.

INDONESIA

Indonesia now has one of the fastest-growing economies in the Asia-
Pacific region. Although it is classified as a lower-middle-income
country, it has an abundance of natural resources. It is now also
a democracy and one of the world's biggest, with a population of
232.5 million, which also makes it the largest Muslim country in
the world. Indonesia was hard hit by the 1997 Asian financial crisis,
which sideswiped many of the world's developing economies. But
as a result of critical reforms to its industrial and financial sectors
in the aftermath of the crisis, the country now boasts one of the
strongest economic growth rates in the developing world and a burgeoning middle class that is growing fast. As the Department of Foreign Affairs, Trade and Development (DFATD) website also reports,
"Indonesia's growth and stability have been bolstered by substantial political, economic, and institutional reforms. The 2009 legisla-
tive and presidential elections were free and fair. Human rights are
improving but certain concerns remain."[51]
Indonesia's economy is highly dependent on the development of
its natural resources, a sector that employs more than 50 per cent
of the Indonesian workforce.[52] It is also a sector that has attracted
significant Canadian FDI, which now exceeds $3.2 billion.[53] Two-
way trade flows between Indonesia and Canada now amount to
roughly $3 billion annually.[54] But Indonesians have not forgotten

that Canada for many years was – and continues to be – an important source of foreign aid to the country, which has bolstered economic growth and political stability. Aid has also helped to alleviate the significant disparities in wealth and income in a country that is fragmented and divided by thousands of miles of ocean. Much of our current aid is now directed to helping one of the poorest regions in the country, the island of Sulawesi, Indonesia's third most populous region.[55] Canada is also a champion of human rights, pluralism, and democracy in Indonesia. Canadian authorities are working closely with their Indonesian counterparts in the area of counter-terrorism cooperation and defence, through Canada's Military Training Cooperation Programme (MTCP).[56] Again, as in Mexico, there is unrealized economic potential to tap in our relationship with Indonesia. And to the extent that Canada wants to be a bigger and more significant player in the Southeast Asian region as a whole and in the region's evolving security architecture, a theme we will take up in chapter 5, Indonesia is a *sine qua non* in that engagement.

VIETNAM

Vietnam had a troubling twentieth century: invaded by Japan in the Second World War and recolonized by a flagging French empire, it was then divided, and suffered through a brutal twenty-year civil war, which killed over 1.5 million Vietnamese. After North and South Vietnam were unified in 1975, Vietnam's fortunes improved only marginally as it was plunged into conflict with the Khmer Rouge, and briefly invaded by China.

Thirty years of conflict left the Vietnamese economy battered and bruised. In 1989, per capita income was barely $600. However, in the 1980s, the Hanoi government began to consciously move away from a centrally planned economy, and launched a series of reforms. By 2012, per capita income had grown to $3,400. When Canada made Vietnam a CIDA (Canadian International Development Agency) country of focus in 2009, Vietnam's economy was actually growing at over 7 per cent a year during the 2000s.[57] The country has gone from the front line of the Cold War to a major destination for FDI and an emerging manufacturing hub. Whereas in 2002, oil, clothing and footwear, and agricultural products made up two-thirds of Vietnam's exports, by 2012 those goods made up around a third of exports, and are being increasingly displaced by electronics, machinery, and other high-value-added merchandise.[58]

Vietnam's future trajectory looks in many ways like China's recent past. With a young, increasingly well-educated population, its once-agrarian economy is rapidly urbanizing. Currently, trade between Canada and Vietnam is quite small (only around $2 billion in 2012), and mostly consists of exports from Vietnam to Canada. However, as Vietnam's population continues to move into its cities (its urban population is growing at 3 per cent per year),[59] and its export sector continues to grow, Vietnam's infrastructure needs, such as railways, access to water and sanitation services, and new port facilities will all increase dramatically.[60] This could create opportunities for Canadian firms willing to take a risk in a so-called frontier market.

With a population of nearly 90 million, and steadily rising incomes, Vietnam could also become an attractive target for joint ventures between Vietnamese and foreign firms. Canada's FDI position in Vietnam is currently very small: less than 0.1 per cent of all Canadian outward investment. Yet, over half of US Fortune 100 companies have operations or subsidiaries in Vietnam.[61] The Vietnamese government has also begun to pass laws and regulations directly designed to attract foreign firms, and has stated that investment in the materials and energy, agriculture, forestry, and infrastructure sectors is particularly welcome.[62] If Canadian firms hesitate to get into Vietnam on the ground floor, we should not expect others to wait as well.

INDIA

The world has waited for the proverbial Indian Tiger to arrive for decades now. India's economy used to be held down by the Licence Raj – the colloquial term for the layers upon layers of regulation and bureaucracy that held back Indian entrepreneurs and made the country an unattractive investment for foreigners. For years, India's economic growth lagged behind its geopolitical rivals Pakistan and China. Even as of the summer of 2013, after a booming decade where annual GDP growth averaged over 7.5 per cent, pundits announced that the Indian economy was dead in the water after the rupee fell to an all-time low against the US dollar and investors fled the country.

While India's economic reforms and growth story have been rocky over the last thirty years, the long-term fundamentals for the country are solid, and its potential is astonishing. India's population today is 1.2 billion, just a hundred million short of being the world's largest. While its economy is only about a quarter of the size of China's (USD$1.87 trillion for India, compared with China's USD$7.32 trillion), India's demographic profile is far more favourable for long-term growth: its old age dependency ratio (the number of people over age 64 per 100 people aged 15–64) is 7.9, compared with China's 11.8. India's working-age population is also increasing and could grow by as many as 9 million people annually until 2020.[63] In fact, India's overall dependency ratio – the number of people too young and too old to work compared with the working population – will decline over the next twenty years, while in most of the world it will increase. Meanwhile, China's working-age population shrank from 2011 to 2012, and China's National Bureau of Statistics believes that it will continue to shrink until at least 2030.[64] In other words, while much of the world gets older, India is still a very young country, and a very big one to boot.

The key to India's economic success will be getting its domestic governance in order. For example, India's labour laws are notorious for making it so difficult to hire and fire workers that many companies choose not to grow rather than deal with the legal troubles involved in expanding their business. One unfortunate side effect of this is the increase in casual employment, which is typically not as productive or well-paying as above-the-board work.

However, if India's government can conquer the regulatory bottlenecks that are throttling the economy, then the country's potential is enormous. The opportunities for Canada are numerous. India's infrastructure is lacking: its railways are decades old and its electricity sector produces insufficient power for the growing population.[65] While this holds back growth on the one hand, infrastructure renewal and growth, on the other hand, is a huge opportunity.

Another area where Canada could profit from focusing its attention on India is in higher education. India's aforementioned demographic trends have created massive demand for universities and colleges, a demand that the Indian education system has been unable to satisfy. The Indian university system is plagued by unaccredited schools, a lack of qualified faculty, and fraudulent degrees, and often produces frustrated graduates who discover that they are unqualified to work in their fields of study.[66] According to India's National Association of Software and Services Companies, 75 to 85 per cent of India's university graduates are unemployable in India's high-tech and outsourcing sectors.[67] With a population hungry to enter the middle class, it may be time for Canadian universities to aggressively target and recruit Indian students.

Besides these two examples, Canada should look at India broadly. Only around 0.5 per cent of Canada's total trade in 2012 was done with India. If India is the next growth story, we cannot afford to miss it.

SOUTH KOREA

South Korea's economy is a tremendous success story, and is ripe for opportunity. Invaded by Imperial Japan during the Second World War, and then ravaged by a civil war, Korea is a relative late-comer to the world economy. South Korea's per capita GDP was a meagre $79 in 1960, and foreign aid made up over 10 per cent of South Korea's gross national product in the 1950s.[68] Despite staring into the abyss of national bankruptcy in 1997 and turning to the IMF for aid, today 50 million South Koreans boast an average annual income of $25,000, making for a trillion-dollar national economy.

Although former president Park Chung-hee typically receives much of the credit for the "Miracle on the Han River" (as South Korea's postwar boom is commonly known) for his state-led, export-oriented growth strategy, the South Korean economy has proven to be highly resilient and innovative. After the 1997 Asian financial crisis, South Korea reoriented itself by investing heavily in information and communications technology (ICT).[69] This has helped South Korea protect itself from increased Chinese competition in the lower-end manufactured exports sector (i.e., clothing, textiles, and the like) and heavy industry. ICT industries grew from 7.7 per cent of South Korea's GDP in 1997 to over 15 per cent by 2000, and the ICT industry alone added an average of 1.7 per cent to South Korea's annual GDP growth from 2001 to 2005.[70] Rather than doubling down on industries that South Korea had already invested in and taking China head-on, South Korea's ICT strategy looked to the future, and carved out a new niche for South Korean firms that relies on R&D (research and development) and high value-added products and creates well-paying jobs. Rather than a race to the bottom of the wage scale, South Korea's ICT rebirth was all about vaulting to the top.

South Korea therefore represents an interesting opportunity for Canadian firms, made even better by the recently concluded FTA. On the one hand, it is a high-wage, high-technology economy: it looks like a competitor. However, South Korea imports large amounts of food and energy, and its enterprising private sector could offer Canadian technology firms partnership opportunities to help them crack the South Korean market and use it as a springboard into the rest of Asia.

Canadians could also stand to update their view of South Korea and learn more about the country. Recent polling suggests that while the vast majority of South Koreans have positive feelings about Canada, 41 per cent of Canadians see South Korea in a negative light, and only 38 per cent feel that South Korea has a positive influence on the world.[71] Why Canadians have such a poor view of South Korea is baffling. It is one of the few stable and open democracies in East Asia. Elections are free, fair, and competitive. Seoul's human rights record has improved remarkably in the last thirty years. It boasts a cutting-edge dynamic economy. Finally, Canada and South Korea share many broader interests, primarily a peaceful and prosperous Asia-Pacific at a time when regional tensions are at a post-Cold War high. As fellow democracies, Canada and South Korea have much in common. A reinvigorated diplomatic and economic relationship is opportune.

JAPAN

Lately, when pundits comment on Japan, the common refrain is that the country is on the wane, due to a self-inflicted lost decade of slow economic growth. Indeed, the Japanese economy has only grown at an average of around 0.9 per cent a year since 2003, a pittance compared with the global average of 2.7 per cent over the same period. While we should not expect Japan's economy to grow at anywhere near the rate of Indonesia, Vietnam, or even Mexico, claims about Japan's inevitable decline are overblown. After all, Japan's greatest challenge is not economic growth, but an aging population. In fact, from 2001 to 2012, Japan's GDP growth per working-age person was the highest in the G7.[72] It is still the third-largest economy on the planet, and the world's tenth-most populous country.

Japan is also still one of the world's most innovative and dynamic economies, despite its shrinking population. In 2011, Japanese companies held three of the top ten spots in terms of patent filings,[73] and from 1997 to 2009, Japan was the world's biggest annual patent filer.[74] The Japanese economy is also very R&D-intensive: Japan spends over 3 per cent of its GDP on R&D activities every year, and over three-quarters of that spending is concentrated in private-sector enterprises, rather than in government-funded labs or universities.[75] All this means that despite Japan's aging population, Japanese firms have been able to diversify and profit by bringing new products, techniques, and technology to market. Japanese companies are also increasingly looking for foreign firms to partner on R&D.[76]

Furthermore, Japan is still one of the world's biggest manufacturing economies and an important investor in Canada. For example, Japanese car makers directly employ over 50,000 Canadians in dealerships, factories, and R&D centres, and Canada exports several times more Japanese-brand cars than it imports. Honda and Toyota alone have invested over $9 billion dollars in Canada.[77]

Finally, Japan is a quintessentially natural-resource-poor country. It has terribly small coal and oil reserves, and consequently imports over 80 per cent of its energy.[78] This means that Japan is the third-largest net oil importer in the world, and the world's largest liquefied natural gas importer. Historically, Japan has imported oil from the Middle East and Iran, which has become a political liability of late as the United States has pressured Tokyo to diversify away from Iranian oil. Canada's oil and gas (and uranium) industries should therefore not just look eastward to China and India for new markets, but keep Japan, and its 120 million consumers, firmly in their sights.

Thus, Japan's boom days may be behind it, but its economy is just as innovative and cutting-edge as ever. Strategic partnerships with Japanese businesses could provide Canadian firms with access to one of the most research-heavy economies in the world, and Japan's consumer market holds potential as an important way for Canada to diversify its energy exports.

What many of these emerging economies have in common is a degree of corporatism – a tight fusion of government policies, notably banking and growth priorities. The most dramatic example is, of course, China, but South Korea, Vietnam, Indonesia, and India in particular, have tried to emulate this government-directed growth – the overriding initial emphasis on export growth being the most common feature. Each has also sought to incubate domestic industries until they were able to compete globally. All had the relative advantage of being low-wage economies that started from a lower GDP base. The most successful countries, such as South Korea, were also able to build on a solid education foundation and a culture that rewarded merit more than lineage.

More advanced economies, like Canada's, do not have the same scope for strict government direction of economic growth, but the lesson we should absorb is that there is a need for greater coherence between government policy and private-sector initiatives designed for growth, and certainly less room for complacency about the extent to which past performance will assure future prospects.

Our trade negotiating strategy is a key instrument of government policy. The success garnered from the CETA negotiations with the EU should embolden more of the same with key emerging markets.

CONCLUSION

The challenges presented by the changing global economy are obvious. And the opportunities are huge. But, as we have discussed, there are risks too. The need for strategy, focus, and leadership is critical. Canada cannot afford to continue to fall behind. Government and business must adapt and move quickly to seize the potential in key emerging markets. The kind of strategy, and new partnerships between the public and private sectors, needed to tap these opportunities are discussed more fully in later chapters. But the key point here is that Canada has the potential to meet the demands of a rapidly changing global economy. What is missing is a determined effort to leverage our strengths and to reshape Canadian policies and priorities to serve our national interest.

4

An Age of Diminished Multilateralism

If the late 1940s and 1950s could be called the "golden age" of Canadian diplomacy as a consequence of our contribution to the creation of multilateral institutions, the second decade of the twenty-first century should be called an era of "diminished multilateralism," one where we cannot place too much stock, or faith, in formal international institutions to deliver critical global public goods. That is because, wherever one looks, global multilateral institutions are in trouble. Climate change negotiations in the United Nations have produced little in the way of concrete results other than heated rhetoric and frequent flier points for the thousands of delegates who attend these meetings on a regular basis. The UN Security Council, after an all-too-brief flurry of activism in the 1990s, has returned to Cold War-style deadlock among its permanent members, with the United States, Britain, and France on one side of the aisle and Russia and China on the other. The Doha Round of trade negotiations in the WTO produced a narrow set of agreements in Bali, Indonesia in December 2013, which will only just barely keep global trade talks alive. Even the G20, after a promising beginning at the end of the last decade, is stumbling badly.

International institutions only work well when there is leadership. However, the kind of leadership that allowed multilateral institutions to function effectively now seems absent on the world stage. The United States is not playing the kind of leadership role that it once did because of its deficits, its debt, and political gridlock in Washington. Europe, with a collective GDP larger than America's, is in the grip of long-standing economic and fiscal woes, including widespread recession and what appears to be a continuing chronic banking and financial crisis. Nor is much leadership apparent from the world's largest emerging economies – China, Brazil, and India – which have been the drivers of global economic growth and expansion in the past decade. China is both defensive and narrowly assertive of its interests.[1] As one close observer argues, when it comes to matters of global governance and multilateralism, "China is likely to repeat what it has done in East Asian regional multilateralism in the past decade: participation, engagement, pushing for cooperation in areas that would serve Chinese interests, avoiding taking excessive responsibilities, blocking initiatives that would harm its interests, and refraining from making grand proposals."[2] Russia is caught between nostalgia and ambition, and is returning to a Soviet-style foreign policy in the Middle East, in countries of Russia's "near abroad," and even in its direct dealings with Washington.

Fiscal deficits throughout the western world have also had their own direct and indirect impacts on global security and multilateral institutions. As NATO struggles with Russia's revanchism and the impact of defence budget cuts, in some cases major, it loses its capacity for influence. Official development assistance (ODA) spending is shrinking throughout the West. During tough economic times, there is also less appetite among politicians and publics alike to attack the causes of climate change through multilateral negotiations or to intervene abroad in countries that are experiencing social unrest or to deal with dictators who are turning their guns against their own citizens.

Sound economic policies are fundamental to national security and international leadership. As former World Bank head Robert Zoellick has argued, when great powers take care to live within their means by carefully managing the public purse, they are better positioned to fight wars, underwrite the provision of key global public goods, and rise to the "Olympian feats" that are sometimes required of them. When they run up massive deficits and become hostage to their creditors, they are in a weak position to do so.[3] Sound economic policy is not simply a *sine qua non* of "hard power" or military power, it is also integral to the exercise of "soft power," the diplomatic and negotiated influence derived through economic dynamism and innovation.

There is no shortage of issues that warrant global and/or regional collective action: from transnational organized crime and terrorism to climate change and pandemic disease, from cybersecurity and social media to financial regulation and economic protectionism. These challenges, by their nature, are best met through combined effort and joint multilateral undertakings. However, in the descriptive phrase of Richard Haass of the US Council on Foreign Relations, we are living in a world of "messy multilateralism" in which the United States in recent years has chosen either to stay on the sidelines or "lead from behind," and cooperation is more like a patchwork quilt of joint undertakings.[4]

The global leadership deficit is hampering the performance and effectiveness of international institutions, which are displaying their own distinctive pathologies. Some, like the G20, after a promising beginning, are stumbling. Others, like the WTO, are fumbling and badly so. While bodies like the UN Security Council are simply dropping the ball, failing to act even when their mandate calls for them to do so.

STUMBLING AFTER A PROMISING BEGINNING: THE G20

To function effectively, large international bodies with universal membership require smaller "minilateral" groupings or organizational structures to lead the common enterprise. That was the original idea behind the creation of a security council of great powers in the United Nations, based on the collective-action failures of the League of Nations in the interwar period of the last century before it succumbed to gridlock among its permanent members. It was also the premise behind the creation of the G20 to deal with the global financial and economic crisis in 2008–09.

The idea of a G20 had its origins among the finance ministers and central bank governors of the world's most powerful economies, who had begun meeting in 1999. That informal arrangement developed into the premier body for consultation on governance of the international financial system. But it would take a major global crisis to advance the idea that the first ministers of the G20 should meet too, even though countries like Canada were of the view that the G8, because it excluded some of the fastest-growing emerging economies of the developing world, was inadequate to the times. Those arguments fell on deaf ears until the 2008–09 financial and economic crisis, when the G20 political leaders' summit was born as an important forum for world leaders to meet, discuss, and address the meltdown of the US financial system, which was sending shock-waves throughout the industrialized world.

The first G20 meeting of world leaders took place in Pittsburgh in November 2008 at the behest of outgoing US president George W. Bush. At that important meeting, and those that followed, the G20 promised and subsequently provided the IMF and the regional banks with new resources to help countries deal with the crisis, issued new Special Drawing Rights (SDRs),[5] undertook a series of measures to stimulate the global economy, and adapted the governance structure of the institutional financial institutions to the changing political and economic realities.

During the crisis, governments also committed themselves to resisting the pressures of protectionism while asking the WTO to monitor lapses. Despite profound differences of opinion between Europe and the United States about the need for greater oversight of financial regulation and the need to stimulate economic growth, these differences did not disrupt the ongoing summitry process. As the *Los Angeles Times* concluded after the second meeting of G20 leaders in London in April 2009, "[t]he measures announced at the Group of 20 summit ... may not constitute the 'new global deal' ... But the outcome still surprised many observers with its unusually substantive achievements."[6]

Since the April 2009 summit, the G20 has met more or less continuously to re-engineer the global financial system to prevent a recurrence of the crisis and maintain the global flow of capital. It has put issues on the table that were once regarded as the exclusive province of sovereign governments, notably monetary policy, exchange rates, and debt levels, thereby taking preliminary steps toward longer-term global macroeconomic governance. It has also continued to counsel against growing pressures for protectionist measures in a period of deep global recession.

But the consensus and political will of this new entity quickly wilted once the initial panic subsided. Differing rates and patterns of economic growth diluted shared fears and common resolve. Domestic challenges, notably those in Europe and the US, gradually displaced attention to broader concerns. Concerns about currency manipulation were aired vociferously but not resolved.

Given the different patterns of growth and the radically different political systems represented at the G20, it is perhaps not surprising that its relevance and capacity for consensus is now very much in question. Annual photo ops for leaders can be attractive in themselves but there is a problem putting an end to summitry, no matter how minuscule the result, because of entrenched bureaucratic and political interests.

Some useful monitoring continues, notably among finance ministries and central bank representatives, and through new mechanisms like the Financial Stability Board (FSB), but there are serious doubts whether, in the absence of overall leadership, the G20 will still serve as the key negotiating forum of world leaders to prevent future financial crises or to inject greater certainty and stability into a highly fluid and complex global economy.

As broad multilateral initiatives fade, a combination of aggressive nationalism – everyone for themselves – and regional or like-minded groupings will undoubtedly fill the power vacuum.

FUMBLING BADLY: COPENHAGEN, DOHA, AND DUBAI

When it comes to the problems of climate change or international trade, or even negotiating new governance arrangements for the Internet, international institutions are also stumbling badly.

Climate Change

To date, ongoing climate change negotiations, which are held under the auspices of the United Nations Environment Programme, have produced little in the way of a legally binding agreement to reduce greenhouse gas emissions. The 2009 Copenhagen Summit was attended by 159 heads of state and no fewer than 40,000 representatives of governments and intergovernmental organizations, non-governmental organizations, and faith-based groups, one of the largest UN gatherings ever. The results were meagre. Though there was agreement on the infrastructure requirements for effective global climate change cooperation, including improvements to the Clean Development Mechanism of the Kyoto Protocol, the rest was fluff. The Copenhagen Accord, much like previous UN conferences on the subject, "expressed clear a political intent to constrain carbon and respond to climate change, in both the short and long term," but little in the way of an actual concrete action plan to combat the problem.[7]

Many saw the 2009 Copenhagen Summit on climate change as the world's last chance to make a deal. However, there were major divisions that stood in the way of a meaningful agreement. Although key developing countries, led by China, India, and Brazil, said they would cut their own carbon emissions, they were all marching to a different drummer in terms of baselines, specific reduction measures, and whether targets should be legally binding.[8] They also wanted rich developed nations to cut their own emissions while providing major funding for technology transfer and adaptation to developing countries. Although the United States said that it would cut its own emissions to 17 per cent below 2005 levels by 2020 – as did Canada – the US Congress was not on board.[9] In contrast, the European Union, which tried to play a key leading role at Copenhagen, only agreed to cut its own emissions by 30 per cent from 1990 levels by 2020 if other countries followed suit.[10] Saudi Arabia, the world's biggest oil producer, was opposed to any kind of new climate change agreement.[11]

The climate change agenda has in a sense been hijacked by environmentalist zealots whose emotional calls for dramatic reductions clash with the problems of sputtering global economic growth. Apocalyptic forecasts of global oblivion may generate headlines and funds for the cause but when electorates are faced with a choice between saving jobs and saving the planet, the immediate challenge tends to be the priority.

Given the highly integrated nature of our economy with that of the US, the most important baby step for Canada would be to design a common approach to carbon emissions with the US, one that neither favours nor discriminates against the economic prospects of either country.

The Copenhagen meeting on climate change underscored the problems with large-scale, unwieldy UN gatherings where many smaller countries have a voice (and vote) equal to bigger countries, who are generally the major source of the problem but also the essential contributors to its solution. Like the earlier Kyoto meeting on climate change, which produced unrealistic and unbalanced targets to reduce greenhouse gas emissions, Copenhagen also underscored the pitfalls of biting off more than you can chew. It is sometimes better to take an incremental approach to a problem, by scaling down ambitious targets to ones that are manageable. Baby steps are sometimes a way to generate momentum and build political support before you do something big.

Copenhagen also showed the need for the international community to work harder to develop effective compliance and verification mechanisms on climate change and to build confidence that countries actually do what they say they intend to do. There was an enormous lack of trust among those sitting at the table at Copenhagen. Many countries feared that others would not honour their negotiated treaty commitments because of the difficulties of monitoring carbon emissions under a voluntary reporting system. President Obama reportedly enraged the Chinese delegates, to the point where they nearly walked out of the talks, when he threatened to use satellite surveillance to monitor Chinese compliance with any agreement.[12] In contrast, the WTO offers a good model for dealing with these problems via its dispute-settlement procedures and monitoring mechanisms for the review of trade policies. Like the WTO, or international security bargains like the Nuclear Non-Proliferation Treaty or the Chemical Weapons Convention, an effective climate-change agreement will also need clear rules, effective monitoring, and penalties for non-compliance.

The absence of leading representatives of the global business community at Copenhagen pointed to another set of problems with the way the international community, and the UN in particular, has approached climate change. The problem can only be tackled by energizing a coalition of business and environmental interests to work for imaginative solutions. Some businesses will clearly benefit from carbon reductions. Others can create new benefits by developing alternative products and processes. The reality is that major change occurs when advocacy and key interest groups in different constituencies come together to support change. That is what produced the Montreal Protocol to protect the ozone layer. It is probably too late to galvanize such a coalition now, and it would take real leadership to do it. Former US vice president Al Gore, who has been a champion of measures to combat climate change, did not succeed because he made less of a pitch to business interests than to environmentalists. Yet, ultimately, such a coalition will be necessary if any agreement is to be reached.

The negotiating impasse at the ongoing UN climate change meetings is not insurmountable. But it is going to take creativity and a lot of hard thinking outside the box of traditional multilateral diplomacy to break it.

Trade

The Doha Round of multilateral trade negotiations began with great fanfare in December 2001 and was seen politically as a potentially strong antidote to the threat of international terrorism in the immediate wake of the 9/11 attacks on America. Since the Second World War, repeated rounds of trade liberalization negotiations have not only galvanized economic growth but provided a measure of stability in a world otherwise embroiled in Cold War rivalries. Trade liberalization was a major differentiator for market economies, epitomized by the US and its allies versus the non-market command economies of the USSR and its Warsaw Pact confederates.

The Kennedy Round of multilateral trade negotiations (1963–67) was the sixth in succession following the Second World War. Its primary purpose was to resolve trade matters between the US and the new EEC (European Economic Community) and EFTA (European Free Trade Association) entities of Europe. Modest steps were also undertaken to reduce barriers to agriculture trade and to increase market access for developing countries. The negotiation's end result was an average cut in tariffs of around 35 per cent across the board for developed countries with exceptions for sensitive products like textiles, steel, and chemicals, and much lower reductions for agriculture.[13]

The Tokyo Round (1973–76) that followed produced tariff reductions by developed countries similar in magnitude to those of the Kennedy Round. More significantly, these negotiations saw the first major effort to bring a range of non-tariff barriers (NTBS) under international disciplines, with agreements on, for example, customs valuation, technical barriers to trade, anti-dumping, subsidies and countervailing measures, and government procurement. Because these provisions required changes to domestic legislation, for the first time the US administration needed to obtain "fast track" authority from Congress to ratify the agreement.

The Uruguay Round (1986–94) was even more comprehensive, creating the WTO and putting the GATT on a more permanent footing. In addition to further tariff reductions, including those on agriculture and textiles, this agreement addressed trade in services (banking and insurance), intellectual property, and investment policy trade distortions. It also strengthened dispute settlement provisions and definitions for subsidies. Developing countries were provided special terms for market access and a slower track for tariff reductions.

It is worth noting that an important strategic objective for the US decision to conclude free trade with Canada and subsequently Mexico (NAFTA) was to pointedly prod the Europeans to a successful conclusion of the Uruguay Round. It certainly helped.

The basic objective of the Doha Round, launched in December 2001, was to bring developing nations more formally into the WTO architecture. To date it has proven a hill too high to climb for a variety of reasons. US leadership on trade – especially absent Cold War rivalries – is not what it once was. China joined the WTO at the meeting that launched the Doha Round. Besides, with 154 members now at the table, the WTO seemed too cumbersome for any substantive consensus. Earlier rounds had been helped by a steering group of sorts, the Quadrilateral group, made up of the US, EU, Japan, and Canada. No such executive group has emerged to help drive Doha. In addition, this round has failed to arouse much support from those who should stand to benefit: the private sector. (For one consultation in Toronto, the Canadian trade minister's venue was the Prince Edward Island Room at the Royal York Hotel – the smallest room available, clearly indicating that the negotiation was not much of a priority for the Canadian private sector.)

Emerging powers like Brazil and India were determined to play according to their new economic strength, demanding better access from the developed world while offering few concessions on access to their own markets. India was often seen as the principal obstacle to progress but the lack of strong US leadership was, according to Jagdish Bhagwati of Columbia University, the real reason negotiations faltered.[14] However, the real problem was, increasingly, China, whose extraordinary economic growth made both developed and developing countries think long and hard before agreeing to liberalize their import regimes. By 2008, the general view had become that the round could only be concluded successfully if there was a genuine meeting of minds between the US and China.

The result has been a paralyzed Doha Round, which is being eclipsed by a flurry of bilateral and regional trade initiatives, notably the TPP negotiations, which appear to be the top priority now for the US. All of this does not bode well for those who hope the world will continue to drop trade barriers and adopt a single set of non-discriminatory trade laws.

With the appointment of the Brazilian diplomat Roberto Carvalho de Azevêdo as director general of the WTO in May 2013, there has been a brief spurt of optimism culminating in consensus at Bali in November 2013 on "trade facilitation" measures. These are aimed essentially at streamlining cumbersome and costly customs inspection procedures and are estimated by the World Bank to save USD$1 trillion over time. Dismantling bureaucratic inefficiencies is, of course, easier than the give and take essential to a meaningful reduction of trade barriers but this modest agreement at least keeps the spirit and value of multilateral trade negotiations more alive than dead.

The world has not been short of new initiatives, but trade liberalization can be a hard political sale in democracies at the best of times. It is even more difficult in a period of prolonged recession, which helps explain why there has been so little actual progress in recent years. Inevitably, the instinct to protect and preserve what a country has is more immediate and more salient to politicians than the promise of growth. To gain support for any trade agreement, governments and stakeholders alike are obliged to demonstrate convincingly how its potential benefits outweigh the risks.

Canada has jockeyed mightily to keep pace with the changes occurring but, until very recently, there have been more trade negotiations launched than concluded.

In October 2013, after almost six years of negotiations, the government concluded negotiations for CETA with the EU – the most significant trade deal for Canada since NAFTA. Although the approval process in all twenty-eight EU member states could still take eighteen months or more, with CETA Canada would be the only developed country with free trade access to both the US and EU markets. Tariffs on more than 9,000 items will be eliminated immediately and the agreement covers new ground in areas such as intellectual property and trade in services. When fully implemented, it is expected to yield lower prices and greater choice for Canadian consumers. The FTA with South Korea will provide more immediate benefits.

Needed next are trade agreements with significant Asian economies like Thailand, Japan, and India, signalling a clear commitment to markets offering real potential to Canadian exporters. Additional trade agreements in Asia would give Canada a basis to diversify away from exclusive dependence on the US market for energy products.

The Internet

Multi-stakeholder multilateralism is another feature of the evolving international system, especially on issues like Internet governance, where a wide variety of state and non-state actors are involved in negotiating, managing, maintaining, and developing rules of behaviour for complex technical systems where many different interests are involved. But it, too, offers no panacea, as illustrated by the growing problems of Internet governance.

At the end of 2012, the nations of the world convened at the Gulf port city of Dubai for the World Conference on International Telecommunications (WCIT) to renegotiate key provisions of the International Telecommunications Regulations, a UN treaty that governs the use of the airwaves, but not, thus far, the Internet. The gathering was fractious and deadlocked because some countries, including Brazil, China, India, and Russia, according to their critics, wanted to bring the Internet, which is currently under private management and ownership through key regulatory bodies like ICANN (Internet Corporation for Assigned Names and Numbers), which assign domain names, under the control of the United Nations in a not-so-secret bid to control and regulate information flows across cyberspace. They were opposed by the United States and many – though not all – western nations, who tend to favour the status quo and a liberal, informal, multi-stakeholder-negotiated regime that is generally free of greater state control and serves the interests of many, albeit from an American base.

WCIT was a frontal assault on the multi-stakeholder model of Internet governance, whose ramifications we are still struggling with and whose consequences will be felt for a long time to come.

There was clearly a wide range of different motives at play: a bid for content control by authoritarian regimes; rent-seeking behaviour on the part of many developing nations or countries where telcos are losing business to the Internet; and frustration on the part of countries with low Internet penetration that they are not getting the kind of assistance they need to build their own IT infrastructure and capacities.

Matters were not helped by the antics of WCIT Chairman Mohamed al Ghanim, who called for a simple majority vote on the proposed treaty framework, contravening a cardinal rule of UN meetings that deliberations should be by consensus.

The issues on the table are complex, but they boil down to the following: (1) granting states new powers of taxation over Internet usage; (2) issues of privacy and whether governments should play a greater role in surveillance and monitoring of the Internet by acquiring access to the real names and identities of online users; and (3) transferring management authority for the Internet from ICANN, the private, multi-stakeholder body that currently oversees the use and operations of the Internet, by, for example, coordinating the assignment of Internet domain names and user protocols to the ITU (International Telecommunication Union) or a new intergovernmental authority.

The multi-stakeholder battle for control over the Internet in Dubai is likely to be a prolonged one in which the December 2012 meeting was simply the first salvo of a difficult and protracted set of negotiations. Although the main protagonists in Dubai are nation-states, they are not the only actors or interests in what is shaping up to be a struggle of epic proportions, which has only been accentuated by the revelations of Edward Snowden about the intelligence-gathering activities of the NSA (National Security Agency). These have not only embarrassed the US government and compromised its relations with some of its closest allies, they have also strengthened the position of those countries that seek to dismantle the current multi-stakeholder model of Internet governance by placing it under national governmental control. The Snowden revelations also underscore a principal challenge for western democracies: how to strike the right balance between surveillance in the name of security and individual rights of privacy.

The other actors in this continuing global negotiation include the major Internet providers (the top twenty companies that field 90 per cent of the world's Internet traffic); movie studios, songwriters, publishers, and other producers of artistic or intellectual content that can be exchanged and downloaded on the Internet; technology companies like Google, eBay, and Twitter that do business with those who operate sites where "free" movies and songs can be uploaded; political activists; the champions of free speech who populate the academy and the legal community; business and commercial interests of every stripe who ply their wares on the Internet, including banks and credit card companies; hackers who challenge computer security systems for a variety of good and bad reasons; criminal elements who exploit the Internet for their own shady ends; law enforcement agencies seeking to protect the public from Internet abuses such as child pornography; and ordinary citizens who have real concerns about their personal safety and right to privacy when they go online.

But the fractious and difficult meeting on Internet governance at Dubai exposed a much deeper problem. As the Internet Society points out, it is not at all clear that "a treaty environment was the best way to address many of the very important Internet policy challenges raised by countries at the WCIT."[15] If the ambitions of some countries are eventually realized we could be moving into a world where the World Wide Web is neither as worldly nor as expansive as it has been, where access is constrained by different Internet rules and protocols, and where the global regime for information increasingly resembles the patchwork quilt we now have in global trade. That is one reason why the ITU should not assume greater control over the Internet – because of the not-so-benign interests of countries like China and Russia.

Canada, a technological leader in the telecommunications field, and one of the most wired countries in the world, is committed to the multi-stakeholder model of Internet governance. Like others, it recognizes that the current governance model – out of political necessity – will have to be adapted to satisfy the needs of developing countries who aspire to develop their own infrastructure and connectivity to the Internet, even as it remains anchored to the kinds of private–public partnerships that currently manage and maintain the Internet. As a credible and independent voice on these matters, Canada is well-positioned to help take the lead in developing a new consensus on how the Internet should be managed and governed. By bolstering public demand for transparency, the Snowden controversy creates both liabilities for Canada (because of our close relationship with the US) and the opportunity to stake out a unique vision of a democratic and liberal Internet.

DROPPING THE BALL IN SYRIA

At the beginning of this century, the notion that western democracies have a responsibility to protect civilians from the ravages of mad dictators and civil war was in the ascendant in the United Nations. Today, it lies in shreds in Syria in the bloody, rubble-strewn streets of Damascus, Aleppo, and many other towns and cities.

Syria's civil war is a clear indictment of the world's multilateral security architecture, and a clarion call for Canada to lead efforts to reform a system that has strayed from the principles of humanitarian intervention, which were given their fullest expression in the 2001 report of the International Commission on Intervention and State Sovereignty. That report argued that the UN should use military force to prevent massive human rights violations and mass killings in civil conflicts and that state sovereignty is conditional.[16] This second, somewhat more contentious proposition, advances the idea that states that indiscriminately kill their own citizens in large numbers, or fail to prevent other actors from doing so, cede their sovereignty, and that the world has a clear moral responsibility to act on behalf of the victims.

The "responsibility to protect" doctrine or R2P, as it came to be known, was the brainchild of Canada's former foreign affairs minister Lloyd Axworthy. Although Axworthy's name never appeared on the actual report – that honour went to the Commission's two co-chairs, Algerian diplomat Mohamed Sahnoun and former Australian foreign minister Gareth Evans – he and officials in the Canadian Department of Foreign Affairs were its chief architects and proponents.

The main principles of the report were subsequently embraced by the General Assembly of the United Nations in 2005 and successive resolutions of the Security Council as well as a number of regional organizations such as the African Union. First in Kosovo, and subsequently in Libya, with NATO's efforts to help unseat Libyan dictator Muammar Qaddafi, it appeared as if the idea of R2P had some currency.

However, the brief precedent set by Libya proved to be short-lived because key members of the Security Council – Russia and China – did not want it followed in Syria. Russia had a major political stake in supporting the al-Assad regime and, along with China, opposed any kind of UN-sponsored military action that would intrude into the sovereignty of states.

The stage was first set for military intervention in Libya when two regional organizations took quick action a few weeks after the public uprisings against Qaddafi's regime began. Qaddafi had few friends in the Arab world so the Arab League's condemnation came as no surprise. In the case of the African Union, Qaddafi had more friends, but his actions clearly did not sit well with the African states that had turned to democracy. The Arab League suspended Libya's membership in late February 2011 and the African Union issued a strong denunciation of the Libyan government.

As the situation in Libya further deteriorated, the Security Council swung into action and authorized member states to "take all necessary measures ... to protect civilians" under Chapter VII of the UN Charter, establishing a no-fly zone (NFZ), an arms embargo, and economic sanctions.[17] The rationale for the imposition of a NFZ over Libya was ostensibly to avert a bloodbath by Gaddafi's forces, specifically in the cities of Benghazi and Tobruk.

On 19 March 2011, the US joined with Britain, Canada, France, and Italy in engaging militarily with Libya and NATO itself took over control of the no-fly-zone operation from the coalition of countries that were already involved in the Libyan operations, which by now also included Belgium, Denmark, the Netherlands, Norway, and Spain. Although the US essentially led from the back seat, this NATO campaign was supported actively by Qatar, Jordan, and the United Arab Emirates, and was also joined by Sweden. By August 2011, the Libyan National Transitional Council, with NATO's support, had taken over the country and killed Gaddafi. Presented to the world as a success, the mission ended on 31 October 2011.

The Libyan intervention involved the ad hoc use of NATO resources, which was negotiated by a coalition of the capable and committed. Moreover, as seen in high-level public statements, agreeing to openly disagree did not, in the end, prevent NATO's activists from mounting an effective air campaign or prevent it from recruiting non-NATO participants, such as Qatar, to join the effort.

However, there were significant underlying rifts between the Security Council and NATO over the operations. UN Security Council Resolution 1973 for the NFZ was notable not by who voted for it, but who abstained: Russia, Germany, India, Brazil, and China. There was clearly little appetite among the so-called emerging powers of the international system for this undertaking. As for the NATO coalition, Turkey and many of NATO's eastern European members shared Germany's reservations about the mission. To add another complicating layer, Turkey also had significant trade and investment links with Libya. The Libyan mission was thus a NATO-led mission without many of its members. NATO à la carte was convenient in this instance, but the alliance was not acting as a whole. Further, the Benghazi bungle, which led to the tragic murder of US ambassador

Christopher Stevens and three of his colleagues, was a colossal intelligence failure that did not inspire confidence in US leadership in the region.

In the Syrian case, the Arab League went straight to the UN to secure a UN resolution, hoping for a similar response and outcome to what had been achieved in Libya, to unseat Syria's unpopular and repressive ruler Bashar al-Assad who had turned his guns against his people as the popular protests of the Arab Spring engulfed the country. The League's proactive overture to the UN complemented its own efforts under the Arab League Action Plan of 22 November 2011 to achieve a peaceful resolution of the crisis, including the deployment of an Arab League observer mission in Syria. The observer mission was unable to carry out its monitoring tasks effectively and was suspended barely a month after arriving in Syria.

The UN Security Council draft resolution on Syria, which had initially been spurred by the League, was months in the making and the result of painstaking, behind-the-scenes negotiations. Nine countries in all voted for it, with Brazil, India, Lebanon, and South Africa abstaining. Although the draft resolution did not call for immediate sanctions, it laid out some clear markers for Bashar al-Assad's embattled regime to change its ways, including harsh measures to follow, such as the possible use of force, if it did not. In the careful wording of the resolution, the Americans, French, and British thought they had finally secured the support of Russia and China. It turned out they were wrong: both Russia and China vetoed the resolution, thus effectively scuttling any future action by the Security Council to unseat al-Assad.[18]

The Friends of Syria initiative was a regionally, and globally, inspired collective response to the deadlock in the UN Security Council over Syria, numbering some sixty countries, including Canada. It was supposed to be a show of unity by the international community on how to deal with al-Assad and help build up Syria's opposition. Although it convened regularly, issued communiqués, and coordinated sanctions by its members, the Friends of Syria grouping has proven to be more of a wailing Greek chorus than a spur to coordinated, collective action to bring regime change to Syria.

UN-sponsored sanctions have hurt the al-Assad regime, but Russian opposition and outright circumvention of the arms embargo against Syria, combined with Syria's porous borders with neighbouring countries, has meant that al-Assad has been able to secure the resources and materiel he needs to keep on fighting and stay in power.

In Syria, the Libyan approach or "model" for intervention ran into trouble because Russia and China believed that NATO had vastly exceeded its mandate in using the NFZ as a pretext to attack Qaddafi's forces and support the opposition in its efforts to topple his regime. The Russians, in particular, did not want a repeat of the Libyan experience in Syria, where they have direct strategic interests and have done everything to ensure that al-Assad remains in power.

Syrian dictator Bashar al-Assad's remarkable comeback when many were writing his obituary is a stark reminder that national self-interest and sovereignty trump humanitarian principles and R2P when really put to the test. The violence in Syria is increasingly looking like a proxy war between Iran and Saudi Arabia, with strong sectarian overtones as Sunni and Shi'ite slaughter one another. Western interventions have, so far, been timid, such as Turkey allowing the Free Syrian Army to set up in its territory while declining to offer any robust support to the Syrian opposition, or the US's limited effort to supply the secular opposition. Even when evidence mounted that the Syrian government had indiscriminately used Sarin gas in the suburbs of Damascus, killing – at a minimum – hundreds of civilians, the global response was tepid at best. While the US pressed for airstrikes, a lack of an appetite for intervention among the US public forced the American government to promise that any action would be an "unbelievably small, limited kind of effort."[19]

Following the 2013 G20 summit of world leaders in St Petersburg, where President Putin allowed Syria to be a topic of dinner table conversation on the opening night, he bested the Americans with his own game plan to dismantle Syria's chemical weapons arsenal – one of the biggest in the world. The agreement took Obama off the hook on military strikes where, had the matter gone to a vote in the US Congress, the president likely would have suffered a humiliating defeat.

As implemented, the agreement takes chemical weapons out of Syria's military equation, which is a laudable result. But it is also important to remind ourselves what the agreement did not do. It did not end Syria's civil war, in which more than 140,000 Syrians have been killed, many of its victims children. Over two million Syrians have fled the country and many are living in abysmal deteriorating conditions in refugee camps in Lebanon, Jordan, Turkey, and Iraq. Another 6.5 million have been displaced internally.

Nor did the agreement see the removal of Syria's leader, something President Obama had repeatedly called for. Assad was not penalized for gassing his own people. Nor is he being hauled before the International Criminal Court, revealing the limitations of that body. Instead, he is more secure than ever, Syria's opposition is sharply divided, and western "support" is in complete disarray. Obama acknowledged that dictators "depend on the world to look the other way" when they commit atrocities, but that is what has happened in Syria as the "diplomatic path" has been pursued. The North Atlantic world did a great deal of hand-wringing, but otherwise sat on the sidelines and watched Syria's fires burn, with few ideas, no will, and no appetite to stop the conflagration.

The Libyan intervention thus stands as a one-off example of a "successful" hands-on intervention, even as that country descends into anarchy and chaos in the aftermath of Qaddafi's overthrow. However, the Libyan intervention is not precedent-setting for the simple reason that some members of the UN Security Council didn't like the precedent, and there was profound disagreement among the P5 (Permanent Five) about how to deal with Syria. But it also points to a much deeper set of problems with the UN's role in the maintenance of international peace and security – the deadlock and paralysis that occur when permanent members of the Council differ on fundamentals and when there is more than one set of hands on the wheel and more than one foot on the brake.

Vladimir Putin's putsch in Crimea, and the threat against Ukraine itself, highlights even more dramatically both the waning influence of multilateral institutions in times of global crises and the diminishing inclination of the US to assert firm leadership. By invoking *realpolitik* tactics to advance Russia's sphere of influence, Putin has exploited the vacuum and accentuated the difficulty that democracies now have: resisting without redress actions that flout the norms of international law and national sovereignty.

CHANGES NEEDED?

Multilateral institutions have long been a key instrument of Canadian foreign policy and a critical vehicle for advancing Canada's interests in the world. We were, to paraphrase Dean Acheson, "present at the creation"[20] of the UN when its charter was signed in San Francisco in 1945. We were also instrumental in the subsequent

formation of the IMF and the World Bank, two Bretton Woods institutions that allowed for the continuing growth of international
financial markets and trade in the postwar years. Our involvement
in the creation of these institutions established Canada's place as a
major player in the evolution of the global political economy of the
postwar era, a role that we have continued to play constructively
right up to the present day.

But one does not have to be a hardened devotee of *realpolitik* to
appreciate that, as the above examples illustrate, international institutions are in trouble and increasingly dysfunctional. This is not to
say that there is no value to the UN. The work it does in development, in providing humanitarian assistance to those in dire need,
and managing and preventing conflict through the good offices of
the secretary general are essential to global security. The UN Charter also remains the basic rule book of international relations, which
most countries see is in their interests to respect. In the words of
Canada's former UN ambassador, Paul Heinbecker, the Charter and
the 500 multilateral treaties negotiated under UN auspices make the
UN "the central operating system" of international relations and the
principal arena for multilateral negotiations.[21]

However, the major bodies of the UN, and the UN Security Council – which is supposed to stand at the apex of the global security
system – are failing to meet the test on the most critical problems
of global security. The Security Council in particular continues to
flounder, though it has long been the subject of repeated attempts
at reform.

For two decades, the Open-ended Working Group on Security
Council Reform has met to review and discuss different proposals,
but there has been only one successful reform of the membership of
the Council. That was during the height of the Cold War in 1965
when non-permanent membership of the Council was increased
from six to ten members by a two-thirds vote of the UN General
Assembly and with the approval of the five permanent members of
the Council itself. That decision was taken to make the Council a
more representative body in the wake of decolonization. It is tempt-
ing to say that the problem with the Working Group is its "open-
ended" nature, which by definition means that it will never reach
closure. However, that is not where the real problem lies. As discussed above, the real problem lies with its permanent members,
some of whom are unreceptive to reform.

Canada's position on the UN Security Council reform has been to not formally endorse any of the proposals that have been advanced on changing the Council's composition. The only exception was during Prime Minister Brian Mulroney's tenure – when Canada formally endorsed Japan's bid for a permanent seat – an endorsement that was later retracted by Prime Minister Jean Chrétien at some cost to Canada's bilateral relationship with Japan.

Until Canada lost its bid for a non-permanent seat on the Council, it is probably fair to say that that the main reason we were not too keen on Security Council reform is that the status quo worked well for us. We got to run for a seat every ten years and, until the last round of elections for which we were eligible, we always won. We were also less keen on the reform proposals that came forward and on which there was greater consensus because they tended to favour regional groupings or major countries in the developing world, who got preference in the allocation of new seats, not us.

Canada, for reasons of its own self-interest, cannot afford to be a passive bystander on the issue of UN Security Council reform any longer. Our position should be no more vetoes for permanent members of the Council. It is laughable that Britain and France, who are both European members, each wield a veto in the Council. Europe should have one voice, not two, on the Council. It is also highly questionable for Russia and indeed China to be allowed to exercise a veto, especially in light of their recent performance on Syria. Perhaps vetoes should be abandoned in favour of a super-majority plurality. Japan, Germany, India, and Brazil should also become permanent members of the Security Council. These countries are simply too big and too influential to be excluded. Japan and Germany, in particular, are also major contributors to the UN's operations and budget.

The number of rotating or non-permanent members should also be increased, perhaps even doubled. Among non-permanent members, a specific number of seats should be reserved on a rotational basis for those countries who are the major financial contributors to the UN. Under the current definition of "major-" and "middle"-level contributors, twenty-eight countries would be eligible. Canada has been the seventh-biggest contributor to the UN's regular budget since 1999. Such a formula would thus guarantee us a seat and on a more regular basis than the formula that exists now.

Table 1 shows the top twenty contributors to the UN's regular budget in 2010, in terms of the percentage of the budget they fund.

Table 1
Top twenty contributors to the United Nations regular budget, 2010

1 *United States* (22%)	11 South Korea (2.2%)
2 Japan (12.5%)	12 Australia (1.9%)
3 Germany (8%)	13 Netherlands (1.8%)
4 *United Kingdom* (6.6%)	14 Brazil (1.6%)
5 *France* (6.1%)	15 *Russia* (1.6%)
6 Italy (4.9%)	16 Switzerland (1.1%)
7 Canada (3.2%)	17 Belgium (1%)
8 *China* (3.2%)	18 Sweden (1%)
9 Spain (3.2%)	19 Norway (0.8%)
10 Mexico (2.3%)	20 Austria (0.8%)
Top 20 account for 86.4% of the regular budget	

Source: United Nations, *Status of Contributions as at 31 December 2010*, 2010, ST/ADM/SER.B/828.

The P5 members of the Security Council, all of whom have a veto, are italicized. Note that nuclear-armed China and Russia, with their privileged veto status, contribute less to the UN budget than Canada and several other countries.

It is high time that the principle "no taxation without represen-tation" was applied to the UN and the membership rules of the Security Council. It is a principle that is fundamental to responsible stewardship and effective governance. But there is also an import-ant precedent to this principle within the UN itself. Current finan-cial contributions to the Bretton Woods institutions, i.e., the World Bank and the IMF, determine the weight of the vote of members of the governing councils in these two bodies. The reform of both is taking place on this basis, as it should in the main organs of the UN itself.

The remaining seats in the Council could be allocated to the devel-oping world but in a way that would ensure that each region (Africa, Latin America and the Caribbean, and Asia) receives fair representa-tion according to the number of states in each region.

If there is no progress on UN reform, Canada, like the British col-onists of the thirteen colonies, needs a "Plan B." We should start reducing our regular budgetary contribution to the UN by 10 to 20 per cent or make a greater contribution to those UN agencies we already support and whose work we deem worthwhile. Such a move would send a strong signal that we are serious about UN reform, and, since we are the seventh-largest contributor to the UN regular budget, others would take note and perhaps even follow our lead.

Canada's financial contributions to multilateral agencies are also in the front rank but lack both coherence and strategic purpose. Almost half of our ODA disbursements are channelled into various global agencies like the World Bank but without much in the way of focus or relevance to Canada's foreign-policy priorities. For instance, Canada contributes more than half a billion dollars annually to the World Food Programme and the Food and Agricultural Organization in Rome but responsibility is scattered across Finance, Agriculture, and what was CIDA to the point where our ability to influence the operations of these institutions in a way that serves Canadian interests is lost in the shuffle. Despite the size of our contributions, in many of these agencies we are little more than bystanders or second-tier monitors. There is a pressing need for structural reform of decision-making in Ottawa on our allocations so that what we spend links more directly with our foreign policy.

Canada also needs to rethink the basis of its involvement in large-scale UN conference diplomacy. The reasons for deadlock are apparent. They include poor problem definition and inadequate understanding of the stakes that are involved for all concerned; poorly assembled bargaining tables, which plague participation; constraints on key participants' capacity to deliver because of domestic opposition; and a failure to agree to deals, owing to the belief that others are conceding less.

We need to be more realistic in our approaches to multilateral diplomacy. In the case of a complex problem like climate change, incremental strategies that break down the issues into bite-sized pieces are the order of the day. Modest steps beginning on our own continent can help to generate momentum and build political support before something big and comprehensive is attempted.

Having too many people in the room can also block the possibilities for further agreement on a more comprehensive settlement because parties are reluctant to move beyond the status quo. Negotiations that go on for too long and continue to break self-imposed deadlines to reach an agreement, such as the Doha Round of trade negotiations in the WTO, should be terminated. Those situations call for drastic surgery and the creation of new forums with fewer countries in the room to discuss issues and develop solutions.

Negotiators – and that includes our own negotiators – also have to recognize the importance of bringing key domestic constituencies

onside, but not in a way that hands them a veto or substitutes endless rounds of public consultation for leadership and action. Major
change occurs when advocacy and key interest groups come together
to support new negotiations and are led by those who are supposed
to lead. Negotiating deadlocks are broken when key business interests and other groups in civil society rally behind a cause and work
with, not against, governments to move issues and negotiating agendas forward.

Finally, the bigger lesson of the G20 is that institutions have a shelf
life and a clear expiry date. They are not always like fine wine, which
gets better as it ages. It is vitally important to be flexible, creative,
and to be prepared to improvise during a major global crisis. That
is why the G20 was created. That is why its forerunner, the G8, also
in the midst of a major global economic crisis, was created. Canada
can take great pride in the development of both institutions. But
when such bodies have done their work and completed what they set
out to do, it is time to shut them down. That is because meetings of
global leaders are hugely costly affairs in terms of time, money, and
political and bureaucratic energy. And if such meetings produce little
in the way of concrete results, it will only feed the frustration of a
public that has grown weary of photo ops and that ultimately takes
the hit in the pocketbook when world leaders assemble, as Canadian
taxpayers know all too well.

Make no mistake. The world and Canada need viable and effective multilateral institutions. But we can't keep on drifting the way
we have, believing that the UN is serving our interests or doing what
it is supposed to. Its reform is urgent. And Canada must act to secure
those reforms while also thinking carefully about how to design
future institutions.

5

Managing New Global Security Threats

Today, citizens and leaders around the world see the world not as a Manichean struggle between two competing political systems – communism versus democracy – but in more immediate if disaggregated terms. International security is broken into many parts as people and their governments attempt to address a wide range of different security challenges and threats. Many of these threats are generated within individual societies, but they also spread across borders to their surrounding environment, and at times become affected by unhealthy regional dynamics. To further complicate the picture, today's security threats encompass a whole series of other factors, such as the rise of Islamic extremism, sectarian strife, terrorism, nuclear proliferation, piracy, narco-trafficking, transnational crime, and mounting challenges to political authority as citizens are mobilized and empowered through the Internet and social networks.

Military and economic power is also increasingly dispersed, but after what George Will called the "holiday from history"[1] after the end of the Cold War, geopolitical rivalries are returning to the world stage. This is in part because the US is suffering a self-inflicted malaise. Without the Soviet Union to focus American energies and create a strategic imperative for US policy, American foreign policy took on a sort of discretionary flavour. Today, the American people, after a decade of wars of both necessity and choice, no longer have the appetite to be the world's security provider of last resort. In many ways, the US has "willed itself into weakness,"[2] and left room for others to flex their muscles. Additionally, while the US is still the world's pre-eminent military and economic power, it now has to share its geopolitical space with ascendant powers such as China,

India, and Brazil, and a resurgent Russia and Japan, not to mention other centres of political and economic power and influence.

The Center for International Development and Conflict Management at the University of Maryland, which tracks global trends in armed violence, points out that, although there was a steady decline in the number of active conflicts around the globe immediately following the end of the Cold War, the trend might now be reversing, with a resurgence of armed conflict and violence in many countries. Furthermore, many of the peace agreements that were concluded in the 1980s and 1990s to end sectarian strife have failed. So, while the number of "new" conflicts in the world has remained low in recent years, old simmering grievances are reigniting in spasms of violence.[3] Since 1982, the number of annual terrorist attacks that have involved the "loss of life, serious injury, or major property damage" has risen steadily,[4] and the horrific attacks on the United States on 11 September 2001 have ushered in a new wave of political violence that has ravaged cities like Baghdad, Islamabad, Kabul, and Mumbai.[5] So too have drone counterattacks against terrorist groups and their leaders.

Many countries are also teetering on the precipice of instability because of persistent social, political, and economic problems. The annual "failed state index," developed by the Fund for Peace and *Foreign Policy* magazine, identifies some sixty countries as being at a high risk for political and economic collapse (see table 2). The fact that so many countries are susceptible to internal conflict and social disintegration suggests that there is still enormous potential for instability in the international system.

These changes in the regional and international security environment are testing the world's capacity to hold potentially devastating threats to peace in check. The international governance systems and institutions, constructed out of the ruins of the Second World War and the Great Depression, as discussed in the previous chapter, have fallen steadily behind the steepening curve of turbulent globalization.

Major powers have been scrambling for politically sustainable and doctrinally coherent strategies. Their search for answers has produced a litany of catchphrases over the years aimed at generating the political will for action – (e.g., "failed states," "cooperative security," "loose nukes," "post-conflict stabilization and reconstruction," "the responsibility to protect," "genocide prevention," "the war on

Table 2
Fund for Peace, failed states index, 2013: Sixty most fragile states[1]

1 Somalia	21 Syria	42 Togo
2 Democratic Republic of	22 Uganda	43 Angola
Congo	23 North Korea	44 Uzbekistan
3 Sudan	23 Liberia	45 Zambia
4 South Sudan	25 Eritrea	46 Lebanon
5 Chad	26 Burma	47 Equatorial Guinea
6 Yemen	27 Cameroon	48 Kyrgyzstan
7 Afghanistan	28 Sri Lanka	49 Swaziland
8 Haiti	29 Bangladesh	50 Djibouti
9 Central African Republic	30 Nepal	51 Tajikistan
10 Zimbabwe	31 Mauritania	51 Solomon Islands
11 Iraq	32 Timor-Leste	53 Papua New Guinea
12 Cote d'Ivoire	33 Sierra Leone	54 Libya
13 Pakistan	34 Egypt	55 Georgia
14 Guinea	35 Burkina Faso	56 Comoros
15 Guinea Bissau	36 Republic of the Congo	57 Colombia
16 Nigeria	37 Iran	58 Laos
17 Kenya	38 Mali	59 Mozambique
18 Niger	38 Rwanda	60 Philippines
19 Ethiopia	40 Malawi	
20 Burundi	41 Cambodia	

1 The full index can be found at The Fund for Peace, "The Failed States Index," 2013 http://ffp.statesindex.org/.

terrorism," "the pivot," and "leading from behind"). But such slogans have too often proven to be a poor substitute for coherent and effective action.

There is no clear readiness to lead or take responsibility in a world where threats to international security can be global, transnational, regional, or local. When the attention of major global actors is focused on countries like Iraq and Afghanistan, many other conflicts in the world are forgotten (e.g., Western Sahara or Congo) or get short shrift because of the sensitivities of key regional (or great) powers and a general unwillingness to tackle them.

TURNING TOWARD THE ASIA-PACIFIC

Canada's security and defence policies have traditionally been wedded to a transatlantic vision of the world and anchored in NATO and NORAD, which have been the main instruments of our engagement in Europe, North America, and "out-of area," as in the cases

of Afghanistan and Libya. We need a new vision for our security
commitments and engagement with the rest of the world that goes
beyond NATO-centrism. That does not mean abandoning NATO,
especially as it deals with a new threat from Russia. But we must
also recognize the clear limits to bending or trying to reshape NATO
into an instrument of global security.

It is now a matter of official government policy that Canada sees
itself as a nation of the Asia-Pacific in what is now commonly known
as the Pacific Century – a century that will be increasingly dominated by China, China's rivalry with Japan and India, and the competing poles of other emerging economies of the Asia-Pacific region
such as Indonesia, Vietnam, Thailand, and the Philippines. The policies of the government of Prime Minister Stephen Harper are slowly
being redirected at developing and strengthening our trading and
investment ties with key countries in this region. Canada's Global
Markets Action Plan, released in November 2013, targets the emerging economies of the Asia-Pacific. Canada is also conducting free
trade talks with India, Singapore, Thailand, and Japan, which has
long been an ally and close friend of Canada.

However, as it courts the different countries of the region, Canada
is fast discovering that there is every expectation that our relations
will also include a strong security dimension. The nascent security
dialogue with Japan that began in 2010 should become more systematic and serious. In the Asia-Pacific, prosperity and regional security
go hand in hand. Our new partners won't just let us "do" economics. They want a much broader and deeper set of engagements in our
evolving partnerships.

In the past, Canada was an energetic and deeply committed security partner in the region. July 2013 marked the sixtieth anniversary
of the armistice that ended the Korean War – a war in which Canada's navy and army were actively deployed in a military action
against an aggressor nation and 516 servicemen gave their lives in
combat.

In the 1980s, under the government of Prime Minister Brian
Mulroney, Canada's creative diplomacy in Northeast Asia laid the
conceptual foundations for what eventually came to be known as
the Six-Party Talks on North Korea, though we were not a party to
that exercise.[6] And, in the 1990s, Canada, with its Indonesian partners, conducted informal diplomacy for conflict prevention in the
South China Sea by fostering dialogue among East and Southeast

Asian nations on a wide range of issues that included putting some imaginative ideas for environmental protection and joint resource development on the table – ideas that were welcomed at the time by senior Chinese participants in those talks.[7]

In the harsh fiscal climate of the late 1990s, our enthusiasm for innovative engagement in the Asia-Pacific region waned. Our security commitments today operate on a much narrower bandwidth that is essentially limited to those areas where we have compelling national interests, such as combatting the scourge of human smuggling, counterterrorism, and nuclear non-proliferation (through our membership in the Proliferation Security Initiative, which was launched under the administration of George W. Bush in an attempt to thwart North Korea's nuclear ambitions).

The major challenge today is that the security dynamics of the Asia-Pacific region are changing dramatically, with uncertain consequences that create their own dilemmas for our future engagement.

In the period 1945–75, the Asia-Pacific region, primarily because of the wars in Korea and Indochina, was the most violent and conflict-ridden on the globe. It has since become one of the most peaceful as the countries of the region have embraced capitalism and economic growth with a vengeance. But will the region's peace and prosperity last? This is an open question. Numerous forces – internal and external – have been set in motion by the region's rapid economic development and its political systems, which are struggling to adapt and accommodate to economic and social change.

The rapid growth of Asia's middle class – to which one billion more will be added over the next five to ten years – will not be satisfied by store shelves filled with goods, but will increasingly seek to participate in political systems where institutionalized avenues for political participation are weak.

Rising nationalism in key countries of the region, like China, Japan, and Vietnam, is playing out as territorial and resource disputes. Many of these disputes are infused by deep-rooted cultural and historical animosities and political opportunism by those in power. It would be a mistake to think that these disputes are simply about sovereignty. The region is also experiencing the political mobilization and, in some instances, the radicalization of ethnic and religious minorities, such as China's perennial tensions with its Tibetan, Uyghur, and Mongol minorities. This too is destabilizing the internal politics of countries in the region.

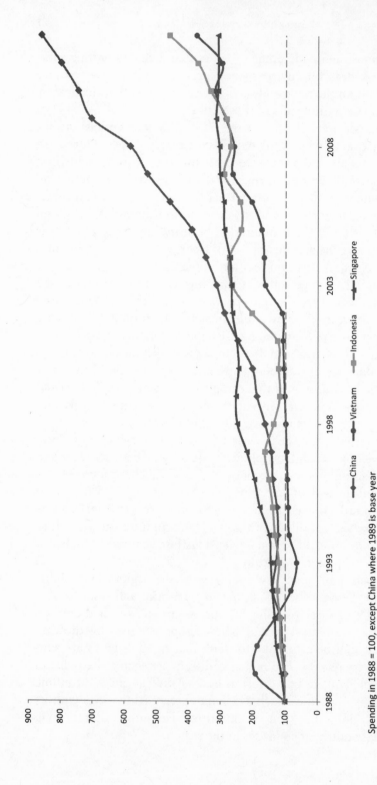

Spending in 1988 = 100, except China where 1989 is base year
Hashed line = 100

Figure 4
Real military spending growth in selected Asian countries measured in constant 2011 US dollars

Source: Stockholm International Peace Research Institute Military Expenditure Database.

The regional balance of power in the Asia-Pacific is also shifting with the rise of its new regional powers. India, Indonesia, Vietnam, and South Korea are challenging the traditional regional power hierarchy, and two of the region's great powers, Russia and Japan, worry about the loss of their power and influence to China. This shift is being accompanied by a major modernization of armed forces in the region (see figure 4), which creates its own competitive dynamic. Most experts say that it is not an arms race yet, but it could become one if political tensions in the region worsen. However, a growing number of incidents at sea involving fishing boats and military and coast guard vessels from rival nations are exacerbating tensions as regional balances shift.

In recent years, relations between China and the United States have been clumsily managed, especially during the Obama and Bush administrations where the so-called pivot (now downgraded to a "rebalancing") is worrying to the Chinese, who see vestiges of Cold War-style containment in US policy. China's own ham-fisted management of relations with its smaller neighbours is also a source of the region's increasing insecurity. As a recent CIGI–ASPI (Australian Strategic Policy Institute) report, "Facing West, Facing North," notes, "Years of emphasizing China's 'peaceful rise' in the region have given way to a confidence since 2009 that makes China more willing to use its economic weight, military and paramilitary power to assert its interests. Methods include, but are not limited to, the deployment of its coast guard vessels to police its claimed but disputed maritime jurisdiction, the application of informal economic sanctions, the encouragement of consumer boycotts and, in November 2013, the unilateral declaration of an Air Defence Identification Zone (ADIZ) in the East China Sea." The ADIZ has no validity or precedent in international law.

However, the most serious potential for catastrophe involves China-US relations. There are clearly many complex factors and dynamics affecting relations between the two countries. They are summarized in the text box on the next three pages.

FIVE REASONS WHY THERE WILL BE AND THERE WON'T BE WAR BETWEEN THE US AND CHINA

WHY THERE WILL BE WAR

1 *The historical curse of great power transitions*
Since the time of ancient Greece and the war between Athens and Sparta, great power transitions in world politics have had deeply unsettling consequences, as Thucydides' account of the origins of the Peloponnesian wars attests. The American strategic pivot toward Asia reflects some of the same fears about China's rise that Sparta felt about Athens. Athens bullied its smaller Aegean Sea neighbours; China is doing the same in its own maritime neighbourhood.[8]

2 *Public opinion*
The overwhelming majority of Americans (66 per cent) see the rise of China as competition for the United States and they don't like it, and another 68 per cent believe that China cannot be trusted.[9] Never mind that China, as an investor, is underwriting much of the US fiscal deficit (including the US defence budget) and debt. America's elites, who really ought to know better, feel that competition even more acutely.

3 *Blame China*
The prospect of a tit-for-tat trade war may be more likely and more ominous – especially if the US economy stays in the doldrums and unemployment stays high. "Blame China" sentiments, especially in the US Congress, could grow.

4 *A return to containment*
The United States is working actively to encircle, if not contain, China by reinvigorating its alliances in the region – notably with Japan and Australia, but also with other Southeast Asian nations, including former adversaries like Myanmar and Vietnam. The much-touted TPP is also part of this containment strategy. Korea is always a tinderbox and an additional potential flashpoint where both China and the US have interests.

5 *Blame the US*
China has taken to blaming America for inflaming regional tensions and creating problems with its neighbours that are largely of its own making. China's claims in the China Sea are legally dubious, but its actions or a crisis could draw in the US in defence of its allies, such as Japan or the Philippines.

WHY THERE WON'T BE WAR

1 *Economic interdependence*
China and the US are two of the most economically interdependent economies in the world. China is heavily invested in the US economy and US Treasury Bills. The US in turn is heavily invested in China. Any kind of major disruption in relations or escalation of tensions would cost both countries dearly. Unlike the US and Russia during the Cold War, or even the relationship between Germany and Britain before the First World War, China and the United States are joined at the hip by mutual trade and investment. They may be strategic rivals, but any kind of surgical separation would almost certainly kill off both of these Siamese twins.

2 *China is militarily in no position to challenge the US*
China's military power and projection capabilities pale in comparison to those of the US, notwithstanding recent increases in Chinese defence spending and China's acquisition of a blue-water navy (an open ocean navy). Nor is it at all clear that China wants to go head to head with the US by challenging its global military supremacy.

3 *Uncertain regional allies*
Most countries of the Asia-Pacific, including ASEAN (Association of Southeast Asian Nations), won't join the US in a formal American-led anti-China coalition. Incidentally, this is one of the reasons why some countries are ambivalent about the security thrust of the TPP and go out of their way to pitch it as a trade deal.

4 *War weariness*
Americans have no stomach for opening up another military
front. Beset by vast domestic challenges and still recovering from
their bloody and inconclusive experiences in Iraq and Afghanistan, Americans will be disinclined to look for fresh conflicts.
The Chinese have their own domestic worries to distract them; if
hostilities open, expect to see them limited to trade disputes, or
to bloodless (and publicly deniable) strikes in cyberspace.

5 *Shared interests and a history of cooperation*
The record of Sino-American relations since the Kissinger-Nixon
opening in the early 1970s has largely been one of cooperation.
China and America cooperated on the withdrawal of Vietnam-
ese troops from Cambodia in the Paris Peace Accords of 1992.
America was a strong supporter of China's entry into the WTO.
American companies have invested hugely in China and now
Chinese companies are trying to do the same in the US (and
Canada). Although China and the US have their differences
when it comes to the Middle East and Persian Gulf (Iran and
Syria), they have shared interests in promoting greater stability
in the Middle East and securing safe passage for the 20 per cent
of the world's oil supplies that pass through the straits of the
Persian Gulf, much of it to China.[10]

On balance, it is our belief that the US and China simply have
too much at stake to replay the war between Athens and Sparta
or between any other great powers from previous eras. Nevertheless, however much major war has been devalued and delegitim-
ized as an instrument of national policy, it is unwise to discount the
chance that major state rivalry, military tests of strength, or sheer
miscalculation could trigger outbreaks of inter-state war, including
in the Asia-Pacific. Tensions will be a constant and containment will
require astute diplomatic footwork.

We also cannot take continued domestic political stability in the
region or in China for granted. It is apparent that the Arab Spring
movement is part of a general global phenomenon that is being
experienced in places as diverse as the post-Soviet states and other
autocracies, including China. The behaviour of authoritarian leaders

around the globe suggests that – whatever we may think of the likely scenarios – they consider themselves to be much more vulnerable than previously to spontaneous pressures from the general populace and may therefore seek to divert popular discontent by manufacturing foreign policy crises with neighbours, especially on territorial issues, about which public sentiment is the most intense.

A careful examination of scenarios that could draw the US and China (or China and various combinations of neighbours, such as Japan, the Philippines, India, or Pakistan) into armed hostilities leads to the conclusion that peaceful coexistence is not assured. And it likewise leads to a heightened appreciation of the importance of managing and deflecting these risks through imaginative diplomacy and regional confidence-building measures of the kind that reduced tensions between East and West during the Cold War and allowed for a peaceful transition when the Soviet Union collapsed and the Cold War ended.

Beyond great power and regional rivalries, there is a wide range of new security challenges, such as terrorism, cybercrime, and espionage, natural disaster management, transnational crime, and drug trafficking that will command policymakers' attention. There is no shortage of things Canada can do with the myriad new challenges of this fast-changing security environment in the Asia-Pacific. But we can't do everything and we are going to have to make some tough choices about where we engage, with whom we work, and, more fundamentally, what we do.

Canada has important security interests in the region, which are defined by the following considerations: as our own economic fortunes and future are increasingly tied to the region we will have a specific and not simply a generalized stake in the region's continuing prosperity and stability. Our economic partners in the region, notably Japan and Korea, but also our new trading partners in Southeast Asia, have signalled that if we want to do business with them and sign new investment and trade deals we have to be more reliable and engaged security partners. We can't simply be carpetbaggers.

We are also going to have to decide what kind of role and defence capabilities are required for a bigger Canadian presence and role in the Asia-Pacific. In the US, the increased focus on Asia implies a very different kind of fighting force than has been produced in the last ten years. No matter how the relationship with China is worked out over the next decade, from a military point of view the focus will probably turn from an emphasis on large land-based forces toward highly mobile naval, air, and special forces and technologically sophisticated cyber-attack capabilities, space-based intelligence and communications systems, and perhaps new anti-satellite capabilities.

Canada will have to decide whether it wishes to follow the US security pivot and rebalance toward Asia, recognizing that as we engage China economically, our own national interests are not necessarily in complete alignment with the US on all security and economic matters. Those countries in the region that are in transition may also need a variety of responses, including help countering violent extremism, talking to unpalatable opponents, strengthening regional organizations and their capacity to manage conflict, and training local police and security forces.

In early June 2013, Canada's former defence minister, Peter MacKay, told delegates at the Shangri-La Dialogue in Singapore, a key annual gathering of defence ministers and other officials, that Canada is keen to join the two key defence and security forums in the region – the ASEAN Defence Ministerial Meeting-Plus (ADMM-Plus) and the East Asian Summit. But what he heard back was that we have to show that we are serious about playing a constructive role in Asia before we are allowed into these organizations. When former ASEAN secretary general Surin Pitsuwan stepped down from his post at the end of 2012, he made it clear that it will be years before Canada gets another chance to join the East Asian Summit,[11] and that, frankly, "Canada knows that it has been rather absent from the region."[12]

Canada is now in the process of increasing its visibility and engagement in the region through, for example, a growing number of ministerial visits, visits to local ports of call by our navy, and participation in joint military exercises such as the Rim of the Pacific Exercise, the annual Cobra Gold exercise in Thailand, and in exercises on the Korean peninsula.

However, there is clearly a lot more we could do to engage and demonstrate that the region is central to our interests. There are relatively easy and non-controversial avenues for deeper engagement such as military medicine, disaster relief assistance and management, and counter-piracy operations. Canada can also help with peacekeeping, police training, and improved civil–military relations. Beyond that, our navy also has an important role to play helping secure sea lines of communication in an ocean that accounts for one-half of the world's cargo tonnage and through which two-thirds of the Asia-Pacific's oil imports pass.

Cybersecurity is also a point of engagement and figures prominently in the agenda of the "5 Eyes," which is one of the cornerstones of our intelligence relationship with Australia, the US, the UK, and New Zealand.

As we deepen our engagement in the Asia-Pacific, our first priority must be to listen to what those in the region see as their main security concerns. Second, before we offer military assistance we need to find out what our security partners want from us, rather than telling them what we think they should do. That approach will gain their respect and trust. Third, in a part of the world where appearances matter, we need to keep a regular pace of diplomatic activity and regularly and actively participate in the region's various forums. But we are going to have to go beyond that, with concrete actions and meaningful activities and forms of engagement.

Finally, Canada must strengthen its bilateral military and security ties with those key countries in the region with which we have had strong historical ties and which are key focal points of our new economic engagement. Korea sees Canada as a kindred middle power and remembers well the vital legacy of our engagement in the Korean War. Japan is also an important friend with whom we have major economic ties that should also deepen in the realm of security. At one time we were Indonesia's major development assistance donor and we continue to do major business in that country's mining sector. As the world's largest Muslim country and the most influential ASEAN member, Indonesia is a natural partner for us.

In particular, we need to deepen security and defence ties with Australia, which increasingly feels exposed in the region and does not simply want to depend on the US as its principal strategic ally. As a recent CIGI-ASPI report put it, "with Britain and the United States taking a more constrained role in security affairs, Canadian and Australian officials are finding themselves the more vocal of the traditional English-speaking security partners. Finding themselves agreeing on a number of issues has caught some by surprise. Yet they have long had much in common, and the shared understanding and altered circumstances are pointing to a renewed interest in collaboration and cross-pollination to enhance regional security and stability."[13] Areas for potential collaboration include cooperation on procuring military hardware, increasing the number of exchanges

of military personnel and joint exercises, and, potentially, a formal
defence arrangement.[14]

REINVIGORATING OUR DEFENCE POLICIES AND DIPLOMACY TO DEAL WITH NUCLEAR THREATS

Thirty years ago President Ronald Reagan went before the American people to declare his bold new vision of a nuclear-free world. Appearing on national television he said, "Let me share with you a vision of the future which offers hope. It is that we embark on a program to counter the awesome Soviet missile threat with measures that are defensive. Let us turn to the very strengths in technology that spawned our great industrial base and that have given us the quality of life we enjoy today."[15] Thus was born the Strategic Defensive Initiative, or SDI, which also came to be known as "Star Wars."

Today, strategic defence goes under a different name, Ballistic Missile Defence, or BMD. Although we are still a long way off from having a perfect defensive system that would shield North America from an intercontinental ballistic missile attack, there has been major progress in the intervening years in developing new technologies capable of shooting down ballistic missiles.

During the first Gulf War against Iraq – known as Operation Desert Storm – Raytheon Corporation's Patriot Missile System was used to shoot down Scud missiles that were launched by Saddam Hussein's army against targets in Saudi Arabia and Israel. However, there was a lot of controversy about the Patriot system's kill rate, with some experts questioning the high interception rates touted by the US government.[16] But as the system evolved, the Patriot's interception rates improved and during Operation Iraqi Freedom (2003), the second Gulf War, Patriots successfully brought down Iraqi tactical ballistic missiles.

The US has also deployed the Aegis Combat System on ships to deal with intermediate-range ballistic missile threats. In a comprehensive series of tests, the system has shown its ability to detect, track, intercept, and successfully destroy its intended target. The US also has a rudimentary missile defence system designed to attack intercontinental ballistic missiles, which consists of thirteen ground-based interceptors in Greely, Alaska, and two more at Vandenberg Air Force Base in California. The US is now in the process of adding more interceptors while refining its BMD systems.

For many years, Canada opposed the very concept of ballistic missile defence on the grounds that such technologies, if deployed, would stoke another arms race. There was also widespread skepticism about the technical limits of ballistic missile defence and its cost.

We should perhaps heed the advice of former US secretary of state Henry Kissinger when he endorsed the idea of limited strategic defence in a syndicated column in 1984, "even granting – as I do – that a perfect defense of the US population is almost certainly unattainable, the existence of some defense means that attacker must plan on saturating it. This massively complicates the attacker's calculations. Anything that magnifies doubt inspires hesitation and adds to deterrence."[17]

Although the logic of Kissinger's case for BMD remains unassailable, the nature of the strategic threat has changed. It no longer comes, as it once did, from the Soviet Union, but from an array of the world's smaller totalitarian regimes. As a 2010 review of the US BMD program by the Obama administration made abundantly clear, the threat of nuclear missile attack against North America is growing. The US government's threat assessment highlighted the growing threat from North Korea and Iran, both of which have developed medium-range missile capabilities.[18]

Western analysts have consistently underrated North Korea's ability to acquire and develop nuclear and missile capabilities. There is a real risk that North Korea might one day be able to put a nuclear warhead on a missile that would be capable of striking targets in the United States, though it still has some distance to go in missile accuracy and intercontinental delivery capabilities.[19] Iran is a threat too. It has the most extensive inventory of short- and medium-range missiles of any developing nation in the world. That includes its solid-fuel Sejil and Ashura missiles, and the Shahab-3 and Ghadr-101 ballistic missiles, which have the range to strike any target in the Middle East, including Israel.

A "thin" ballistic missile defence capability could provide much-needed protection against a North Korean missile attack or an attack by some other third party or even an accidental missile launch. It would also, in Kissinger's equation, plant a seed of doubt in an attacker's mind about his ability to successfully launch such an attack, thereby strengthening long-standing deterrence policies.

Whether we like it or not, geography makes Canada a target. The flight path of any missile fired at North America from North Korea (or perhaps, one day, Iran) would take it over Canada, especially if it was directed at cities on the US eastern seaboard, such as New York or Washington. North Korea doesn't have that capability now, but one day it could. So too could other powers who harbour similar ambitions. A missile could thus easily land on a Canadian city by accident or design.

In 2005, the Liberal government of Paul Martin, through Foreign Minister Pierre Pettigrew, rejected an offer by the Americans to join their missile defence program, apparently because the US was unwilling to give Canada the kinds of guarantees it sought over how the program architecture would be implemented. As a consequence, however, the opportunity to rebrand NORAD into a meaningful security instrument of the twenty-first century that would deal with the full spectrum of threats to the North American continent, including ballistic missiles, was missed.

A major priority for any Canadian government is the preservation of national security. The risk of nuclear proliferation is, if anything, greater today than it was a decade ago, not just from North Korea but from other radical regimes. New initiatives are already underway to quash the threat from terrorists, including the homegrown variety. Far more lethal, however, is the looming missile threat against which Canada has no practical defence other than to hope that the United States will act in its own interest and defend us against an attack, accidental or otherwise.[20]

That is simply not good enough. The best antidote to the antics of North Korea, as Nicholas Eberstadt contended in *The Wall Street Journal*, is a "threat-reduction strategy," a combination of sustained military and civilian actions designed to degrade North Korea's military capabilities and lessen its ability to blackmail its neighbours.[21] Such a strategy also means not repeating offers of dialogue when North Korea makes "bait-and-switch" extortion demands in its attempts to gain rewards for bad behaviour from all-too-gullible western powers.

Intensified Canadian diplomacy in nuclear non-proliferation is the necessary accompaniment to any actions we take to boost North America's defence capabilities against rogue states and their aspirations to acquire long-range ballistic missile capabilities. While some may dismiss the notion of arms control as quixotic, focused and timely efforts can produce tangible results. When the USSR collapsed, Russia was awash in chemical weapons, unsecured nuclear materials, and atomic bombs. Russia's chemical weapon stockpile, for example, amounted to 40,000 tons of nerve agents (such as Sarin, VX, and Soman) and blister weapons (such as mustard gas) stored not just in warehouses, but in rockets and artillery shells as well. Given the dilapidated state of the Russian economy, and the epidemic of corruption and poor morale in Russia's security services, the risk that these weapons could spread far beyond Russia's borders and into the hands of other countries and even terrorists and guerillas was very real. Similar concerns abounded when it came to Russia's nuclear weapons and materials.

Part of the solution to the problem of unsecure weapons is to destroy them. To that end, Canada launched the Global Partnership Program (GPP) at the G8 in 2002, which got like-minded countries to work with Russia to secure and destroy its surplus radioactive materials and chemical weapons. The GPP has also helped secure funding to build facilities to destroy chemical arms. Canada has contributed over $60 million to the building and operation of the Shuch'ye chemical weapon destruction facility, located at a depot with over one million artillery shells and rockets with nerve gas payloads. By 2012, over half of Russia's nerve gas and blistering agents had been destroyed.

Through the GPP, from 2004 to 2011 Canada also helped Russia dismantle fifteen surplus nuclear submarines and defuel seventeen others. Getting the reactors and fuel out of these boats not only reduced environmental risks to Russia's Arctic, but also secured a large source of highly enriched uranium, which would otherwise have posed a serious proliferation risk.

While Russia ultimately has to take charge of the safe destruction and cleanup of its Cold War legacy, putting money into these efforts does not mean that Canada was getting fleeced or that Russia was shirking its responsibilities. In the long run, Canada benefits from any effort to mop up deadly weapons and nuclear waste. Talking about disarmament is one thing, but we have to put our money where our mouth is if we want results. The GPP demonstrates that it can be done. The GPP also worked because Canada reached out to other countries that shared our concerns and interests, and offered to share the burden in an effort to secure those interests. If Canada wants to bolster its credibility with the US and increase our national security, then it is time to put money and diplomatic capital into serious arms control projects.

Appearing before the US Senate for her nomination hearings, former US secretary of state Hillary Clinton identified the "the gravest threat" facing America as being "the danger that weapons of mass destruction will fall into the hands of terrorists."[22] To address this threat, the Obama administration signalled early on that it would negotiate reductions in nuclear stockpiles with Russia. It also upped its diplomatic efforts to strengthen the nuclear Non-Proliferation Treaty (NPT) regime, revive negotiations on the Fissile Material Cut-off Treaty, and, less successfully, to urge the US Senate to ratify the Comprehensive Test Ban Treaty (CTBT). One of the biggest problems with the current nuclear non-proliferation regime is that countries like Iran are trying to remain within the NPT by blurring the distinction between possession and non-possession of a nuclear weapons capability.

The problem with the NPT's "grey zone" is painfully apparent in the interim nuclear deal that was struck between the P5 plus Germany and Iran on 24 November 2013, in which Iran agreed to temporarily "freeze" the development of its nuclear program and stockpile of enriched uranium in exchange for USD$8 billion in sanctions relief.

The geopolitical or strategic logic of such a breakthrough for the US with Iran was compelling. Those defending the negotiations and the agreement viewed it as the "least-worse" of a bad set of alternatives where a continuation of the status quo would inevitably lead to war. Equally, the Iranians were desperate to get relief from the sanctions that are having a devastating impact on their economy. However, without some element of trust and without stringent terms of certification, the agreement won't be worth much unless Iran ultimately agrees to substantially reduce the number of its advanced gas centrifuges and its plutonium production capacity. As two former secretaries of state, Henry Kissinger and George Shultz, wrote in *The Wall Street Journal*, "Any final deal [with Iran] must ensure the world's ability to detect a move toward a nuclear breakout, lengthen the world's time to react, and underscore its determination to do so. The preservation of the global nuclear nonproliferation regime and the avoidance of a Middle East nuclear-arms race hang in the balance."[23]

Canada is a leading exporter of uranium and has been a major supplier of nuclear reactor technology. In addition, Canada has numerous service contracts to do maintenance on existing CANDU reactors. We are also a long-standing champion of nuclear non-proliferation and have been a key supporter of the International Atomic Energy Agency (IAEA), the NPT, and the development of other nuclear safeguards. Canada is especially well-positioned to work closely with the Obama administration to strengthen and preserve the integrity and structure of the NPT regime so that there are proper firewalls in place for countries that have (or intend to pursue) nuclear energy programs. This is especially important because nuclear power use is going to grow. According to recent estimates, even in the wake of Japan's Fukushima nuclear accident, global nuclear energy consumption could double by 2030.[24] As new markets emerge in unstable corners of the globe, Canada and other providers of peaceful nuclear energy, including the US, will have to ensure that they strike the right balance between exporting nuclear technology and preventing nuclear weapons proliferation. With the revived use of nuclear power, multilateral governance of the nuclear fuel cycle is an important way to reduce proliferation risks.

DEALING WITH THE NEW AGE OF TERROR

For a time, it looked as if the "age of terror" was finally behind us. During the presidency of George W. Bush there were no further attacks on American soil after 9/11 – something for which his much-criticized administration could take real credit. When the decade-long hunt for Osama bin Laden finally ended with his killing by US Navy Seals in May 2011, it looked as if al-Qaeda was on the run. Americans were finally beginning to feel more secure as life returned to the new normal of a post-9/11 world.

The murderous terrorist attacks in Boston during the Boston Marathon on 15 April 2013 changed all that. The age of terror returned with a vengeance – a stark and painful reminder that we cannot let down our guard.

In Canada, the successful apprehension only days later of two suspects, Raed Jaser and Chiheb Esseghaier, who were allegedly plotting to blow up a VIA passenger train bound for New York, also served to remind Canadians that we are also on al-Qaeda's hit list.

Much has been made of the fact that these new attacks came from a "B" team of so-called homegrown terrorists who are not nearly as well-trained as bin Laden's henchmen. But even B-teamers get lucky – as the Boston marathon bombers demonstrated.

Some of the members of this new B-team are individuals, like Raed Jaser, who managed to get into Canada because of our lax immigration and refugee laws. But others – like Xristos Katsiroubas and Ali Medlej, two young Ontario men who were involved in leading the terrorist attack on a gas plant in southeastern Algeria, or the Toronto 18, who were a mix of immigrants, native-born Canadians, and teenagers – certainly don't fit the stereotype of Islamic extremists.

More troubling is the sloppiness of police and intelligence officials on both sides of the Canada-US border. In spite of the billions poured into the Department of Homeland Security, the FBI apparently repeatedly ignored warnings from Russian intelligence services that Tamerlan Tsarnaev, the elder brother in the Boston Marathon attack, was a terrorist suspect and had to be watched closely.[25] We have also learned that the RCMP had Medlej and Katsiroubas in their sights for two years before the Algerian gas plant attack, suggesting that there may have been a partial failure of intelligence in Canada too.[26]

The one piece of good news is that the foiled VIA Rail attack was the result of unprecedented levels of cooperation among Canada's security and intelligence agencies – a pattern that will be critical going forward. Both events also demonstrate the importance of individual actions by community members: the Chinese immigrant whose car was hijacked in Boston, the boat owner who alerted police, the videos shot by those watching the marathon, and, reportedly, the initiative of an imam in Toronto.[27]

The openness of western societies is a source of vulnerability in the face of blatant, seemingly mindless, terrorist actions. The balance between liberty and order in a democracy will never be perfect. But the innate sense of responsibility and the resourcefulness of individuals, as demonstrated spontaneously in Boston and Toronto, offer some assurance that the vigilance of ordinary citizens, acting on values we all cherish, will be our best defence.

For those who like to speculate about the "root causes" of terrorism, it is worth bearing in mind that conflicts in far-off places are ultimately the incubators of terrorist movements. It is not simply a matter of perennial disaffection of youth. Tamerlan Tsarnaev likely learned his trade at the hands of Islamic extremists in Chechnya and Dagestan. And if Canadians reflect for a moment on their own history, they may remember that the FLQ (Front de libération du Québec) terrorists who operated in Quebec in the 1960s were trained by Algerian rebels in the techniques of guerrilla warfare.

As the US and remaining NATO forces prepare to disengage from Afghanistan, they are sowing the seeds for the next generation of terrorists and religious extremists, who will almost certainly try to seek amends for the injustices they believe were wrought by the West on their country. The more failed and collapsing (or collapsed) states there are in the world – no matter how distant or obscure – the greater the likelihood that they will export their problems, their religious or ethnic extremism, to Canada. That's the harsh reality of a deeply interconnected globe, where problems and movements don't respect national boundaries.

FOCUSING ON CONFLICT PREVENTION TO DEAL WITH FAILED STATES

Western democracies, including Canada, have grown weary from the costly military interventions of the last decade. If military intervention is not an option, or, at best, a blunt instrument to deal with conflicts in fragile and failed states, then we need to focus on alternative policy instruments. In many western capitals, including Washington, greater attention is now being paid to conflict prevention. Broadly speaking, conflict prevention refers to actions or measures taken that are directed at thwarting the eruption of violence. However, the relationship between means and ends is a complicated one, and conflict prevention is no exception. Very often, international actors have made matters worse with their so-called peaceful interventions. It is also difficult to identify which actions prevent conflict, and even more so to prove that they were effective, given that successful conflict prevention is often a non-event.

It is equally important to note what prevention is not. Conflict prevention is not intervention or military engagement per se, but rather an attempt to forestall the need for forceful intervention with humanitarian aims and other forms of "fire-fighting" action that tend to be dangerous and expensive, and often simply come too little, too late. What preventive efforts do or can do, nonetheless, is seek to foster the peaceful management of disputes, typically (and ideally) with the consent of the parties to the conflict.

Although every conflict is complex and unique, contemporary violent conflict has several common characteristics that are relevant to policy development. The first is the importance of economic factors in contributing to and prolonging war. Resource scarcity due to high population growth, the legacies of land distribution, uneven food distribution, and a lack of access to fresh water are all potential sources of conflict. Conversely, an overabundance of natural resources can also increase the probability and duration of violent conflict as actors enrich themselves through illicit means, for example those engaged in massive looting of treasuries, embezzlement of state revenues from oil exploration, small-arms trafficking, and the mining of minerals such as diamonds, coltan, and gold.

The second common characteristic is the role of belligerent groups and the manner in which they foment and perpetuate violence. Their ability to manipulate populations through the instruments of ethnicity, religion, history, and myths is one of the key factors that determine how a conflict will unfold, and hence what can be done to arrest it.

The third characteristic is the fungible nature of contemporary conflict. So-called civil wars permeate easily across existing territorial borders to form "regional conflict complexes." Conversely, regional conflict dynamics can impact rapidly on the internal processes of neighbouring states. Conflicts have a nasty habit of spilling over (as in Africa's Great Lakes region since 1997, Liberia/Sierra Leone/Guinea in 1999–2001, and Syria/Lebanon/Iraq today) and spilling in, as demonstrated by the extensive external involvement in the Democratic Republic of Congo's civil war or Pakistan's involvement in Afghanistan. The role of neighbours is extremely important. They can act as important perpetrators of violence just as easily as they can fuel and prolong it. The term "civil conflict" is, in fact, often a misnomer.

The kinds of preventive measures that might usefully be undertaken by Canada, along with its key democratic allies – a theme we take up in greater depth in the next chapter – to address the underlying causes of violence include comprehensive development assistance programs that focus not just on lower-income countries, but also on the most politically troublesome and unstable states in the world, which are known in development lingo as MICs (middle-income countries) and LMICs (lower-middle-income countries). These countries typically suffer from wide disparities in wealth and income between different regions, lack of state control over areas where there are local insurgencies, and chronic but enduring state fragility (Pakistan is a good example). LMIC and MIC countries are generally ineligible for development assistance according to poverty-level benchmarks.

Additionally, as part of an effective conflict prevention strategy, our development assistance and diplomacy must also include initiatives that focus on the promotion of human rights, pluralism, and freedom of religious expression. These are critical to promoting long-term political stability and good governance, since that allows aggrieved people to seek political reform and redress grievances through peaceful political competition, rather than having to resort to taking up arms. We also discuss this theme at greater length in the next chapter.

Canada's diplomats, development professionals, and armed forces must begin to think and plan for conflict prevention as a proactive central plank in our global security policy. Analysts, academics, and governments know much more today about when, why, and how large-scale armed conflict happens than they did even fifty years ago (which is not to say that there is no room for improvement!). It is time to take that knowledge and begin applying it to serious, deliberate, and active efforts to forestall and stop civil wars before they start, rather than continuing the dismal post-Cold War trend of intervening when it is too late to stop the killing except through large-scale, long, and costly armed interventions.

INNOVATIVE DIPLOMACY TO ADDRESS BORDER DISPUTES

Contested borders and territories lie at the heart of many of the world's most difficult and troubled hot spots – East China Sea, Kashmir, Israel versus Palestine, Crimea, the Western Sahara, Gibraltar, North Sudan versus South Sudan, Somaliland, the list goes on. Canada has its own territorial disputes with the United States over the ownership of the navigable waters of the Northwest Passage, and until it was recently resolved, a piece of rock in the Davis Straits called Hans Island, which Denmark claimed. In all, there are more than a hundred major unresolved border and territorial disputes between sovereign entities that could one day escalate into something bigger. While no definitive list of territorial disputes exist, we can offer a few figures to illustrate the range of the phenomenon.

Using data drawn from the CIA *World Factbook*, we counted 149 ongoing disputes between sovereign countries over land borders,

Table 3
International Territorial Disputes, 1946–2013

Ongoing disputes over land and river borders	At least 75[1]
Ongoing disputes over maritime boundaries and ownership of islands	At least 60[2]
Armed conflict between states over territory since 1945	47[3]
Number of territorial changes from 1946 to 2008	275[4]
Number of territorial changes from 1946 to 2008 that involved armed conflict	44[5]
Number of territorial changes since 1991 that involved armed conflict	7[6]

1 Authors' calculations using data from the Central Intelligence Agency, *The World Factbook* (Central Intelligence Agency, 2013).
2 Ibid.
3 Lotta Themnér and Peter Wallensteen, "Armed Conflict, 1946–2012," *Journal of Peace Research* 50.4 (2013): 509–21.
4 "Territorial Change, 1816–2008 (v4.01), see Jaroslav Tir, Philip Schafer, Paul Diehl, and Gary Goertz. "Territorial Changes, 1816–1996: Procedures and Data," *Conflict Management and Peace Science* 16.1 (1998): 89–97.
5 Ibid.
6 Ibid.

river borders, ethnic enclaves, maritime boundaries, and sovereignty over inhabitable islands. While many of these disputes are relatively calm affairs that are being actively resolved via dialogue and negotiation, others are far more tense and involve multiple parties, which complicates any attempt to negotiate a solution. For example, it is not just China that claims parts of the Spratly Islands, a cluster of shoals and reefs in the South China Sea, but also Vietnam, the Philippines, Taiwan, Malaysia, and Brunei. Fashioning a deal that will satisfy six parties is far more difficult than brokering an agreement between two! Other disputes, such as those along China and India's Himalayan border increasingly involve shows of military force, suggesting that at least one party thinks that it can get what it wants through muscle rather than diplomacy. Table 3 summarizes some of the characteristics of current territorial disputes, and the relationship between territorial disputes and international conflict since the Second World War. While the number of territorial disputes causing armed conflict has declined in recent years, it remains clear that when governments disagree about who rules where and who owns what, the risk of escalation is very real.

Borders are one area of global conflict management where Canada has much to contribute, partly as a result of our experience effectively managing what has been referred to as the world's longest unprotected border between Canada and the United States. More recently, our diplomacy on the Afghanistan-Pakistan border, which has deployed the skills and know-how learned along the Canada-US border, has much to commend to the kind of role we could play in other border disputes, such as those between South and North Sudan, or Haiti and the Dominican Republic, where we already have engaged and committed players in development assistance and diplomacy.

The war in Afghanistan, begun in the aftermath of the 9/11 al-Qaeda attacks and the overthrow of the Taliban government in Kabul, imparted to the Afghanistan-Pakistan border an urgent new international significance – not least to Canada. By early 2006 the Canadian Forces (part of the NATO-led International Security Assistance Force [ISAF]) were deployed and responsible for security in Kandahar province, next to Afghanistan's southeastern border with Pakistan. For ISAF, and for Canada in particular, the infiltration of insurgents and weaponry from safe havens in Pakistan was a continuing and deadly threat.

Generations of hostility, warfare, criminality, and nationalist politics have characterized cross-border relations between Afghanistan and Pakistan. The very existence of the border – called the Durand Line and decreed in 1893 by the British government and the king of Afghanistan – is not recognized as legal or legitimate by the Afghan government. Pakistan recognizes the Durand Line as the international border, but many Pakistanis do not; Pashtuns and Baluchis regard the border areas as their own tribal lands and exercise their freedom to cross the invisible line whenever and wherever they choose. Running more than 2,500 kilometres through remote and mountainous territory, most of the border is neither monitored nor controlled by either government. Drug and arms smuggling, the traffic in insurgents, and movements of terrorists in the border area have been common, and they menace the security of people in both countries and abroad. Afghan and Pakistani security forces have lacked the capacity to police or even to watch the border effectively. Border-region poverty and the intensifying war of insurgency and counter-insurgency in Afghanistan have interacted to create their own incentives for violence and disorder across the borderland's forbidding terrain.

On a visit to Islamabad in February 2007, in a discussion with then-president Pervez Musharraf, the Canadian foreign affairs minister at the time, Peter MacKay, offered Canadian technical assistance to strengthen security along the border with Afghanistan. That offer, reiterated in Kabul and developed in fact-finding missions by Canadian officials to both countries, led to a meeting attended by Afghan and Pakistani officials from 30 October to 1 November 2007 in Dubai. The venue was chosen by consensus as neutral, safe, and convenient.[28]

In Dubai, through negotiations facilitated by Canadian officials, Afghan and Pakistani delegations agreed to an action plan that dealt with five subjects: social and economic development; customs (including trade, revenue collection, and security); managing the movement of people; law enforcement; and counter-narcotics. Under each heading, the two sides agreed to work together on cooperative, practical initiatives – the establishment of customs posts, for example. The parties also accepted Canada's offer to facilitate more such meetings. In the years since, other sessions have taken place in Dubai, Pakistan, Afghanistan, and Canada.

The five working areas of what is now referred to as the Afghanistan-Pakistan Border Process have been part of an internationally-recognized process that not only promotes dialogue and negotiations between Afghan and Pakistani officials but also to advance cooperation. Importantly, the process has also engaged and mobilized a wide range of partners and stakeholders not only in the two countries, but also at the international level, including the US Border Management Task Force in Kabul and Islamabad, the United Nations Office on Drugs and Crime, ISAF Regional Command (South), the World Bank, the United Nations Assistance Mission in Afghanistan (UNAMA), the United Nations High Commissioner for Refugees, the International Organization for Migration, other organizations working on border management, and key donors, such as Germany and Denmark.

The Canadian interest in the initiative was to achieve improved management of the Afghanistan-Pakistan border so as to reduce flows of insurgents, arms, and bomb-making materials, and to promote Afghan development. To succeed, Canadian officials would have had to address the mixed motives evident in Islamabad and Kabul.

By all appearances, Pakistan's initial primary interests in the Dubai Process were to increase border security, regulate flows of migrants (including refugees) more effectively, speed transportation, and attract foreign aid. Pakistani authorities seized the chance to take part in a dialogue with Afghanistan that would have been difficult or impossible without the third-party facilitation offered by Canada.

For Afghans, the chief interest seems to have been the maintenance of an open border essential to the Afghan economy. (Landlocked Afghanistan relies on land crossings for access to Karachi and other ports, and for practically all its imports and exports.) Pressure from Canada – a major aid donor and important ISAF troop contributor – may also have influenced Afghan attitudes, along with the access to international funding implied by Dubai Process participation.

These asymmetries of interest (like the asymmetries of power and capacity) between Afghanistan and Pakistan – and the distrust that divided them – affected the course of the process and shaped some of the obstacles to progress. Nevertheless, meetings between the parties have continued in various combinations of subject-matter working groups and steering committees. To a remarkable degree, participants have reported that Afghan and Pakistani delegates have taken ownership of the process – and responsibility for its progress.

Canada has had – and demonstrated – several advantages as sponsor-facilitator of the Dubai Process. Our G8 membership permitted Canadian officials to help shape G8 commitments to border-region development, while informing process participants about G8 priorities and intentions.

As a non-great power, Canada could win acceptance by both Afghans and Pakistanis as a truly neutral and honest broker without geostrategic ambitions. Pakistanis and Afghans in the process have credited Canada for encouraging a bottom-up development of agendas and solutions, and for avoiding the top-down imposition of negotiated subjects or outcomes.

As a significant member of the ISAF coalition and development donor in Afghanistan, Canada could also claim a certain standing in the region, with a real stake in the improvement of Afghanistan-Pakistan relations. Indeed, Canadian officials sought to focus the process on the Baluchistan-Kandahar border area – to improve Kandahar's security and development, and to avoid overlap with US and British projects elsewhere along the Afghanistan-Pakistan border.

Canada likewise brought to the process a professional foreign service respected for its competence and reliability. These attributes proved crucial in fostering the trust and ownership that were essential as Afghans and Pakistanis assumed management of the process and made it their own. Canadian officials assigned to the process have displayed commendable diplomatic skill and energy.

All these Canadian assets served to offset any weaknesses in Canada's performance. One such weakness – especially in early phases of the process – may have been the lack of Canadian expertise contributed from any department other than the Department of Foreign Affairs and International Trade; customs, policing, and other technical and legal expertise was brought to bear later from the Canada Border Services Agency, the RCMP, CIDA, and other reaches of the Canadian government.

Ultimately, the fate of our efforts to promote greater cooperation and stability along the Afghan-Pakistani border is out of our hands and depends on the overall relationship between Pakistan and Afghanistan and the outcome of Pakistan-supported Taliban insurgency, which shows few signs of abating as the US begins to withdraw from this conflict. When the final chapter on Afghanistan is written (if indeed there is a final chapter), our diplomacy may prove to have been a heroic exercise that produced little of direct lasting substance and consequence. That being said, if we make no effort to help resolve conflicts where we have a vested interest, we can hardly complain while they fester without any resolution in sight. Part of taking action to help resolve difficult problems is accepting the risk that your efforts may ultimately fail for reasons beyond your control. Furthermore, our experience in the Dubai Process does point to a variety of Canadian advantages and strengths, and the kinds of qualities that might be valuable to others attempting to manage their border disputes, whether they are in sub-Saharan Africa, South America, or the Caribbean.

ASSERTING OURSELVES GLOBALLY

O.D. Skelton, who served as undersecretary of state for external affairs and as a close adviser to Prime Minister Mackenzie King during the interwar years, was "largely responsible," in the words of Canadian historian Norman Hillmer, for "pushing Canada onto the world stage" and for Canada's evolution as an independent nation.[29] However, his premature death in 1941 meant that the active strategy of Canada's diplomatic and political engagement was not sustained. King was far too mild-mannered, shy, and conciliatory to assert himself – and by extension Canada – in the great war councils of the allies, especially when dealing with the outsized personalities of British Prime Minister Winston Churchill or US President Franklin D. Roosevelt. As a consequence, his influence was not commensurate with that of South African and Australian prime ministers of the day on the critical political and military decisions that shaped the Allied strategy, notwithstanding the fact that Canada was the third-largest troop-contributing country to the Allied war effort. Instead, King played, at best, a cameo role. Even when Canada was titular host for the Quebec Conference in 1943, though he appeared in a few photos, he attended no meetings of substance. His main interests, as recorded in the diaries of our high commissioner, Charles Ritchie, seem to have been to request regularly that ruins from the London bombings be retrieved and shipped to his estate at Kingsmere, just north of Ottawa.[30]

As the memoirs of Churchill and others attest, King's unfortunate reluctance to engage in strategic discussions about the war and its aftermath stands in dismal contrast to the valour and sacrifice of the many Canadians who fought on the front lines. The net result was that Canada's substantial military contribution was subjugated, in a somewhat humiliating fashion, to the whim of British commanders.

To this day we suffer from a similar affliction as a nation. We worry unduly about whether the Americans will thank us when they thank others for their military contribution to global security, be it Afghanistan or Libya. And when we fail to get mentioned, as we often do, our sense of national pride is wounded and affronted.

Because of our lopsided relationship with the United States, as the late Margaret Thatcher observed, we are inordinately sensitive and generally tend not to assert ourselves. Our engagements with the world are typically driven more by emotion and a desire to be present, or to have a symbolic seat at the table, rather than substance. But in the turbulent new world we find ourselves in, we must be strong, bold, committed, and driven by interest and real conviction. That must be the basis of our engagement in the Asia-Pacific and our redoubled efforts to deal with the world's new security challenges.

6

Restoring the Allure of Pluralistic Democratic Values

On 14 August 2013, Canadians and the rest of the world woke up to the news that hundreds of Egyptians had died when security forces stormed two encampments where supporters of ousted Egyptian president Mohamed Morsi had been holed up to protest his overthrow by Egypt's military. The television scenes of hundreds of dead Egyptians, many of them young teenagers, were appalling. Yet the bloodshed that day was simply the beginning of an escalating pattern of violence that has engulfed the Arab world's most populous country. Marking a return to repressive rule in the style of Egypt's former dictator Hosni Mubarak, the government declared a state of emergency, giving Egypt's security forces the license to use whatever means they deemed necessary to crack down on the Muslim Brotherhood and its Islamic allies.

Egypt's military coup, which no one wanted to call a coup, was a coup in everything but name. It underscored the difficulty of moving seamlessly from dictatorship to democracy, a challenge affecting not only the Middle East but governance around the globe. People may want pluralistic values but they also want stability and the two do not always go together.

The Arab Spring, which began when a fruit vendor set himself alight in Tunisia after being berated by a female police officer, has dissolved into a pattern of violence and volatility. Tunisia has witnessed the assassination of key opposition leaders and growing divisions in its polity that have delayed the drafting of its constitution. Although Libya has resumed pumping oil, which is the lifeblood of its economy, production is down to a fraction of its 2012 postwar peak, and the security situation has deteriorated rapidly since

Qaddafi's overthrow.[1] In the absence of any kind of effective military or police force, local militias and armed gangs now control many of Libya's cities, towns, and villages. (The worsening security situation was underlined by the attack on the US diplomatic compound in Benghazi and the brutal murder of the US ambassador in 2012.) Syria is engulfed in a brutal civil war. The war has spilled over into neighbouring Lebanon, which itself is now teetering on the brink of civil war. Syria has become a proxy regional and global conflict. The constellation of players includes Russia, Iran, Iraq, Turkey, Qatar, and Saudi Arabia, who are jockeying erratically for influence. Since the departure of President Ali Abdullah Saleh, Yemen still smoulders in recurring tensions among its different tribal factions and long-standing divisions between the country's north and the south, which loyalists of al-Qaeda have exploited to their own advantage. Bahrain, following the brutal crackdown by its Sunni monarchy on political dissenters, faces continuing opposition from its Shi'ite majority. And Iraq, following the withdrawal of American troops, is being shaken by escalating sectarian conflict and violence between its Shi'ite majority and Sunni minority populations. As *The New York Times* ominously reported after a series of terrorist bombing attacks in August 2013, "Across the country, the sectarianism that almost tore Iraq apart after the America-led invasion of 2003 is surging back."[2]

When the Arab Spring first began, many in the West saw it through the prism of the French and American revolutions and as being motivated by liberal values and a desire to establish a new political order based on human dignity, justice, equality, democracy, and the rule of law. As we have now seen, there were other motivations clearly at play, such as a desire simply to get rid of bad leaders and dynastic regimes that had lost their legitimacy and grip on power, as well as deep currents of Islamist extremism and sectarianism. But there is also another narrative at play with broader implications for the West and its support for democracy and nation-building, not just in the Arab world, but throughout the developing world.

Democracy is not the automatic outcome of the so-called "global political awakening" of the newly mobilized populations of the developing world who are throwing off the yoke of years of tyranny and repression. There are other political values and models out there in the world that rival democracy's affections because western democracies have sullied their copybook through clumsy military interventions in the developing world and the mismanagement of their own economic affairs, as in the case of both the United States and Europe in the run-up to the 2008–09 financial crisis and recession, and its aftermath.

Although Islam offers its own political alternative to western values, China stands out increasingly as a beacon for a very different, and, thus far, successful political system, and in recent decades, an even more successful economic model where individual rights are subjugated to the policy direction and control of an all-powerful Communist (at least in name) party. As long as the economy continues to grow and the benefits are spread throughout society in reasonable balance, the desire for stability and continuity will prevail. While Chinese youth can work around blockages on the Internet, they act with self-restraint on the three taboo Ts – commentary on Tiananmen, Tibet, and Taiwan – and rarely chafe at these restrictions.

Military intervention is a blunt unwieldy instrument to promote political change and install democratic values and practices. If western countries, including Canada, are serious about promoting pluralism and democracy in the world they will need a new strategy that relies on concerted diplomacy and much greater levels of cooperation among them to promote stability and advance democratic values in the world's trouble spots.

THE GREAT AWAKENING HAS NOT LED TO DEMOCRACY

According to the liberal tradition, one of the pillars of a stable international order is the embrace of democracy. As Immanuel Kant argued in his essay *Perpetual Peace*, democracies typically do not go to war against each other, and the norms of negotiation, adherence to the rule of law, and respect for human rights that govern relations within democratic states also apply to relations between and among them.[3] Kant's seminal observation about the preconditions for a "democratic peace" is confirmed in a wealth of research by scholars on this matter.[4]

But the evidence that the world as a whole is moving in the direction of Kant's "perpetual peace" is at best inconclusive. On the one hand, since the overthrow of Portugal's dictatorial regime in April 1974, the number of democracies in the world has indeed multiplied dramatically. Before the start of this global trend toward democracy, there were roughly forty countries that could be classified as more or less democratic.[5] Today, Freedom House designates ninety countries, representing 43 per cent of the global population, as free and democratic, and says another sixty are "partly free."[6]

On the other hand, as Freedom House also reports, democracy is under assault in many different corners and regions of the world. Some "27 countries showed significant declines, compared with 16 that showed notable gains" in their democratic development, marking "the seventh consecutive year that *Freedom in the World* has shown more declines than gains worldwide" and there has also been "a stepped-up campaign of persecution by dictators that specifically targeted civil society organizations and independent media."[7] The declines are most evident in the Middle East and Eurasia: "the gains for the Arab Spring countries triggered a reaction, sometimes violent, by authoritarian leaders elsewhere in the Middle East, with resulting setbacks for freedom in Iraq, Jordan, Kuwait, Lebanon, Oman, Syria, and the United Arab Emirates ... Russia took a decided turn for the worse after Vladimir Putin's return to the presidency. Having already marginalized the formal political opposition, he enacted a series of laws meant to squelch a burgeoning societal opposition. The measures imposed severe new penalties on unauthorized demonstrations, restricted the ability of civic groups to raise funds and conduct their work, and placed new controls on the internet ... Kazakhstan, Russia, Tajikistan, and Ukraine all had notable declines."[8]

Massive military interventions in Iraq and Afghanistan aimed at nation-building using a democratic model have backfired on the targets and on the appetites of the US allies for more "democracy by forceful import."

There are now serious questions about whether the West's, and in particular Washington's, zealous penchant for democracy promotion and the terms on which it has been delivered is not, in fact, counterproductive. As Georgetown scholar Charles Kupchan argues, "even if liberal democracies do tend to provide good governance at home and abroad, rapid transitions to democracy historically have had the opposite effect: disorder at home and instability beyond the countries' borders. In nations that lack experience with constitutional constraints and democratic accountability, electoral victors usually embrace winner-take-all strategies; they shut out the opposition, govern as they see fit and unsettle their neighbours. In one case after another – Bosnia, Russia, Ukraine, Iraq, Egypt – newly democratic governments have demonized opponents and ruled with an iron fist."[9]

Sarah Chayes astutely observes that time and again westerners have vested "incautious hope in the notion that [elections] will somehow produce ... a 'more legitimate government.'" She points out that "Afghanistan fits a pattern of transitioning countries that have rushed to elections before their polities were sufficiently constituted. And the results, from Nigeria in 2004 to Egypt and Libya in the wake of the Arab Spring, have [also] been dire." That is because the "rush to elections ... before the development of broadly agreed-upon frameworks to govern political competition helped spark subsequent upheavals. Partisan majorities determined to capitalize on power shirked the more neutral and farsighted responsibilities incumbent upon them as framers."[10]

Such reservations go right to the heart of a long-standing debate in democratic political theory about the virtues of popular sovereignty and whether or not, given the opportunity to do so, men and women will join together in a civil society where the rule of law and a live-and-let-live ethos prevails. This is a classic question, and one that matters as much today as in the nineteenth century.

Like the great English democratic political theorist John Locke, some put their faith in the powers of human reason which, in Locke's words "teaches all Mankind, who will but consult it, that being all equal and independent, no one ought to harm another in his Life, Health, Liberty or Possessions."[11] Locke's doctrine of natural rights and his views about the origins of self-government had enormous appeal among America's founding fathers, especially Thomas Jefferson, but also among more recent American presidents such as Woodrow Wilson, John F. Kennedy, and George W. Bush, who have championed the virtues of democracy and self-determination in America's international affairs.[12]

But others, following in the tradition of John Stuart Mill, are more skeptical. Although Mill believed that democracy is the best form of government because it allows individuals to pursue their self-interest and maximize their own personal happiness, he worried openly about the tyranny of majoritarian rule and "the tendency of society to impose, by other means than civil penalties, its own ideas and practices and rule of conduct on those who dissent from them."[13] According to Mill, unleashing majoritarian rule in societies where there is no tradition of democracy – as in the case of France under Jacobin rule in the early nineteenth century or, for that matter, Egypt today – poses just as much of a threat to personal liberty as authoritarian rule. Mill was not alone in expressing this concern. Alexis de Tocqueville expressed similar reservations about majoritarian rule, as did James Madison and Alexander Hamilton in *The Federalist Papers*.[14]

In stressing the importance of individuality and the exercise of personal freedom, Mill argued that any political system has to protect minority opinion and culture so that they are not trampled by the will of the majority. Mill was also one of the first writers to champion federalism as a form of government that would protect minority rights, especially in the British colony of Canada after the rebellion of the French minority in 1837, as indeed it has. He and other utilitarian philosophers also stressed the importance of a professional, merit-and-career-based public service that was immune to class privilege and political pressure and that would administer the government in the interests of the citizenry as a whole.

CHOOSING THE RIGHT INSTRUMENTS OF INTERVENTION

Today, we should heed Mill's warning that efforts to transplant democracy to societies and cultures that have no real history or experience of it is a problematic enterprise and one where there is a real risk that the outcome will be tyranny or mob rule (or some alternating combination of the two) where elites manipulate and exploit popular prejudices for their own selfish ends, what Fareed Zakaria has referred to as "illiberal democracy."[15]

The widespread belief at the beginning of this century that military force can be used to weaken (or overthrow) oppressive regimes and install democratically elected leaders and institutions in their place has also been cast in doubt by the events of the past decade and the wars of liberation in Iraq, Afghanistan, and Libya. The Bush administration's intervention in Iraq and the lack of emphasis on postwar planning followed clearly from the view that the democratization of Iraq would evolve naturally and quickly in the wake of the Ba'ath Party's ouster.[16] That did not happen. Similarly, the belief that Iraq's "liberation" would spread democracy like toppling dominoes throughout the Middle East proved to be ill-founded. Dominoes did fall. But new democratic structures have not been erected in their place. Instead, there has been chaos.

Afghanistan and Iraq together stand out as flawed military adven-
tures guided by erratic, politically motivated decisions which, in
turn, ultimately reflected democracies' lack of stomach for lengthy,
inconclusive, and lethal military engagements. As events in Syria dis-
mally demonstrate, the US and its allies are most unlikely to volun-
teer for any peacemaking enterprise in a faraway land for a long,
long time.

The other lesson is that, in the absence of a tangible threat to
security and without clearly defined goals and timeframes, injections
of foreign military forces into the affairs of a distant country – no
matter how noble the initial intent – cannot resolve what is essentially a domestic political, as well as security, problem. To be successful, military strikes need to be quick and surgical. They may stop
something temporarily but they are unlikely to be instruments for
long-term solutions. Foreign forces can certainly help but nation-
building is not part of any military tool kit.

Existential threats to national security will have to be dealt with
by means other than occupying forces. A political–diplomatic effort
is the indispensable instrument for success, and this, more than anything, is what the Afghan conflict never witnessed, from America,
NATO, or the UN. Rhetoric is no substitute for hard-headed leadership, commitment, or patient negotiation. The biggest impediment
to "success" in Afghanistan was the inadequacy of all three.

From Iraq to Afghanistan to Libya, where the initial intervention
was prompted by a combination of humanitarian and/or national
security considerations, subsequent efforts to restore political order
and lay the foundations for democratic political processes through
the promotion of elections and the development of legal institutions have not succeeded. Those countries have been the objects
of what Marina Ottaway refers to as "coercive democratization,"
where externally led efforts to hold elections, write new constitu-
tions, and form political parties encounter "stiff opposition from
traditional political authorities."[17] Nowhere is this more apparent
than in Afghanistan where, notwithstanding the thousands of lives
and billions in treasure that have been devoted to rebuilding, it is
still a mess, riddled by a corrupt government, its stability threatened
by a growing Taliban insurgency stoked by Pakistan.

Ultimately, nation-building means the creation or re-creation of a
single national identity as the foundation of common national political institutions. However, in divided societies that have experienced

violent conflict, oppression, or war, narrow clan-based tribal, ethnic, or religious identities can harden, destroying any semblance of
a broader national identity.[18] Further, the notion of "building" democracy in such societies, where mistrust and insecurity are acute, is
particularly illusory. Democratization is a slow process of cultural,
social, and political development that does not simply revolve around
the exercise of the franchise and the holding of free elections. It also
involves the establishment of a civic culture where citizens learn to
become active and responsible participants in the political life of
their country and where negotiation and dialogue becomes a custom
and a rule, rather than the exception. Successful transitions from
dictatorship to democracy also require various leadership groups to
cut deals that help reduce the risk of violence and retribution. Some
scholars have called this "pacting," where newly empowered leaders of a democratic movement strike a deal with the outgoing elites,
promising to respect their core "vital interests."[19] This could include
limited immunity from prosecution, arranging exile for a deposed
leader, or agreeing upon rules by which the deposed party can still
participate in politics. This was the case in apartheid South Africa,
where key social and economic groups such as businesses, labour
unions, and even elements of the government learned to deal with
each other through processes of bargaining and negotiation before
free and open elections were held in 1994. This has not been the
case in Egypt, where the die was cast in early 2011, when Hosni
Mubarak was pushed from office and then put on trial, setting the
tone for the coming conflict in Egyptian politics, where whoever can
bring the biggest crowds to the street rules the day.

Critically, democracy can only develop in societies with a strong,
well-functioning administrative state apparatus that is generally
responsive to the public's needs and welfare. Providing essential services and public goods are critical elements of good governance, as is
a proper understanding of the requirements for governance at both
the national and local levels. Ultimately, the measure of successful
nation-building is the creation of a viable functioning administrative state apparatus, not necessarily full-blown democracy itself. As
Larry Diamond asserts, "a country must first have a state before it
can become a democracy."[20] Or, in the words of Charles Kupchan
again, "Incremental change produces more durable results; liberal democracies must be constructed from the ground up. Constitutional constraints, judicial reform, political parties, economic

privatization – these building blocks of democratic societies need time to take root ... the best way to do that is to go slow."[21]

A lack of a strong civil society is often the Achilles heel in the transition to democracy, especially in countries where civil society has been actively repressed by autocratic regimes. As we have seen in the Arab world, notwithstanding their power to bring people into the streets and topple dictators, popular social protest movements have shown little ability to shape the course of subsequent political events and participate in critical negotiations to construct new institutions and a new political order because a culture of negotiation did not exist during the era of autocratic rule. For example, it is one thing for Egyptians to agree on negative goals, such as getting rid of a dictator. It is much harder to agree on positive goals, such as what the future of their country will look like, who will wield power, who will make the rules, and how minority rights will be protected.

However, external actors and interests should be careful about jumping to the conclusion that what underdeveloped civil society in the Arab world needs are generous doses of hands-on support to strengthen and grow. Wariness in a country like Egypt toward entrenched elites and traditional power structures extends to foreigners, especially Americans, who are generally seen as having played a key role in propping up the *ancien régime*. It is therefore important to listen, respect, and understand the local situation before extending a helping hand. As the Council of the Community of Democracies urges in a recent study: "It should be mandatory at the outset to seek advice from local civil society on how best to support their efforts. Respecting and understanding the different roles and interests of all partners in the democratic development process is a basic requirement for productive relationships and successful support. Outsiders also have to understand and respect the ways in which the local reform process needs to take account of traditional values: social and political practices common in one country can be abrasive in another."[22]

CANADA'S ROLE

The Canadian government's decision in the Spring 2013 budget to fold CIDA into the Department of Foreign Affairs and Trade was long overdue and welcomed by most. Even *The Globe and Mail*, whose editorial page is not always charitable to the Conservative

government, applauded the decision.[23] Save for a few predictable
critical voices, there was surprisingly little gnashing of teeth in Canada's development community, with most NGOS (non-governmental
organizations) preferring to take a quiet, wait-and-see attitude to
the bureaucratic restructuring and reordering of priorities that will
soon follow.

The truth of the matter is that CIDA had increasingly become a
feeble instrument of ODA, rendered increasingly obsolete by the
changing global context of development assistance and a growing awareness that development is not really about poverty alleviation per se, but, instead, about using economic growth, investment,
good governance, and the empowerment of marginalized groups like
women and youth through education and access to opportunity as a
means to end poverty.

The poverty-alleviation narrative has also become less persuasive
as the actual number of low-income countries (LICS) continues to
shrink. China and India, which on a per capita basis aren't major
aid recipients, have lifted themselves out of the poverty trap by their
own bootstraps and the workings of the global economy. LICS are
understandably the priority target for ODA, but in foreign policy
terms some of the most politically troublesome and unstable states
are LMICS like Pakistan, for example, where there are wide disparities in wealth and income between different parts of the country, a
lack of state control over areas with local insurgencies, and chronic
but enduring state failure. These countries typically receive less aid
on a per capita basis than their poorer peers, despite being substantially more fragile at times.

With the stroke of a pen, development assistance moves from the
periphery of government (CIDA had become an orphan in our foreign-policy machinery) to the centre (that, at least, is how DFATD
would like to see it itself). Canada's three principal instruments of
foreign policy will now be concentrated in what should be a more
coherent, more complementary, and more effective whole, provided
the change at the top is not undermined by bureaucratic turf wars
at other levels.

The devil is in the details and the manner in which the restructuring of Canada's roughly $4 billion aid program will be imple-
mented. Questions persist about the effectiveness of virtually all
bilateral ODA efforts by governments. Various models for delivery
have been tried. The aid business is plagued by the ebb and flow of

new fashions and fads as the cottage industry built around the study of development processes criticizes old ways of doing business and constantly tries to offer something new. With an ever-changing cluster of programs, taxpayers are left wondering what is being done and whether programs are having the desired impact. Genuinely independent approaches like that of the Gates Foundation and some select NGOs tend to get higher accolades, but the track records and analyses of results are chequered.

By becoming an integral part of DFATD, and with at least one senior minister to call on, development assistance has a chance of being more relevant and more effective. But this should not be left to chance alone. During the 2006 transition to the Harper government, an attempt was made to move CIDA organizationally into what had become by then a bifurcated DFAIT (Department of Foreign Affairs and International Trade). The move was resisted by senior bureaucrats in a manner that would have made the writers of the *Yes Minister* series proud. "Too complicated, likely to arouse negative reaction, too technical and not worth the agony," etc. Those sentiments prevailed in CIDA. The *Yes Minister* problem will still be there in the implementation of this new reorganization unless the government fights bureaucratic inertia and makes a concerted effort to fundamentally change the way we target and manage our ODA.

In the end much will depend on the leadership given to Canada's ODA programs by ministers and officials wherever they reside, but if more of what we do is presented as reflecting or reinforcing our foreign policy principles and priorities, that is as it should be.

In recent years much of Canada's development assistance policies have focused on public sector outputs and the requirements of good governance, such as improving systems of public finance in developing countries, providing budgetary support, strengthening systems of accountability, ending corruption, and promoting democracy, human rights (especially gender equality), and the rule of law. This emphasis is well placed because it recognizes that state building is a prerequisite to democracy building. However, such efforts should not be limited to LICs because many LMICs face similar challenges in their institutional development. In some of these countries, such as Kazakhstan and Mongolia, Canada has growing investments where there are major problems in local governance and the rule of law. Canada needs to strengthen its trade, investment, and development agenda for these countries and reach out to Canadian companies who are operating in these markets about enlisting their support in promoting better systems of governance and the rule of law in the countries in which they operate.

A case in point is the experience of HudBay Minerals in Guatemala. HudBay, which purchased a Guatemalan nickel mine in 2008, became embroiled in the front lines of the global debate over the extent to which private corporations must strive to ensure that they do no harm and that they share the benefits of their business with local populations when engaging in overseas investments. Tragically, in 2009, during negotiations to relocate households living near the mine, community leader Adolfo Ich was killed by Guatemalan security officials.[24] Protesters alleged that security officials had committed other abuses, such as rape, in and around the site. Today, HudBay is facing civil lawsuits in an Ontario court, as the victims of the abuses seek compensation. Ultimately, every company that does business overseas cannot insulate itself from the political risks of investing in foreign countries. But Canadian firms can also be a force for positive change that increases the security of everyday people in developing countries if, as a matter of policy, we engage with local governments and insist that good governance and respect for human rights and dignity are a standard condition for investment.

The Middle East and North Africa are tricky regions for Canada. In much of the region the weakness of political institutions, or simply their absence, is why the military still retains power. However, the Arab Spring, as discussed earlier, is democracy undefined as opposed to liberal democracy. It has degenerated in some countries into civil unrest, instability, and a series of developments that could have adverse consequences for the West and Canada. It will be hard for many of these countries to institutionalize large-scale social movements into democracy and to hold elections when the ground has not been properly laid beforehand. The chief risk facing the Arab world right now is that elections will simply bring to power governments riding a wave of populism whose commitment to pluralism and the accommodation of different political and religious values is skin deep.

Canada could play a constructive role in advancing religious freedom, pluralism, the rule of law, and human rights, especially in those countries where the risks of religious extremism and intolerance run high. The key foundations of Canadian foreign policy were laid more than sixty years ago by then-secretary of state for external affairs Louis St Laurent in the Gray Memorial Lecture at the University of Toronto on 13 January 1947. It was a truly magisterial speech and like all great pieces of oratory on such weighty matters it identified clear principles that would serve as a guide for future action. It was not partisan. Instead, it spoke to the heart of Canadian values and interests by identifying a number of key principles for action. Among them, "we dare not fashion a policy which is based on the particular interests of any economic group, of any class or of any section of the country. We must be on guard especially against the claims of extravagant regionalism no matter where they have their origin ... a disunited Canada will be a powerless one."[25]

St Laurent's speech underscored that our "conception of political liberty" which "is an inheritance from both our French and English backgrounds" should "shape our external policy." It also stressed the importance of basing our foreign policy on a "conception of human values." And it stressed our "willingness to accept international responsibilities." However, in today's world we will have to tread carefully, recognizing that our sources of leverage are limited. Whatever we ultimately decide to do to promote pluralism will have to be done with allies who share our democratic values.

Although there was much criticism when the Government of Canada established an office of religious freedom in February 2013, the decision to do so was entirely consistent with Canada's long-standing leadership in advancing human rights and taking "principled positions to promote Canadian values of pluralism and tolerance throughout the world."[26] The office's mandate to "protect, and advocate on behalf of religious minorities under threat; oppose religious hatred and intolerance; and promote Canadian values of pluralism and tolerance abroad" is in fact sound, provided the office is properly resourced and staffed.[27] In fact, a similar office exists in the US Department of State, where it has been operating for many years.

Canada has also supported the Global Centre for Pluralism, established by the Aga Khan, which describes itself as "an independent, not-for-profit international research and education centre located in Ottawa, Canada."[28] The Centre was "[i]nspired by the example of Canada's inclusive approach to citizenship" and "works to advance respect for diversity worldwide, believing that openness and understanding toward the cultures, social structures, values and faiths of other peoples are essential to the survival of an interdependent world."[29]

Both of these instruments, along with others, can serve as important tools of Canadian foreign policy and our own efforts to promote and restore the allure of democratic pluralist values. But it will be a tough uphill battle that will require patience and perseverance. To be effective, Canada will have to work alongside other countries that are also prepared to speak out against violations of freedom of religion and defend basic human rights. We should not try to do everything ourselves, given our limited resources and capacities for influence.

THE D10 — CREATING A COUNCIL OF DEMOCRATIC NATIONS TO WORK TOGETHER

Canada should work closely together with other western democracies to promote pluralistic values and secular traditions as the tidal wave unleashed by the Great Awakening spreads through the Arab world and into other regions. What's happening in Egypt, Syria, and elsewhere in the Middle East and North Africa speaks to a struggle that will envelop other countries in the Eurasian and Pacific regions for years to come. It is a struggle between tolerant forms of secular democracy as practised in the West and religious (Islamic) zealotry – or theocracy, as in Iran – along with authoritarian brands of state-sponsored capitalism, as in the case of China, and, to a lesser extent, Russia, both of which are anxious to exploit perceptions of western weakness.

Leadership in support of western values and ideals must begin with the United States. However, in order to lead, the US first has to listen to others. It has been remarkably inept throughout the Arab world's continuing crisis. On the Morsi regime it blew cold and then hot. The Obama administration convinced itself that it could do business with Morsi when he signalled that he would not try to renegotiate Egypt's peace treaty with Israel. There was also little overt criticism of Morsi by the Obama White House after he rewrote Egypt's constitution to elevate sharia law and empower himself and the Muslim Brotherhood. When Coptic Christians were attacked by Islamist extremists or when Morsi subverted civil rights, Washington's response was mealy and meek. But now that Morsi is out and the military is back in power, Washington is playing a different tune. It cancelled joint military exercises when security forces turned their guns on the Brotherhood and its supporters, but other than voicing expressions of disdain has done little else.

The US has both leverage and influence, given the billions it funnels to Egypt's military. Carefully nuanced press statements may straddle diplomatic imperatives, but the situation calls for firm but quiet diplomacy, led by the one power with real influence – the United States – and supported by its like-minded allies.

Canada has little scope for direct influence in the Arab world. We should, however, quietly urge the US to focus on the bigger challenges of political accommodation and pluralism, and not just the perennial problem of Israel–Palestine. The US continues to have major interests in Saudi Arabia and the Gulf, where messages of secular democracy have little resonance. But surely it and its western allies can all endorse more opportunities for free expression and free assembly.

Some of this may be wishful thinking as the situation in the Arab world's most populous nation becomes increasingly polarized and dangerous. But unlike the case of the Algerian coup of 1992, when the military took power to thwart the political ambitions of Islamists who had won national elections, the US and its western allies can't simply turn a blind eye this time.

In a social media universe, dissent in authoritarian societies cannot be suppressed as easily as in decades past. Progress will never be linear. Situations will not be black or white – but even grey can have texture. The West is going to have to work harder if wants to be on the right side of history in the Middle East and elsewhere. That means encouraging consistent steps toward pluralistic secular democracy while recognizing that values, unlike flowers, are not easily transplanted.

Western leaders should also talk less about the need for democratic elections and instead encourage societies in transition that are experiencing turmoil and upheaval to move in the direction of a genuinely inclusive process of national dialogue and reconciliation. This too is a challenge for Canada's own forms of engagement, which have traditionally focused on monitoring elections. There is clearly much more that has to be done in terms of the formation and strengthening of political parties, the engagement of civil society, and the healing of divided societies by developing habits of negotiation. For example, although Canada is providing extensive humanitarian assistance to Burma (Myanmar), if Burma is to make a successful political and economic transformation, our assistance will have to extend to a long-term strategy that includes promoting human rights, embedding the right to free expression, enhancing government accountability, popular participation in ongoing peace processes, and the development of a democratic culture.

Canada should also lend its strong support to a "D10" initiative that would bring together the ten leading democratic nations of the world. These include the US and its closest democratic allies, including Canada, the UK, Germany, France, Japan, Italy, Australia, South Korea, and the European Union.

The concept of a D10 was developed recently by Ash Jain and David Gordon as a means for like-minded democracies to assert their values and work more effectively around the blockages in existing institutions such as the UN Security Council, the G8, and even the G20, where the conflicting positions of Russia and China prevent consensus and action on global problems.[30] Jain argues for the D10 because "as a "unique community of values," NATO has long served to promote cooperation among allies ... But the alliance lacks the ability to serve as a broader venue for like-minded coordination. Its mandate remains limited to defense and security cooperation, whereas current threats and challenges often require a wider set of coordinated foreign policy actions, including those related to sanctions, foreign assistance, and public diplomacy. At the same time, other important political challenges, such as the promotion of democracy, human rights, and transnational justice, remain largely outside of NATO's purview."[31]

The specific functions of a D10, as outlined by Jain, include the following:

- STRATEGIC CONSULTATION. As Jain argues, "[f]irst, the D10 would offer a standing framework for consultation at the strategic level, allowing the like-minded to collaborate on analyzing global challenges and defining strategies for advancing a rule-based international order, countering terrorism, preventing nuclear proliferation, promoting democracy and human rights, protecting civilians against state violence, and defending the global commons. The D10 could focus on production of a joint security strategy setting .... Among the range of challenges that could benefit from such collective analysis are China's activities in the South China Sea, and more broadly its role as a rising global power; the future of political Islam in the wake of the Arab Spring, the promotion of democracy in an increasingly difficult Russia, and the protection of Internet freedom."[32]

- POLICY COORDINATION. According to Jain, "[t]he D10's second function would be to facilitate policy coordination on specific political and security challenges. Among trusted allies, participants could share relevant intelligence and sensitive information, discuss the merits of various policy options, and, work to coordinate diplomatic actions on such challenges."[33]
- CRISIS RESPONSE. Finally, says Jain, "the D10 could provide a venue to formulate collective responses to future political or security crises. In the wake of a new North Korean provocation in East Asia or an Iranian escalation against Western interests in the Persian Gulf, for example, the like-minded could come together through this venue to forge a rapid and unified response to address such a crisis."[34]

The attractiveness of the D10 concept is that it does not call for the creation of yet another new international organization. Rather, it is intended to serve as an informal coordinating mechanism among leading democratic nations, who must recognize that it is in their collective interest to work together in a world in which there are other competing political models and belief systems that have their own powerful poles of attraction.

CONCLUSION

As noted earlier, Prime Minister Louis St Laurent in his Gray address argued that Canada's foreign policy should be based on a "conception of human values," while stressing our "willingness to accept international responsibilities." However, to use St Laurent's own words, we should be more than just "present" in international councils. We must be active and committed global citizens defending our democratic values and traditions of tolerance while recognizing that such values are not easily transplanted from our soil to others. However, we must also overcome our own cynicism, which is cancerous and cripples our inclination to act.

7

Managing Internal Fault Lines

Not all the challenges facing Canada are external. As a nation with more geography than history, and often more points of differentiation than cohesion, internal management poses difficulties which, at times, seem insurmountable.

THE MACKENZIE VALLEY SAGA

In March of 1974, the Mackenzie Valley Pipeline Inquiry, also known as the Berger Inquiry after its head, Justice Tom Berger, was commissioned by the Government of Canada to investigate the social, environmental, and economic impact of a proposed pipeline to transmit gas through the Yukon and Mackenzie River Valley of the Northwest Territories. The inquiry cost $5.3 million.[1] The report compiled 40,000 pages of text and evidence in 283 volumes.[2] The verdict was that no pipeline should be built through the northern Yukon and that a pipeline through the Mackenzie Valley should be delayed for at least ten years, allowing time for the settlement of Aboriginal land claims and decisions on key conservation areas to be safeguarded.

Ever since, major energy companies have attempted to gain approval for a 1,200 kilometre pipeline from the natural gas fields of Canada's north to the energy heartland of Alberta, not only to bring gas from the Arctic to market but also to help fuel the expansion of Alberta's oil sands.

The project would have employed thousands of people in depressed northern communities, particularly Aboriginal ones, and brought additional economic benefits to First Nations in exchange for the right to construct pipeline across their lands. Even though the federal government granted provisional approval in March 2011 to what had become a $16 billion project – more than twice the original estimate – the Mackenzie pipeline fell under the combined weight of intractable and costly regulatory oversight (which may have cost more than $600 million in total),[3] environmental and Aboriginal concerns, declining gas prices, and the more attractive economies of other transmission alternatives, particularly for liquefied natural gas exports from the West Coast.[4]

While some may cheer the failure of the Mackenzie pipeline, it is a pointed example of constipated decision-making in Canada, of process overwhelming substance. Without an efficient process for resolution, conflicting claims, some more pertinent than others, pose a real threat to any major energy project. If the building of the TransCanada pipeline and the St Lawrence Seaway two decades before the Berger Inquiry underscore action-building infrastructure at its best, the Mackenzie Valley saga epitomizes the opposite.

The difference highlights one of Canada's greatest challenges – managing internal fault lines in a balanced manner to sustain prosperity while safeguarding our environment. Consensus on needed infrastructure poses a chronic challenge for our federation.

INFRASTRUCTURE

If Canada expects to export our products to markets where demand is growing, we need to bolster much of our antiquated transport and transmission infrastructure – from power grids to pipelines, from ports and bridges to roads, railways, and border crossings. The benefits of new pipeline infrastructure alone would be huge. Three pipelines (Trans Mountain, Northern Gateway and West–East) would generate $1.3 trillion for our GDP through to 2035, or $52 billion per year. They would also contribute almost $300 billion in government revenues during the same period.

This should be a higher priority for nation-building and for federal–provincial collaboration. What we can ill afford is a repeat of the Mackenzie Valley fiasco – after almost four decades of costly on and off regulatory wrangling, not one inch of pipeline laid.

And yet, what we are still seeing are provincial rivalries frustrating pipelines to the West Coast and historical grievances stymying hydro developments on the East Coast. Aboriginal grievances and environmental pressures are multiplying as well, providing an impressive amount of work for lawyers but chilling the interest of investors and producers alike. Adding to the burden of decision-making is regulatory overlap between often competing federal and provincial authorities.

The shortage of pipeline capacity in Canada for oil shipments has prompted a dramatic increase in crude oil exports by rail (up more than ten times in recent years, and up four times if we compare the first half of 2012 with the first half of 2013),[5] which is not only more costly and has larger carbon emissions but, as demonstrated tragically by the explosions in Lac Mégantic, less safe than pipelines. A test case going forward is whether Energy East – a project carrying oil from West to East to serve both domestic consumption and exports – will gain the necessary approval.

To reinforce and refurbish aging transmission and distribution systems for electricity, it is estimated that nearly $300 billion in investments will be needed to meet Canada's demand for reliable electricity in 2030.[6] The problem is, that kind of funding requires an assured rate of return for utilities and for others paying the infrastructure costs. Yet the provinces, notably those, like Ontario, that have invested heavily in questionable Green Energy subsidies, are reluctant to saddle taxpayers with even higher rates than those already planned.

Many politicians are calling for needed reforms, including steps to mitigate against severe weather. Risk mitigation is the name of the game but the political courage to make the needed investments is as uncertain as the reliability of our aging power grid. In the absence of a national commitment, a major electricity outage, like the one in 2003 (or a catastrophe of similar proportions) may be what is needed to jolt attention and action.

There is no easy way to reconcile the serious and often conflicting positions involved in debates over infrastructure. The federal government is trying to streamline regulatory approvals. Immediately after Confederation, similar obstacles had to be overcome to build transcontinental railways. These involved controversy, even some chicanery, but in each case the single ingredient for ultimate success was the vision and firm leadership from Ottawa that made things happen.

That is the lesson for government today. The government either succumbs to the pressures seeking to delay or frustrate essential infrastructure or it charts a vision and clear priorities to enhance the

well-being of the nation with equal parts of courage and determination. The only viable solution to the infrastructure morass is strong
compelling federal leadership.

NATION-BUILDING IN THE ARCTIC

Nowhere is the need for infrastructure development more urgent
than in the Arctic. Canada sees itself as an Arctic nation and yet, as
the Mackenzie Valley saga and decades of broader neglect demonstrate, we do little more than assert sovereign claims to the territory
from time to time. Other Arctic nations, notably Russia and several Scandinavian countries, are moving ahead to capture the enormous economic and human development potential of this region,
deploying the infrastructure and resources needed to adapt to the
changing climate and the melting ocean. Even the Chinese, in con-
junction with the Russians, are becoming active.[7]

Prime Minister Harper has shown commendable interest in Canada's Arctic, paying annual visits to the region and announcing our
intention to expand our territorial claims right up to the North
Pole. But effective stewardship requires commitment that extends
beyond such high-level visits and announcements. What is needed
is consistent leadership and a plan of action, both of which break
out of the existing bureaucratic morass and commit to the construction of efficient and environmentally sensitive infrastructure
and transportation facilities that will support energy and mineral
development, promote eco-tourism, and enhance livelihoods in
local communities.

Canada's Arctic and the challenges it faces are vast. Isolated,
thinly populated communities confront a wide range of social and
economic pressures as they struggle to sustain traditional values and
a viable future. The federal government's span of responsibility is
equally vast, but modestly resourced, and scattered across several
departments and agencies with little cohesion among them.

Significant climatic changes open the door to new socio-economic
potential but they also pose negative ecological challenges. The shipping season is getting longer but the weather is becoming less certain,
with unpredictable implications for wildlife and for the traditional
way of life in the region.

A policy report published by CIGI in the summer of 2013 identified a "significant transportation deficit" affecting all communities

in Nunavut and proposed that the federal government develop an "Arctic Maritime Corridor and Gateways Initiative" for the region modelled after the Asia-Pacific Initiative launched a decade earlier.[8] Whether or not more interdepartmental institutional process is the right answer, Canada's Arctic and the prospect of an enlightened twenty-first-century economy should be addressed urgently as an example of progressive nation-building.

There is a defence dimension to the Arctic as well. Again, simple claims of sovereignty ring hollow in the absence of resources to monitor activity in the Far North. Modest steps have been taken, including the promise of twenty-first-century icebreakers for the Arctic to give life to the historic Northwest Passage. The use of drones for surveillance is one example of what should be instituted. Another would be to make the Arctic an integral part of naval strategy. Canada's navy is modest by any measure and certainly not capable of more than a minor support role in either the Atlantic or the Pacific. But it should have a presence in the Arctic, giving substance to our sovereignty and ensuring that we will have a more credible voice in the growing network of multilateral councils in the Arctic.

What we need, in short, is a balance of soft and hard power to give substance to our stewardship and to integrate the Arctic into the culture and well-being of Canada, as opposed to empty space at the top of our maps.

ENERGY

It is one thing to claim to be an energy superpower but quite another to establish policies, a regulatory framework, and infrastructure to support such a claim. In an ironic twist of history, Alberta, which fought tooth and nail against the National Energy Program – and with good reason – is now in the vanguard of those calling for a National Energy "strategy" in Canada. Regardless of the merit of a "strategy" (or a "program"), these calls underscore the frustration about our inability to turn a comparative advantage – our energy resource base, much of which lies in Alberta – into a national asset. Whatever we call it, we need greater political coherence on how this asset can best be developed in a manner that enhances our prosperity while sustaining principled standards to safeguard our environment. The debate should not offer a stark and false choice of one versus the other.

SECURITIES REGULATION

Efforts to establish a national securities regulator in Canada have been stymied by obstreperous provincial fiefdoms and a limp Supreme Court ruling. Canada is alone among G7 countries without a single securities regulator in a rapidly globalizing world. Companies – Canadian and foreign – are left to contend with excessive and costly procedures involving thirteen different agencies (yes, even the territories play the game) despite the fact that very few of these mini-regulators have sufficient expertise. Most often, they follow in lockstep with the Ontario Securities Commission. Ottawa's creation of a cooperative securities regulator in partnership with British Columbia and Ontario is a long-overdue step in the right direction, but only a partial step, nonetheless. "Going for bronze" is not a salutary objective for financial regulation of any kind in the twenty-first century.

Given the quasi-market nature of many of these markets, the government needs to consider non-conventional approaches to negotiations and seek additional binding mechanisms for the adjudication of disputes, as well as strong protection for intellectual property and for technology transfer as matters of priority.

ABORIGINAL ISSUES

The squalid conditions on many of Canada's Aboriginal reserves are a national embarrassment. The pattern of gross neglect and counterproductive jurisdictional, even constitutional, squabbling has done little to address basic problems of health, education, and employment. It is the most glaring fault line in the country today. Pressures are mounting, as is the Aboriginal population of Canada – the fastest growing by far of any population segment.[9] It is always easier to find fault than to design solutions and there is a distinct lack of coherence on all sides of this debate. As a country we can choose to be hobbled by history while searching for constitutional nirvana or we can undertake to tackle issues at a practical level, one by one, using examples of successful adaptation and economic well-being as models for broader implementation. What we can ill afford to do is sidestep or ignore a glaring problem at home while we attempt to implement an imaginative global agenda. Our Aboriginal communities should be able to benefit from such an agenda but they will not be able to if they remain locked in nineteenth-century straitjackets that impair development.

Land claims disputes and constitutional challenges have a life of their own that may only be resolved by the courts, but the severe deficiencies in education and basic health facilities on the reservations are eminently fixable. We cannot expect Native peoples to benefit from the quality of life available to most Canadians if they are denied the wherewithal and the responsibility to acquire what others take for granted. Neither the federal government nor the Aboriginal leaders can continue to sidestep their shared responsibilities.

IMMIGRATION

Immigration is primarily a federal responsibility. The policy itself is subject to periodic debate and the role of the provinces is one element of the debate. Canada is known as a nation of immigrants and one that has been welcoming around 250,000 new immigrants and refugees a year since 2001, one of the highest rates in the world.[10] In addition to immigrants and refugees, Canada has also welcomed at least 160,000 temporary foreign workers every year since 2006. With a population more than ten times the size of Canada's, the US takes in about 1,000,000 immigrants (legally) each year.[11]

Opinions vary sharply as to whether the annual intake is good or bad for the Canadian economy and for the well-being of Canada's society. Some contend that too many of the most recent entrants become a drag on the country's social safety net and are placing an excessive burden on major cities like Toronto and Vancouver for which there is no adequate recompense. There is also concern that the quality and the volume of immigration should be better attuned to the needs of our society.[12]

Others argue that the volume is necessary to offset declining birth rates and employee shortages from an increasingly aging population.[13] Ethnic communities in support of larger intakes tend to resonate powerfully at election time.[14] Many in both camps recognize that there are abuses in the system as a whole which includes refugee admissions and more than 200,000 temporary foreign workers in 2012 alone.[15] Ironically, larger numbers of temporary foreign workers are needed to fill vacancies not being filled either by new immigrants or by unemployed Canadians!

Recommendations are made regularly to provincial governments to expedite and streamline professional accreditation for landed immigrants but few reforms along these lines have been implemented at the provincial level, where much of the responsibility lies. That is just one example of how jurisdictional overlap between levels of government also complicates immigration.

Quebec has demanded and obtained a greater say in the selection of immigrants, using its unique need to bolster the French fact through immigration. But, at a time of increasing security concerns these provincial downloads raise doubts, especially in the US, about the effectiveness of the vetting process.

Unquestionably, immigration has been a net benefit to Canada over time, and our ability to assimilate people of different races, religions, and ethnicity from around the world peacefully and responsibly enables us to assert with confidence that we walk the talk on the values of pluralism. But immigration is more than a numbers game. The problems of abuse, the economic costs for major urban centres, and the systemic weakness of security checks by different levels of government – with varying capabilities to conduct each check – all require prudent analysis and realignment. What is needed most is a comprehensive strategy on immigration, one that pragmatically reconciles our need, notably for skilled immigrants, along with the capacity of our major cities to accommodate significant annual intakes. It calls for a spirit of cooperation, coherence, and discipline at all levels of government.

The federal government cannot subcontract its responsibility to lead both the policy and the delivery of future immigration. At minimum, during periods of high unemployment there should be a greater effort to match Canadians to jobs that are in demand before resorting to temporary foreign workers.

EDUCATION

Above all else, the provinces need to spend more and better time addressing policy areas that are predominantly their responsibility – namely health care and education. Much has already been written about the problems of health care in Canada and it is not a subject pertinent to the theme of this book. But education is critical to our ability to compete and succeed in a more uncertain world.

The problems in education are even more glaring than those in immigration. As Ken Coates and Bill Morrison observed in a 2012 *Walrus* essay, "Canada's post-secondary education system is failing our students and our economy."[16] We no longer live in a world where, if you work hard and play by the rules, you will be assured a decent life. Technology and globalization are wiping out lower-skill jobs faster than our institutions are adapting to raising skill levels for new jobs. There is a fundamental conflict between access and quality. Governments relentlessly pursue the goal of universal access to higher education but the more they provide, the more diluted the standards of quality become.

We have one of the highest rates of post-secondary graduation – second only to South Korea – but not all degrees are of equal value or relevance to today's economy. In Canada, there is a serious misalignment between what graduates have learned and what they need to know in order to find productive employment. Those seeking to fill advanced manufacturing, IT, and skilled construction jobs are in strong demand, whereas those with bachelor's degrees in English, outdoor recreation, psychology, sociology, or education itself are hard-pressed to find employment. We are graduating too many of the latter and not enough of the former. The imbalance explains why companies and provinces – particularly those in Western Canada – are clamouring for increases in temporary foreign workers to fill jobs in demand.

It is why Jason Kenney, as minister responsible for the temporary foreign worker programs, lamented in April 2012 that "one of the things that frustrates me is that culturally perhaps in our education system we have devalued basic work and trades."[17] That is a major reason why we import some 160,000 temporary workers annually. That is also no doubt why, in the summer of 2013, Jason Kenney was handed what the government believes is its single biggest challenge – aligning skills training and education to jobs in demand.

At the turn of the century, supporting a knowledge economy became the mantra for higher education. Money poured in from governments for research and innovation, along with a push for mass participation. "If you want more money, take in more students" became the rallying cry.[18] So the post-secondary institutions did, but with little attention to what should be taught. Instead, students were given the luxury of choosing whatever they wished. Meanwhile, the knowledge economy did not produce the anticipated job growth. Technology enabled outsourcing to places like Mumbai rather than Waterloo. Higher education should be about future careers, and yet students get little practical counselling on potential job prospects.

And now, at a time of fiscal restraint, our bloated post-secondary institutions are strapped for funds. They are busy competing with one another for higher-paying foreign students to fill the budget gaps, while desperately dispatching increasing numbers of Canadian graduates to teach English abroad, regardless of their academic training. Too many university graduates are obliged to take employment that requires no post-secondary qualifications while, at the same time, employers complain that there are too few properly skilled individuals available for jobs in demand. Action is needed to reconcile the sharp imbalance.

Part of the problem is that the private sector is unwilling or unable to invest in adequate training for employees so they can obtain needed skills. Canadian companies not only have a dismal record of innovative investment, they are also reluctant to invest in the human dimension of their potential success.

Educational institutions are a crucial element of future prosperity. Unfortunately, as former Harvard president Derek Bok observed in *Higher Education in America*, university administrators these days spend more time trying to keep the peace with and between faculties, departments, governments, and fundraisers than on implementing changes that would help students.[19] The same can be said about university administrators in Canada. Academic deans and university presidents are more concerned about increasing enrolment, hence funding, than about the standards of education being offered or the imbalance between academic disciplines being served in an increasingly competitive post-secondary system.

Former US education secretary Bill Bennett offers a radical prescription, suggesting in *Is College Worth It?* that students who choose anthropology rather than engineering should pay a premium for their personal choice – either higher tuition or higher interest rates on student loans.[20] Not likely, of course, in the US or Canada. The answer is not more but better education, focused more on the needs of our economy and our society and less on the personal preferences of students. In China, more than one in three graduates have degrees in engineering disciplines.[21] In Canada, it is one in fourteen![22] It is hard to be innovative if you lack the basic skills to develop new concepts.

Other countries appear to be doing a better job of directing students into the fields in greatest demand. Canada should do no less. Children in Estonia start to learn how to develop software code in school in Grade 1.[23] Too many students the same age in Canada spend most of their time on video games. As Amanda Ripley pointed out in her book *Smartest Kids in the World*, the most important aspect of education is "a pervasive belief in rigor. Shared expectations that tests will measure results along with policies that attract, train, and pay for top teaching talent are ingredients that enabled Finland, Korea, and Poland to move from the bottom to the top in a generation or less."[24]

It is time our governments – provincial and federal – used their funding of academic institutions more as forceful prods than as gentle nudging to bring about reforms more in line with the needs of our society. Instead of essentially aimless incentives to universities to fill enrolment numbers, allocations of government funding should be weighted heavily to what is needed as opposed to what is desired.

Regrettably, as Coates noted, what we have seen most recently, and notably in Quebec, is that students are demanding greater access and lower fees. Precisely the wrong direction on both counts and yet governments cave in, inevitably worsening the quality and the value of undergraduate education and compounding the problem of skills shortages in the country. Everyone agrees that we have a problem and that quantity should not trump quality but prescriptions for change inevitably emphasize more process, more consultation, and more study than action. Excessive comfort and complacency is at the root of the challenge Canada faces on education. Universities are uncomfortable with the reality that, for most students, they are primarily job-training institutions.

Our post-secondary institutions should be a magnet of excellence, not only to train and equip Canadians for a better future but also to attract the best students from emerging markets. They should not be an expedient perch for expanding enrolment numbers. Like immigration, education should be more than a numbers game, with a higher accent on excellence and a sharp focus on disciplines that will enable graduates to contribute to a more prosperous, more decent way of life.

The most recent OECD report on education was a source of dismay for Paul Cappon, a former head of the Canadian Council on Learning. Canadians between the ages of sixteen and twenty-four, i.e., the most recent graduates, ranked fourteenth out of twenty-one on literacy and fifteenth out of twenty-one on numeracy. "Not only," said Cappon, "is Canada mediocre at best, we now know that our future in learning, and therefore our prosperity, is more clouded than ever."[25]

Educational reform proposals being contemplated in BC seek a "child-centered, less structured way of learning." These are modelled after the lamentable Hall-Dennis recommendations from the 1968 that put Ontario's educational system on a downward slide for more than a generation before a degree of common sense prevailed. Experimental theories may be fine for the bureaucrats in our education ministries but the record shows that they have done precious little to advance the learning of our most precious assets.

The OECD report should ring alarm bells for education and administration alike and they should be held to a standard of accountability higher than "mediocre."

INTERNATIONAL REPRESENTATION

Although the British North America Act was designed to clearly distinguish between the powers of the federal and provincial branches of government, those responsibilities have, since Confederation, become more blurred, not more precise. This is particularly the case in the conduct of international affairs, despite the fact that the power for foreign affairs, for defence, and for trade and commerce is explicitly federal.

The blur is evident from the patchwork quilt of Canada's external representatives. Along with over 260 embassies, high commissions, consulates, and other overseas offices, we have a growing number of separate provincial offices, and individual provincial representation housed in several embassies. Many of these work more or less hand in hand with their federal counterparts. Some operate independently, as offices of the Quebec government customarily do, which, as a matter of principle, operate independently from their federal colleagues and sometimes (notably in Paris) at cross purposes.

When, in the name of fiscal restraint, the federal government acted recently to reduce Canadian representation abroad, several provinces, including some, like Quebec, Ontario, and Alberta, with serious budget deficits of their own, have been quick to fill the vacuum. For example, British Columbia has opened more than ten foreign offices since 2007; Alberta has ten trade and investment offices around the world; Manitoba has opened five foreign offices since 1987 (including one in Brazil in 2012); Ontario has ten offices in three continents (though all are co-located in Canadian government sites); and Quebec has twenty-six foreign offices around the world. (What this escalating provincial representation does, of course, is fuel demands from the provinces for greater involvement in trade negotiations.) Meanwhile, in 2012, DFAIT's (now DFATD) budget was cut by $350 million, spread over three years. Canada has also closed several overseas offices in recent years, including an office in Cape Town, South Africa and our high commission in Malawi.[26] Our diplomatic representative in Baghdad is housed in the UK Embassy.

The provinces allege that federal representatives are often incapable of providing adequate support to the particular priority sectors of each province – energy for Alberta, potash and agriculture for Saskatchewan, fish exports from the Maritimes, etc. The same logic reinforces regular junkets by premiers and their ministerial colleagues to various international capitals, often more frequent than visits to remote parts of their provinces, ostensibly to promote trade and investment opportunities.[27]

The image presented for and about Canada is often as confused as the impact. If the aim is to play coherently as Team Canada, some reordering of roles and responsibilities is essential.

The trend to increased international representation by the provinces is completely ad hoc and self-directed. There should be a more rational basis for the allocation of scarce resources. A proper process of consultation and implementation should be an integral feature of a coherent global trade and investment strategy, one that sets priorities for negotiations and for a recalibration of representation. Scarce resources should be concentrated on markets with significant growth potential where they can be most effective in delivering tangible results for Canadian firms.

The shifting economic landscape in Canada – with power moving from the centre to the West – parallels the global economic transformation. Future equalization and other federal transfers will have to accommodate this change and should be reflected more tangibly in trade and investment policies and priorities as well.

More broadly, both levels of government should give a sharper focus to matters that are predominately within their jurisdiction and reduce wasteful overlap. The federal government should take the lead, defining a national vision for trade and investment, one that recognizes the legitimate role for provinces in areas of their jurisdiction but keeps the responsibility for leadership clearly with federal representatives.

INTERPROVINCIAL TRADE

The provinces should, first and foremost, make the perennial promise of interprovincial free trade a reality within a fixed time frame (three years). The existing barriers are estimated to cost Canada $21 billion annually – clearly a problem worth fixing.[28] The western provinces have already provided a model that the others should emulate. To encourage more than rhetorical commitments to the task, interprovincial free trade should be a conditional part of pending equalization discussions. Given that the onus to contribute to equalization payments is shifting dramatically to the West, the potential for leverage would seem axiomatic.

In an extraordinary move, the federal government invited the provinces to participate fully in the CETA negotiations, thereby adding an additional layer of complexity to the process. It is incongruous to see provinces demand a full role in liberalizing international markets while steadfastly refusing to dismantle interprovincial barriers at home.[29] On a more positive note, one potential bonus from the CETA negotiations may be reductions in some interprovincial trade barriers, actions that, if consummated, would help validate provincial participation in these negotiations.

In the face of increasing global competition, it is imperative that the federal and provincial governments collaborate closely with each other and with the private sector to align domestic and global policies and strategies to bolster Canada's ability to capture opportunities in emerging markets. To that end, governments and business need to share market data and analyses and success stories to inspire a more concerted and more targeted approach by Canadian firms in new markets.

Domestic policies should be tailored to the growth of competitive outward-oriented firms, recognizing that success at home is the best model for success globally. We should not handicap the success of Canadian firms in our own market nor manipulate market regulations to favour foreign firms. Conversely, governments should, where possible, bolster the prospects for success by Canadian firms both at home and in global markets. In particular, we need smart procurement policies and timely regulatory approvals of infrastructure proposals that do not place Canadian firms at a competitive disadvantage in our own market.

Removing barriers to interprovincial trade and labour mobility, and investments in infrastructure and innovation, along with a greater harmonization of tax regimes, are among the obvious remedies but these require coherent strategies and collective political will. They are prescriptions that go against the grain of "I'm all right Jack" attitudes at the provincial and federal levels. However, if we continue to hobble ourselves with silo approaches to national problems and continue to coast on our resource base, we will inevitably fail to be sufficiently competitive to sustain, let alone increase, economic growth.

EXPORT FINANCING AND TRADE

The Export Development Corporation can play a vital role in facilitating access by Canadian exporters and investors alike to foreign markets. It provides loans to Canadian companies with export contracts and to foreign companies looking to buy goods and services from Canada. The EDC also offers loans and insurance to help Canadian firms invest abroad, along with insurance to protect our businesses against a variety of risks, including non-payment.

The EDC was given a strong boost in funding by the government in the midst of the financial meltdown in 2008–09. This provided the capacity for broader global engagement at a time when project financing by the chartered banks was anything but robust. Traditionally, the EDC had often been as conservative as the chartered banks when deciding whether to lend into relatively unknown markets. More recently, however, the EDC has become less risk averse and more active in supporting Canadian businesses in dynamic, emerging markets. (In 2010, $24.4 billion out of a total of $84.6 billion helped stimulate business in emerging markets. By 2012, the amount exceeded $26 billion, from a total of $87 billion; the top five recipient markets were China, Mexico, Brazil, India, and Turkey. In 2013, the total is projected at more than $27 billion to facilitate business in emerging markets.)

The EDC is also giving more attention to the export potential of small- and medium-sized enterprises (SMEs) – $8.9 billion was targeted at SMEs in 2010, rising to almost $12 billion in 2012.

Not surprisingly, the government's latest "Global Markets Action Plan" emphasizes not only the need to concentrate resources in emerging markets with real potential but also stresses the need to encourage more SMEs to take advantage of opportunities in those markets. So export financing and trade promotion are acting in a concerted and coherent fashion to support global growth by Canadian firms. That is as it should be. All we need are more companies active in global markets.

This emphasis on more focused trade promotion is hardly revolutionary, and certainly not, as some persistent critics of this government lament, a signal that other instruments of Canadian foreign policy will be diminished or downgraded as a result. Canadian ambassadors and many of their embassy colleagues have often been their country's chief trade promotion officers, more so than those from countries that are not as dependent on trade for their livelihood. That is also as it should be but there is nothing that suggests that this emphasis is, or should be, exclusive of all others.

Although negotiating free trade agreements, first with the US and then with Mexico, were central pillars of the Mulroney government's foreign policy, that did not prevent the prime minister from playing a leadership role in combatting apartheid and supporting Nelson Mandela's remarkable transition role in South Africa.

Trade is one component of our foreign policy in which our scope both for relevance and influence is actually commensurate with our comparative advantages, hence our voice and leverage in trade negotiations. As the saying goes, we must "play to our strengths." While trade promotion has a prominent supporting role to play in assisting Canadian firms abroad, it is the history of successful trade negotiations that has given Canada the essential foundation to promote, enhance, and protect our economic interests around the world.

From the early postwar period, senior Canadian diplomats were at the forefront of major multilateral trade negotiations, beginning with the launch of the GATT negotiations in 1947, running through subsequent rounds, and culminating with the creation of the WTO in 1994. The FTA with the US, NAFTA, and, most recently, with the European Union and South Korea, are also significant diplomatic achievements which involved many of Canada's top diplomats. All of these agreements delivered tangible gains to the Canadian economy, with benefits for producers and consumers alike, and with rules governing trade that enabled us to compete more effectively in global markets.

Negotiations are now underway primarily with Japan, Thailand, and India, as well as under the broader Asia-Pacific umbrella of TPP, priorities that link directly to the thrust of the "Global Markets Plan." If successful, these negotiations would give Canada privileged access to markets with significant prospects for growth. They also offer the added advantage of diversification. The more diversified our exports become the more competitive and efficient we will be in a rapidly globalizing economic environment.

FOREIGN INVESTMENT

The government confronted the challenge of SOE investments in late 2012 with its decisions on Petronas's $6 billion acquisition of Progress Energy, and the much more sensitive $15.1 billion acquisition of Nexen by CNOOC (China National Offshore Oil Company), the largest foreign acquisition at that time by a Chinese SOE. After months of hand-wringing, the government approved both, but also established stringent guidelines restricting future control stakes by SOEs in oil-sands companies, and some degree of uncertainty about just how welcome SOE investments would be in other sectors as well. The verdicts represented a balancing act between economic necessity – Canada needs foreign investment to develop its resources base – and political acceptability, namely fundamental Canadian fears about losing "crown jewels" through foreign acquisitions. The problem is that the more the government tries to clarify the rules on investment, the more it circumscribes its own capability to render political judgment on such decisions. That is why a broader understanding with like-minded, resource-rich countries like Australia on how to deal with SOE investors would be worthwhile.

It is understandable that the government would have some concerns about the manner in which SOEs (or at least some SOEs) conduct their affairs – particularly in terms of cost of capital, competitiveness, transfer pricing and taxation, and transparency considerations, all of which could be assessed under the opaque "net benefit" clause, as well as the SOE and national security provisions, of the existing legislation. But not all SOEs behave in the same fashion. Several, including Petronas and CNOOC, were already investing and operating in Canada's resource industries. They have provided millions if not billions of dollars in project development with positive effects for the communities where they operate, including Aboriginal communities. Foreign investors are also obliged to adhere to Canadian laws and regulations.

Making choices in a turbulent highly competitive global economy is not easy but blocking investments that respect existing Investment Canada criteria offers few long-run economic or political rewards. Canada needs, and ordinarily welcomes, foreign investment to develop its oil and gas potential. Former Natural Resources minister Joe Oliver has estimated that we will need $650 billion in natural resource investment by the end of this decade, and much of it will need to come from foreign sources.[30] Much of the available foreign capital lies in emerging market countries like China and Malaysia and much of that is state-controlled. The oil industry on a global basis is hardly the hallmark of free enterprise for open-market theoreticians. State-owned oil companies are the dominant players and the OPEC (Organization of the Petroleum Exporting Countries) cartel sets world prices. Political considerations are a constant factor affecting oil markets.

That the announcement on Petronas and CNOOC was made and explained by Prime Minister Harper at a Friday news conference as most Canadians were heading home for the weekend underscored the sensitivity and complexity of the issue. There was significant opposition to CNOOC's acquisition among members of the Conservative caucus, mirroring public opinion polls.[31] (At one time, more than two-thirds of Canadians were found to be opposed.)[32] The prime minister acknowledged that the decision would have "broad" (i.e., not unanimous) support from his own caucus.[33]

The review process carried a lot of unwieldy baggage, including security concerns about the activities of Chinese telecom giant Huawei Technologies, problems with temporary Chinese workers at a British Columbia mine, concerns about human rights generally and, more fundamentally, rank Sinophobia among the Canadian public, which is borne out in public opinion polls. The issue was equally an acid test of sorts on whether the government really intended to diversify and concentrate strategically on emerging markets that are growing, rather than being exclusively dependent on traditional markets that are stagnating or sinking.

The government approved the CNOOC proposal without divulging the extensive undertakings offered by the company to pass the net benefit test and SOE criteria of the existing Investment Canada requirements. Pointedly and correctly, it adjudicated the transaction under the terms of existing Investment Canada legislation. The onus is now on CNOOC to meet or exceed commitments on capital to be invested, employment, transparency, governance and so on, and on the government to ensure that it does.

Most importantly, the prime minister set very tight guidelines that restrict future SOE attempts to gain control of oil-sands companies. Although the bar for reviews of acquisitions by private-sector acquisitions was raised to $1 billion, it remains at $330 million for SOEs. The prime minister stated bluntly that the decision on CNOOC was "not the beginning of a trend, but rather the end of a trend."[34] He stressed repeatedly his concern about the degree to which the global oil market is already dominated by SOEs and where government policy, not market principles, reigns supreme. Further control and/or ownership of oil-sands companies in Canada by foreign SOEs could jeopardize the extent to which market forces would determine outcomes. It was obviously no accident that a confidential report to the prime minister underscoring this basic point about the impact of SOEs on the global market was released expeditiously under an Access to Information request just before the CNOOC decision.

However, the prime minister's express preference for free enterprise principles and exclusively private investment may be wishful thinking if Canada hopes to attract foreign investors. The manner in which he straddled both economic and political imperatives is certainly preferable to former Reform Party leader Preston Manning's insistence that any decision had to "carry the judgment of the Canadian people."[35] The essence of leadership, after all, is not to follow popular whim, but to lead and shape it.

To bolster public support and understanding of its decisions, however, the government must spend more time articulating to Canadians precisely how dependent we are on foreign investment for the development of our resource base – and not just the oil sands. As noted above, we will need an estimated $650 billion in capital, mostly foreign, by the end of this decade in the resource sector alone. Canadians need to better understand not just the degree to which our prosperity relies on foreign investment but also the investments that Canadian companies make abroad. This two-way street is critical to our prosperity and growth.

Significantly, in the Nexen decision the prime minister also signalled that Canada will seek comparable reciprocal access for our
own investors and exporters from countries seeking to invest in our
resources, especially from China, where the economic relationship is
currently sharply imbalanced. The relative openness of our market,
our reputation as a secure source of supply, and our strict adherence
to the rule of law constitute real comparative advantages for us and
should be deployed accordingly in any broad trade and investment
negotiation.

The "only in exceptional circumstances"[36] caveat to the blocking guideline on future SOE control stakes in the oil sands leaves an
element of constructive ambiguity available to the government on
future investment decisions. It recognizes that not all SOEs are necessarily cut from the same government cloth. More fundamentally, it
allows Ottawa to retain the whip hand on foreign investment decisions, as it should. Canada is certainly not alone in establishing limits and a degree of ambiguity in this regard. But perhaps it is time
for us to work with like-minded countries such as Australia and the
United States to establish a more common, as opposed to a competitive, approach to SOE behaviour.

The government may also be understandably concerned about
opening the floodgates to foreign investment to the point where even
crown jewels in the oil sands are taken over, leaving Canada with
minimal involvement in, let alone control of, our natural resources. But neither Progress nor Nexen would qualify for such concern.
And, given the vastness of the oil sands, it is difficult to see how any
one firm could dominate production.

Neither economic purists nor economic nationalists were satisfied
by the government's decisions. But there is still some uncertainty
about the degree to which restrictions on SOE control stakes of oil-
sands companies would serve to chill the appetite of foreign investors more generally. In 2013, investment in the oil sands slumped to
a nine-year low.

Our policy on foreign investment must inevitably balance economic necessity and political acceptability. That is the reality. Canada will need large amounts of foreign investment, especially to
develop our oil and natural gas resources. Yet Canadians are concerned about head offices being hollowed out by foreign acquisitions
and about undertakings offered, but not fulfilled, by foreign investors. "Net benefit" should have a precise meaning and undertakings

volunteered by putative foreign investors should be fully respected. Access should not be unfettered but adjudicated prudently and geared specifically to the need to maintain Canadian texture at the management level and, in the resource sector, to ensure maximum benefit for Canada from the extraction process. We should not hesitate to seek, as well, comparable access for Canadian investors in the markets of those seeking to invest in Canada. We may need clearer, more exacting rules, not as walls but as efficient filters, to ensure that such investments are fully compatible with the standards for corporate behaviour in Canada.

The economic rationale for foreign investment is indisputable. Canada's growth depends on it. The challenges posed by SOEs in particular and foreign acquisitions in general are inherently political. A one-size-fits-all guideline is certainly not the answer. In fact, tighter guidelines may not resolve what is essentially a political management challenge for the government. The real dilemma here is that the more government attempts to clarify or codify its approach to foreign investment, the more it circumscribes its capacity to exercise political judgments.

The fact that foreign investments in Canada's resource base dropped sharply in the year following the verdict (i.e., from $27 billion in 2012 to $2 billion in 2013) signals that the decision added more uncertainty than clarity into the investment climate. Combined with similar doubts about Canada's capacity to approve necessary infrastructure – pipelines, terminals, etc. – in a timely fashion, the hesitation shown by foreign investors, who do after all have other choices available, undercuts Canada's ability to exploit a major comparative advantage in the global economy.

Governments will always want to retain political discretion to rule on major investment foreign decisions and cannot blindly override the domestic mood. But, by "sucking and blowing" on resource investments, they risk the worst of both worlds – not satisfying their critics and yet hobbling the prospects for necessary resource development.

The government should confirm that the restriction on control states by SOEs applies only to the oil sands and not, as many fear, to other sectors as well. A filter or informal sounding board to test the mood would also be a constructive addition to the investment review process, one that would have particular merit for Asian investors who, for reasons of face, are otherwise reluctant to embark on a formal process that concludes with an embarrassing rejection.

The government may also prefer a strategic framework based on clearly stated principles (not a checklist) as the foundation for investment decisions. Instead of a national security test, it might also consider a clearly defined national interest test, modelled after that used by the US (Committee on Foreign Investment in the United States), that includes close examination of the market capitalization and transparency of foreign firms, a determination of the degree of access permitted by the investor's country, an analysis of the effect of the acquisition on Canada's global competitiveness, as well as the national security implications. And if it wishes to preclude outright takeover of crown jewels, it should establish equally clear hurdles to that effect. But new prescriptions should be proscriptive, not retroactive or cobbled on the fly. Pending applications should be adjudicated on their merits, free of any phobias.

Especially in the case of China, the government should also reach out politically and negotiate terms that will provide better access for Canadian firms and rectify the "imbalance" in the economic relationship cited publicly by the prime minister.[37] It is a matter of leverage and enlightened self-interest.

However, the bigger lesson here is that when a government loses control of its own agenda or changes the ground rules as investment applications are being considered, it creates damaging uncertainty and magnifies the challenge of finding a balanced solution, one that respects our economic needs but also provides a basis for sensible political management. Ultimately, the government will have to reconcile Canada's need for foreign capital with the political desire to be seen to be controlling our national destiny. Furthermore, when it comes to foreign investment, this is no time to embrace an "igloo" mentality. Constructive rather than destructive ambiguity should be the goal, and the sooner the better. The government's strong suit is its sensible stewardship of the economy. Uncertainty and confusion over foreign investment rules threaten to undermine that solid reputation.

THE SASKATCHEWAN MODEL

The one province that does have its act together in terms of both fiscal rectitude and strategic vision is Saskatchewan, whose government's basic objective is to secure a better quality of life for its people. The six core growth activities identified in the *Saskatchewan Plan for Growth: Vision 2020 and Beyond* are:[38]

- Investing in the infrastructure required for growth
- Educating, training, and developing a skilled work force
- Ensuring the competitiveness of Saskatchewan's economy
- Supporting increased trade, investment, and exports through international engagement
- Advancing Saskatchewan's natural resource strengths, particularly through innovation, to build the next economy
- Ensuring fiscal responsibility through balanced budgets, lower debt, and smaller, more effective government.

All of these are underscored with a clear stipulation that the government "will not directly intervene in the economy or undertake direct investment in business."[39] (Ontario and Quebec take note!) Against this broad outline, in 2012 the government also set more precise goals, including:[40]

- A population of 1.2 million by 2020
- $2.5 billion to be invested in infrastructure over three years
- Transfer of $150 million into a new SaskBuilds Fund to drive innovation in infrastructure financing, design, and delivery, including public–private partnerships
- 60,000 more people working in Saskatchewan by 2020
- Reducing the difference in graduation rates between Aboriginal and non-Aboriginal students by 50 per cent
- Increasing the cap on provincial immigrant nominees from 4,000 to 6,000
- Lowering the business tax rate from 12 per cent to 10 per cent by 2015
- Doubling the value of exports by 2020
- Increasing crop production by 10 million tonnes by 2020
- Balancing the budget annually and cutting debt in half by 2017 (from the 2007 level)
- Reducing surgical wait times to no more than three months by 2014 while eliminating wait times in emergency rooms by 2017
- Offering scholarships for students to study business at an international institution if they agree to return to Saskatchewan for at least five years after graduation.

The basic plan includes specific measures to increase innovation and strengthen regulation in energy, minerals, and forestry – prime sectors of Saskatchewan's economy.

The *Plan for Growth* offers comprehensive explicit goals – many of which other provinces would do well to emulate – but with a clear focus on provincial responsibilities and a "supportive" role in areas of federal jurisdiction. Overall, it strikes a healthy balance between prudence and vision!

THE WAY FORWARD

Our fundamental argument is that on each of the above issues, there needs to be a sharper division of labour between levels of government in Canada, greater cohesion on areas of shared jurisdiction, and stronger leadership from Ottawa. We coast on our laurels at our peril. We need to address, not ignore, serious fault lines that jeopardize our future prospects. The Saskatchewan model could be a template for a national vision.

Above all else, Ottawa needs to take a clearer leadership role, assert confidently what Canada should be doing to meet contemporary global challenges while engaging the provinces and all stakeholders to contribute appropriately on mutually beneficial goals. A revamped structure for decision-making on global policy in Ottawa with the prime minister consistently in charge will be essential to establish clear direction, ensure timely action to facilitate systematic consultations, and to ensure accountability. This is precisely what was done to galvanize our negotiating effort vis-à-vis the US in the 1980s. A separate negotiating office was created in Ottawa to cut through the jurisdictional overlap among departments. It reported through a special cabinet committee chaired by the prime minister and served as the primary consultative mechanism throughout with the provinces and with stakeholders in the private sector. The prime minister engaged personally and directly with the premiers and with the US administration at the most senior level to keep matters on track.

The global challenges facing Canada today oblige a similarly consistent personal commitment by the prime minister supported by whatever structural reform will actually deliver more than incremental results.

Structures beyond trade policy are in need of reform. The foreign policy/securities dimension of decision-making is as diffuse as that on trade policy. Cosmetic changes bringing CIDA closer to Foreign Affairs need to be anchored in more basic organizational changes that give greater cohesion to implementation, including greater authority for ambassadors to oversee *all* departmental operations within their purview. Immigration, Agriculture, and Finance should not operate as independent silos on the international stage. They need to be sensibly integrated under a policy umbrella that serves and enhances Canada's national interest.

National unity, along with security and prosperity, is a perennial priority for any government in Ottawa. The separatist pressures from Quebec ebb and flow with the fortunes of the Parti Québécois and they pose a nagging threat, one that finds spasmodic resonance outside Canada as well as inside. History suggests that constitutional dialogue is unlikely to provide a solution. But evidence or neglect is not an adequate response either. What we do need is an imaginative vision for the future, one that will attract interest from all regions, including Quebec, and inspire Canadians to engage and meet the challenges of global transformation with confidence, commitment, and a spirit of adventure.

8

Invigorating and Engaging the Private Sector

Governments alone cannot meet the challenges posed by the global transformation. The private sector has to be a full and committed partner. Business executives have to move out of the "cocoon of comfort" that our resource base and proximity to the world's largest market has provided for decades. In some ways, Canada is too much like the man who was born on third base and thought he had hit a triple.

Canada is endowed with abundant natural resources – from energy to minerals and agriculture, along with huge reservoirs of fresh water – and yet the crutch of geography hobbles our inclination to search for new market opportunities beyond our continent.

Even when the dollar was at or near par, and despite lower tax rates, and taxpayer-funded health care, Canada's retail sector underperforms US competitors. According to a 2012 Senate report, a major reason for the price discrepancy is the chronic Canadian malaise – complacency. Retailers and wholesalers alike recognize that Canadians are willing to pay more. By way of example, Cadillacs and Camaros manufactured in Oshawa cost several thousand dollars more in Canada than in the US.[1] German automobiles can command a 20 to 25 per cent premium in Canada, compared with the US market.[2] But it is not just automobiles. The discrepancies cover the entire retail sector. The only safety valve for frustrated consumers is the uniquely Canadian buying practice – cross-border shopping. Whether it is for better airfares, wireless rates, or groceries, Canadians, especially those living near the border, will opt for bargains in the US. When it comes to pocketbook issues, national pride has its limits. Because of perceptions about a lack of competition in the wireless telecom market, the government is gerrymandering auctions of spectrum for wireless telephony and decisions on acquisitions in an attempt to induce lower prices for consumers. But the competition problem is much broader in scope and unlikely to be remedied by ad hoc government fiat to manipulate markets.

Canada's chartered banks were prevented by tighter regulations from following their American counterparts down the disastrous money trap of dubious financial instruments to support equally dubious mortgages. By concentrating now on wealth management, however, these banks see little reason to support innovative product or marketing concepts, especially by small Canadian companies. In fact, most of their profits are now derived from government-backed CMHC (Canada Mortgage and Housing Corporation) mortgages.

The combination of resource riches, docile consumers, lethargic competition regulators, and ultra-conservative banks spawns a pervasive sense of complacency in Canada which is a serious drag on both economic growth and entrepreneurial spirit.

Entrepreneurship *is* a Canadian strength, but follow-through is a problem. As John Manley, CEO of the Canadian Council of Chief Executives, notes, Canada is near the top of the G20 when it comes to founding businesses, and a top five economy for starting a new business, due to our simple tax regime, deep capital markets, and relatively low-cost labour.[3] Where Canada fails, says Manley, is that of all these start-ups, "very few of those firms ever go on to acquire significant scale. In other words, as a country we do a poor job of nurturing what economists call "gazelles" – high-growth firms that can make a significant contribution to economic growth and job creation."[4] Of course, Canada has produced some big players in a few industries, but, as Eric Reguly wondered in *The Globe and Mail*, why is it that, compared even with smaller countries like the Netherlands and Sweden, we have "pathetically few global superstars?"[5] We have many positive attributes – globally competitive tax rates, a skilled work force together with heavy R&D expenditures by governments, and a quality of life that invariably ranks at or near the top.

Many see complacency as the basic problem which, in turn, spawns a risk-averse culture among Canadian CEOs, one conditioned to ride with the prevailing tide rather than strive for something different. Reguly offers an even more pungent critique. Examining the trend of foreign takeovers in Canada of everything from beer companies like Molson's and Labatt to resource giants like Inco, Falconbridge, and Alcan, he blames "the sellout culture, nice-guy directors with a propensity to protect the wrong executives at the wrong time and Canada's classic lack of corporate self-confidence!"[6] Don Argus, the former chairman of BHP Billiton, echoed this blunt sentiment, stating that, with the steady loss of mining head offices in recent years, "Canada has already been reduced to an industry branch office and is largely irrelevant to the global mining stage."[7] Overstatements by both to be sure but with some kernels of truth.

Elyse Allan, CEO of GE Canada, offered a different but equally telling reason as to why Canadian firms shy away from global prospects. In her view, Canadian firms are known for excellent quality when it comes to manufacturing but they tend to operate "with their windows closed to the outside world market." GE's acquisition strategy in Canada reflects that analysis. Small firms are bought and assimilated into GE's global platform – windows wide open to the opportunities that can be derived from an efficient world-wide value chain of production and distribution.

NOTABLE EXCEPTIONS

There is little doubt that too many Canadian CEOs are cautious and prefer to coast with what they have rather than tackle new challenges. But there are also some major notable exceptions.

CAE

In the summer of 2000, Dave Barette of CAE was assigned to Dubai to conclude a joint venture with Emirates Airlines on a flight training centre – one that would combine CAE's sophisticated technology for flight simulators with Emirates' increasing need for pilot training. Neither side really knew what enormous potential would accrue from this initial agreement.

What began as a six-unit training centre in Dubai evolved rapidly to house fourteen simulators with an annex for an additional twelve now in the works. CAE has also moved beyond Dubai in the region to open training facilities in Kuwait, Qatar, Saudi Arabia, and Oman. Dave Barette has been at the centre of this remarkable growth. When asked in late 2012 why few other Canadian companies had experienced similar success, his answer was poignant.

"Actually, many have visited Dubai. They kick the tires looking for instant success and when it does not happen, they go home and rarely return for a second look."

He then added, even more tellingly: "Do you know how long it took us to break into the Saudi Arabian market? Five years. Repeated visits and steady networking to find the right combination."

CAE made a major strategic shift in 2000, moving beyond the sale of simulators in a market that was becoming saturated into the pilot-training business, buying and building centres around the world, some in joint ventures with airlines like Emirates and China Southern. Although the 9/11 attacks in the US had a paralyzing effect on many airlines, and those reliant on them like CAE, the move into training, especially in countries that could no longer send their pilots to the US to learn how to fly, was, according to the current CEO, Marc Parent, "what saved the company."[8] CAE is now, under Parent's determined leadership, number one globally in commercial simulator sales and in independent pilot training.[9] As the company's own website reports, "CAE offers civil aviation, military and helicopter training services in more than 45 locations worldwide and trains approximately 100,000 crew members yearly ... With customers in more than 190 countries, CAE has the broadest global reach of any simulation and training equipment and services company on the market. Ninety per cent of CAE's annual revenues are derived from international activities and worldwide exports."[10]

There are also other examples of globally successful Canadian firms. Along with CAE, Bombardier, Linamar, GardaWorld, and Manulife, each offer interesting lessons about why and how they diversified beyond the Canadian market and positioned themselves for global success.

Bombardier

The world's only self-described "manufacturer of planes and trains," Bombardier Inc. is today the world's third-largest commercial aircraft manufacturer, and has major lines of business in mass transit, building locomotives as well as train and subway cars, and made over $16 billion in revenue in 2012.[11] Bombardier's business is also geographically diverse, with eighty manufacturing and engineering centres spread across twenty-six countries, aircraft customers in over 100 countries, and train customers in over sixty.[12] (Table 4

Table 4
Bombardier around the world in 2012

Theatre	Revenue	Personnel
North America	$6,265 million (37%)	36,500 (51%)
Europe	6,864 million (41%)	31,400 (44%)
Asia-Pacific	2,130 million (13%)	3,000 (4%)
Rest of the World	1,509 million (9%)	800 (1%)
Totals	16,768	71,700

Source: Bombardier Inc., *Stepping into the Future*. Annual Report. Fiscal Year Ended December 31, 2012. Numbers are in US dollars.

shows the global breadth of Bombardier's operations.) According to former CEO Laurent Beaudoin in 2008, in a world characterized by growing demand for oil and rising incomes, "China, India and Russia with half the world's population are our immediate future."[13]

Joseph-Armand Bombardier, who built his first snowmobile in 1937, owned an Imperial Oil garage in the town of Valcourt, Quebec, and tinkered in his garage throughout the winter months, since no customers could reach his business by car due to Valcourt's snow-bound roads. Bombardier eventually hit on a design that he believed would work as a wintertime replacement for the automobile, and founded his eponymous firm in 1942.

By the 1970s, Bombardier was still a snowmobile company, but a profitable one, earning $200 million in sales in 1970. Then geopolitics intervened. The OPEC oil embargo of 1973 gutted Bombardier. The entire snowmobile industry's sales fell from 500,000 units in 1972 to 250,000 in 1974.[14] Bombardier went from making over 200,000 snow-mobiles to half that number in a little over a year, and posted its first annual loss – approximately $8 million.[15] Beaudoin and Bombardier's response to the crisis was to diversify not just their product line, but their customer base as well. While the oil crisis destroyed demand for snowmobiles, it also created incentives for a renewal in mass transit. By happenstance, Bombardier inherited a streetcar company when it purchased the Austrian firm that made the engines for its snow-mobiles. That legacy asset created an opportunity for Bombardier, not only to halt the decline of its business, but also to break into a new sector, and begin selling trains, subways, and streetcars.

Bombardier was able to win a contract to supply new rolling stock to the Montreal metro. The company applied the same attention to detail, cost-control, and quality it had used building Ski-Doos to designing and pricing their Montreal bid.[16] This initial success bolstered Bombardier's confidence as it sought out new markets, from Portugal, to Tanzania, to New York and Mexico City.

Getting into the aerospace industry in 1986 was in many ways a natural extension of the original 1973 strategy: diversification is strength, and so too is quality. Bombardier's CSeries jet epitomizes this philosophy: Bombardier hopes to challenge entrenched aerospace giants Airbus and Boeing (and perennial competitor Embraer) with a superior product rather than by offering deep discounts and cheap financing to potential customers. Bombardier claims the technologically advanced CSeries will be 20 per cent more fuel-efficient than its Boeing and Airbus competitors in the mid-size jet class. Early adopters of the aircraft are very enthusiastic. Trygve Gjersten of Sweden's Braathens Aviation claims the CSeries will be an environmental revolution in the 120- to 150-seat aircraft, while airBaltic, another company that has ordered the plane, estimates that they will save $30 to $50 million a year by switching their fleet from Boeings to Bombardiers.[17]

Linamar

Founded by Hungarian immigrant Frank Hasenfratz in the basement of his Guelph, Ontario home in 1966, Linamar is another rare example of a Canadian company that has managed to compete on a global scale. Today, Linamar has forty facilities in ten countries. While Canadian operations provided 62 per cent of revenues in 2012, the rest was well diversified between Europe (17 per cent), Mexico (9 per cent), the US (8 per cent), and the Asia-Pacific region (3 per cent), marking a slow and steady diversification away from the US and Canada, which together had accounted for over three-quarters of revenues in 2007.[18] Linamar's modest size ($2.6 billion market capitalization, 17,000 employees) has helped it compete and thrive in the highly globalized and competitive world of industrial manufacturing.

Linamar is fundamentally a precision machining firm. Its subsidiaries make parts for automobiles, off-road vehicles, the energy sector, and other industries. That means Linamar's customers include firms like General Motors, Ford, and Chrysler, who are in a remarkably competitive industry, and due to their size have the option to seek out suppliers around the world. Consequently, they can and do demand that suppliers regularly lower their prices. If parts suppliers can't meet their price and quality needs, "you're dead in the water," says Linamar CEO Linda Hasenfratz.[19] This means that Linamar fundamentally competes on the basis of productivity and seeking out value-added niches. During Canada's grim recession of the early 1990s, Linamar took the opportunity to hire in a depressed labour market. As Hasenfratz put it at the time, "as we look ahead, the most critical competitive advantage for Ontario is going to be in its well-trained and creative workforce," and as long as applicants have the right attitude and are willing to learn, "the training we can do."[20] In other words, Linamar took control of its own destiny and trained workers to meet their specific standards and needs, rather than bemoaning the lack of tailor-made workers in the general labour market.

To quote the founder again: "My view of it is our industry is competitive where the managers are competitive. Your plant is only as good as your manager. A manager will surround himself with good people that works all the way down to the floor ... The dollar going up does not hurt us. Why does an American produce better than us? They cannot. They use the same equipment. It only depends on management. People like to cry."[21]

Linamar focuses simply on making things well – competing on quality rather than on being the lowest bidder. Again, as Hasenfratz puts it, "the Chinese are very good workers. But we can beat them with high precision, goods that require skilled labour."[22] Like Bombardier, Linamar's success is also a function of a willingness to change with the global economy. What started as an auto parts maker now builds components for a range of industries, including the oil and gas sector, wind and solar energy, and the agricultural sector. Rather than rely on a single product or industry, Linamar has expanded deliberately and carefully in a way that has allowed them to leverage their core competency – high-quality precision machining – into lines of business (like agriculture and energy) that are increasingly driven by emerging market growth. In short, Linamar is a testament to the wisdom of doing what you know best, but doing it well, and continuously looking for new ways to do it.

GardaWorld

In a similarly entrepreneurial vein, Stephan Crétier has built Garda-World (GW) into a major position as the leading cash-logistics provider in North America (surpassing Brinks) and a significant security services player in some of the world's most difficult and dangerous business environments. Starting in 1995 with a $25,000 second mortgage on his Montreal home, Crétier has grown GW into a privately-owned enterprise, with 45,000 employees worldwide and annual global revenues of $1.4 billion.[23]

Crétier's initial vision was to create a Canada-wide platform that would become the premier security provider. Following the successful integration of Sécur in Quebec, he set his sights on consolidating the US market, establishing operations with more than 200 service points and 3,000 armoured vehicles. Garda has overtaken Brinks, serving many of the largest US banks, notably JPMorgan Chase, Wells Fargo, the Bank of America, and the Federal Reserve, as well as several major retail chains. GW's growth in the cash logistics business has been generated by both acquisitions and a highly efficient customer-friendly business model serving major banks and financial institutions in the US and Canada.

For the past decade, Crétier has also pressed the industry to raise its operational standards, particularly through improved training and enhanced codes of conduct. (Because the entry barriers are low, many small firms offer services that do not meet the professional quality standards that are used by GW). GW became a founding signatory of the International Code of Conduct for Private Security Providers adopted in Geneva, Switzerland in 2010.

Crétier explains his success in cash logistics in the following way: "I do not want to insult anyone but when I started in the Company, it was security people in business instead of business people in security ... people trying to build a police-type model. We tried to replicate a model that existed in Europe since the 1970's (in response to terrorist attacks in Europe)."[24]

In the wake of the tragic events of 9/11, the Canadian government created a major public–private partnership designed to protect passengers and enhance national security at Canada's eighty-nine airports. This prompted GW to bid and win contracts for pre-board screening – a service now provided by GardaWorld at twenty-seven airports. Guarding and physical protection services are offered by a separate branch of GW to government agencies, including embassies and military bases, and to private-sector resource firms in places like Iraq, Libya, Yemen, and Afghanistan. These are not markets for the faint of heart or for those who are risk-averse.

Crétier favours a "one-stop shop" approach for each business. "Before the model was when you wanted a security guard, you called one company. When you wanted an investigation or an armoured truck, you called another. I wanted a model where you call one number and find everything without having to pay a premium."[25] He sees himself as a true entrepreneur. "Every morning I get up and get to work at building a great company,"[26] one he runs on a hands-on basis and with a 25 per cent stake in the business. Crétier has demonstrated a unique capacity to flourish in both the most sophisticated markets of the world and those at the other end of the spectrum. His entrepreneurial acumen, his appetite for risk, and his attention to the need, above all, to generate cash flow are what underpin his record of achievement and serve as a compelling model for aspiring entrepreneurs.

Manulife

Founded as Manufacturers' Life Insurance Company by an Act of Parliament in 1887, Manulife first cracked foreign markets in 1893, when it began selling insurance policies in Bermuda. The company continued to expand into the Caribbean throughout the 1890s, did its first business in China in 1897, and had entered the US market by 1903. The logic driving this aggressive expansion was simple: Canada had too many life insurance firms in far too small a market. In 1887, Canada had at least eight life insurance companies (including Manulife) competing for fewer than five million customers. Rapidly diversifying its customer base allowed Manulife to thrive, despite the Canadian market's limited potential at the time.[27]

Manulife continued to grow throughout the twentieth century, and was, for a time, Canada's largest insurance company. It was generally a profitable business, and by most measures compared well with its peers. However, by the early 1990s, year-over-year profits were declining, and an anxious board of directors began to fret about what seemed to be a lack of strategic direction.

To turn Manulife's fortunes around and enable it to survive in an increasingly crowded North American market, senior management returned, in a way, to the 1893 playbook: grow the business by entering emerging markets. Despite not being allowed to sell any policies in China in the early 1990s, Manulife opened several representative offices in the country, provided training programs for

Chinese bankers and actuaries, and contributed to philanthropic projects, such as orphanages.[28] In 1994, two years before Chinese regulators granted Manulife a licence to sell policies in Shanghai, vice-president Victor Apps estimated that Manulife was planning to spend $20 million dollars in its Chinese operations, and anticipated that it would take at least seven years before the effort would break even.[29] In other words, Manulife took the consummate long view, and as one company executive put it, "we probably won't see a big return for 10 years, but as capitalism takes hold it will be a very big market."[30]

Manulife sold its first (new) life insurance policy in China in 1996 as part of a joint venture with the state-owned Sinochem. All told, it took five years from Manulife's re-entry to the market to its first sale, and the campaign cost tens of millions of dollars. Dominic D'Alessandro, then CEO, reflecting on the time and costs, noted, "of course it's been a frustrating time, but now looking back, it was understandable. We were the first joint venture so all the rules were new, and everything moved very slowly."[31] The competition to get access was also fierce. AIG was the only foreign insurer that Beijing granted a licence to before Manulife, and by 1995 over eighty foreign insurers had set up representative offices in China in a bid to enter the market.[32] However, as Sui Hui, the official in China's Ministry of Foreign Trade and Economic Co-operation who helped broker the joint venture deal between Sinochem and Manulife, put it, "it is not important to be big or biggest. It is important to be first. And Manulife was first. You have to set up the friendship first. You have to have good relations first for mutual trust."[33]

Today, Manulife's revenues ($2.8 billion in 2012) are broadly drawn from its three core markets: 29 per cent from Canada, 33 per cent from Asia, and 38 per cent from the United States.[34]

LESSONS

These examples illustrate how some Canadian companies and business leaders have met the challenge of a changing global economy and found ways to succeed. There are of course others, including many in the resource sector, like Barrick, Suncor, and Canadian Natural Resources Limited, Magna, and Air Canada, but we need many more strong performers who can operate just as effectively on the global stage.

What ties these Canadian business stories together is a greater tolerance for risk, a willingness to diversify, and the discipline to follow a long view, while accepting the occasional failure. What is certain is that the existing comfort zone is shrinking and short-lived. It will not sustain future prosperity for either our companies or our country.

Those who have successfully penetrated dynamic emerging markets have followed prescriptions that blend persistence with perseverance. It does take time and patient commitment to understand the cultural mores of specific markets and to cultivate and nurture personal relationships with potential partners, suppliers, and customers. But instant gratification is not the name of the game. Executives and their boards must take the long view and not be mesmerized by quarterly returns. Part of Bombardier's success, for example, has been attributed to the fact that the Bombardier family has historically held a large stake in the firm. That has helped insulate management from short-term shareholder pressures, and given the company the freedom to focus on long-run strategies.[35]

TOLERANCE FOR RISK

When it comes to risk, the problem for Canadian business leaders is attitudinal and cultural. We are not known as risk-takers nor as people with a high degree of tolerance for failure. Americans see occasional failures or setbacks, conversely, as vital experience. Fast-moving markets will involve higher risk. Doing business in Shanghai is markedly different than doing business in Cleveland.

It would be most unfortunate if the new emphasis on corporate governance produced little more than a check box mentality of process, obliging boards to staunch appetites for risk by management. Proper governance practices should enable, not frustrate, reasonable, balanced risk-taking by competent managers. We need to emulate and celebrate the success of our entrepreneurs and inculcate work habits that will deliver more success in the future.

The willingness to take risks is learned best by trial and error experience in global markets – more a matter for the stomach than the head to absorb. You cannot teach executives or boards to accept higher degrees of risk. It requires a change of mindsets comparable to what happened in the early 1990s when Canadian firms were obliged to adapt to the forces of stronger competition in North

America induced by the Free Trade Agreement. Business leaders at all levels now have to expand their vision of what is possible, recognizing and accepting that some missteps along the way are essential elements of experience.

Whether it is access to risk capital or an appetite for risky markets, the problem for too many in Canada is a cultural resistance to taking a chance. There is no magic cure for excessive caution. For one thing, those who are prepared to take some risk can go elsewhere and, often, many do.

The best risk mitigator of all can be diversification. It works for investors and can have the same stabilizing effect for exporters venturing into and spreading the risk across several markets, recognizing that each will inevitably grow at a different rate and will be impacted differently by global trends of the day. It can be the distinction between a passive reactive business and one that chooses to play a winner's game of diversifying market expansion in order to balance risk.

R&D AND THE PRODUCTIVITY GAP

One of the most persistent criticisms of Canadian business is its inability to transform substantial R&D investments by government (at or near the top of all OECD countries) into commercial success. Complaints about Canada's low productivity performance highlight this gap as a major contributing factor.

Unfortunately, much of Canada's R&D spending perversely delivers benefits outside of Canada, suggesting that foreign firms spend more time analyzing R&D spending by government – mostly in academic institutions in Canada – than our home-grown firms, who have steadily left the R&D field more and more to government. Since 2005, R&D spending by business as a percentage of GDP has shrunk by more than 1 per cent a year; in 2011, no doubt in part because of the recession, it stood at only 0.91 per cent.[36] On that OECD scale, Canada fell from eighteenth to twenty-fifth out of forty-one countries, and the lowest by far of the G7.[37] (Given the plethora of studies, the forest industry is probably the only beneficiary of Canada's dismal productivity performance.) Canada's annual rate of labour production growth from 1998 to 2011 was a mere 1.01 per cent, half that of the US (which averaged 2 per cent productivity growth per year over the same time period).[38]

The perennial lament about the lack of innovation in Canada is that we are strong on "inventing" but fall short on implementing or executing ideas for change. Michael Bloom, who heads the Conference Board Centre for Business Innovation, observed, "We punch above our weight in idea generation but, the further you move toward commercialization, the weaker we get as a country."[39]

A 2012 OECD study pinpointed the paradox of Canada's innovation record. Despite our high levels of education, easy access to the market of the global technology leader – the US – and ample public spending in support of innovation, "activity is by any aggregate measure, lack lustre."[40] The weak quality of management, restrictive banking practices in Canada, and the "closed windows" attitude mentioned earlier were among the factors cited for this dismal performance.

The government has tried several approaches to address this problem but with few tangible results. One recent attempt was the diversion of R&D tax credits from big successful global players like CAE, Bombardier, and Pratt & Whitney to create a special fund for SMEs – a populist move that struck some as a method for suppressing success in order to enhance mediocrity.[41]

The fact that fracking and horizontal drilling technology for extracting non-conventional oil and gas reserves were pioneered in Canada and have revolutionized this sector world-wide is a rare exception to the norm but offers lessons for other sectors, such as the industrial value-added services and technology sectors, where Canada has gained little traction and the culture of complacency still runs deep.

ACCESS TO CAPITAL

According to Derek DeCloet, in the *Report on Business*, "the biggest single problem for doing business in Canada is getting money. Canada ranks 26th in ease of access to loans" ... DeCloet added pointedly, "Despite our vaunted banking system, we're 11th in affordability of financial services. Foreign competition is limited."[42]

Another chronic lament is that Canadian firms lack access to venture capital that would support innovation. For the most part, our large banks have little interest in providing this financial capital to high-risk, high-potential companies in their early stages of development. Among OECD countries, Canada has the third-largest venture capital market in absolute terms, but ranks fifteenth in terms of venture capital measured as a share of GDP.[43] Canada's venture capital market is less than half the size of that of Finland, Belgium, Ireland, Switzerland, Sweden, or the US, and one-third the relative size of Israel's (see figure 5). SMEs that are going to bring new unimagined products to market and be tomorrow's global competitors do not need to be coddled, but they do need access to finance.

Spending on R&D is of little good if companies cannot access investors with the right risk tolerance and long-term view needed to turn ideas and prototypes into products with customers. There is also some evidence that small companies that rely on government-sponsored venture capital perform poorly compared with those that rely on private or private and public venture capital.[44] The federal government's commitment of $400 million to Canada's venture capital markets, announced in 2012, is therefore no panacea, and might be best used if it was directed to promising firms by private markets on behalf of the government, rather than by politicians.[45] In the long run, young Canadian firms will need angel investors to make the leap from being prospects to top performers.

BIGGER IS SOMETIMES BETTER

Governments tend to see small- and medium-sized enterprises as the engines of growth and employment in the economy and yet, without R&D investments and global success from flagship companies, our SMEs will become orphans deprived of innovation and growth. Many tend to forget that the relationship between our bigger and smaller firms is a symbiotic one. For example, more than 100 small firms in Quebec depend heavily on the continued global success of Bombardier, CAE, and Pratt & Whitney.

There is also strong empirical evidence that large firms are, in fact, the drivers of productivity and innovation in the Canadian economy. Overall, a mere 0.3 per cent of all Canadian firms account for one-third of all private-sector jobs in Canada.[46] Furthermore, as a 2013 Statistics Canada study points out, "In 2008, the level of productivity, as measured by nominal gross domestic product (GDP) per hour worked, was much greater for large ($72) than for medium-sized ($42) and small businesses ($35). The gap is widest in industries where large firms are more prevalent. For capital-intensive industries (mining and oil and gas, utilities, manufacturing, transportation, and

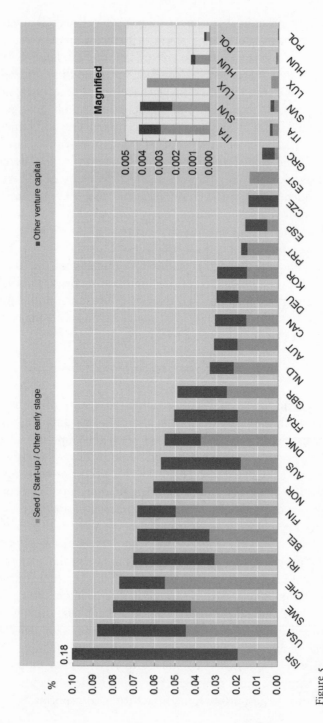

Figure 5
Venture capital as a percentage of GDP, OECD countries, 2009

Source: OECD Entrepreneurship Financing Database, June 2011.

information), nominal GDP per hour worked in large businesses is relatively higher than in medium-sized and small businesses."[47]

The reasons for the higher levels of productivity in these particular sectors nonetheless remains something of a puzzle.[48] Firm size is obviously an important factor, along with the ability to marshal capital and other resources, but so too is the appetite for large-scale innovation in these sectors. As an earlier study, which compared the performance of Canadian mining companies with those in the US, noted, "The key reasons for higher levels of productivity in Canada versus the US had to do with the focus of Canadian mining companies on 'breakthrough' as opposed to 'incremental' innovations in an adverse economic climate characterized by "low commodity prices, consolidation, globalization and regulatory constraints."[49]

There are also some things that government and regulatory authorities have gotten right to support success, such as the creation of Venture Exchange, which was the result of an agreement among the Vancouver, Alberta, Toronto, and Montreal exchanges in 1999 to restructure Canadian capital markets along the lines of market specialization, and which is now an important source of capital for companies in the mining and oil and gas sectors. Also, tax-advantaged flow-through shares have been a critical source of capital for resource companies and highly effective in directing equity capital to this sector.

MENTORING PROGRAMS

Those companies that have proven to be successful should also be powerful magnets for others to follow. To that end, Quebec has instituted a mentoring program – QC100 – in which veteran business executives share their experiences and their business practices with young entrepreneurs in small- and medium-sized firms anxious to spread their wings on a more global scale. This type of mentoring should become national in scale, led possibly by the Canadian Council of Chief Executives and/or the Canadian Chamber of Commerce, and with consistent support from government agencies like Export Development Canada, Business Development Canada, and the Department of Trade.

What we do not need are more studies or task forces to consult and then produce recommendations on innovation that simply gather dust.

EDUCATION AND TRAINING

While we like to celebrate the highly-educated calibre of our work force, we should not go overboard with a sense of false pride. As mentioned earlier, a growing challenge for Canada, one recognized repeatedly by the government in budget documents, is the chronic shortage of skilled people for jobs in demand and its corollary – a surplus of young people with talents not in demand. There is not simply a shortage of technologically skilled employees – computer scientists, physicists, and mathematicians – but managerial deficiencies – on marketing, on organizational logistics, and on how best to adapt to increasingly global value chains.

Our academic institutions could also play a crucial role in changing the culture of business executives, especially if business and international affairs schools were to use case-study examples of Canadian success stories as part of their curriculum, introducing the successful CEOs of today regularly to the executive talent of tomorrow. Equally needed are courses that move beyond conventional theories of trade and investment and take into account approaches and risk analyses required to negotiate with economies run more by government edict than by customary market rules.

However, responsibility for tackling Canada's education challenge should not fall solely on the shoulders of the provincial and federal governments. The private sector must also play its role in training Canadians and nurturing their talents. As several studies have highlighted, Canadian firms, while on the one hand bemoaning a shortage of skilled labour, simply do not, on the other hand, invest enough in their employees.[50] One study notes that Canadian companies spent 40 per cent less on employee learning and development in 2011 than they did in 1993.[51] Canadian firms also do not compare well with their peers on this issue. Canadian companies spend somewhere around $600 to $700 on annual per employee training, compared with over $1,000 per employee in the US.[52] Even according to Canadian business leaders, Canada lags on employee training. The World Economic Forum's 2013 *Global Competitiveness Report*, which analyzes responses from surveys of businesses in 148 countries, ranks Canada thirty-fourth in adequacy of employee training. This places Canada not just behind highly innovative economies like Switzerland, Singapore, and the United States, but also behind emerging markets like South Africa, Malaysia, and Indonesia.[53] When asked why Canadian firms don't spend more on employee training, businesses respond that they fear other companies will poach their employees, and also cite that it costs too much, it is not their responsibility, and that government assistance is inadequate.[54] These are not satisfying responses.

Margaret Wente of *The Globe and Mail* points her finger at business firms who have become "risk averse about new hires" observing that "It's hard to prove that you can do the job if nobody will give you the first one." As Wente points out, few companies do training any more, even to break in someone new. "Today, there's hardly any way to learn on the job, except through unpaid internships." Companies also set requirements so high that only a very few qualify. One consequence is that more students stay longer in university, piling up degrees in the hope that will better qualify them for employment when what they really want is the opportunity to work.

Canada's various levels of government, individual citizens, and private sector all need to be proactive and take control of our collective destiny if we are going to secure Canada's economic future. This means that Canada's business community has to cultivate and nurture its own talent, rather than expect others to do it for them.

At the same time, the private sector should not allow provincial ministries of education to operate as silos, detached from assessments of what types of education are in demand for our future prosperity. Business leaders should take the lead in establishing a systematic dialogue with provincial administrators, including university and community college presidents, to ensure better linkages on training and research priorities. As many emerging market countries are demonstrating, an educational system and methodology in tune with twenty-first-century challenges will be critical to Canada's future well-being.

ENGAGING THE BUSINESS COMMUNITY IN TRADE POLICY

The private sector should be fully engaged in the government's trade and investment negotiating strategy. What is striking to date is the extent to which they are not publicly encouraging results on CETA or for that matter on prospects with Japan, Korea, India, and China. While associations like the Chamber of Commerce and the Canadian Council of Chief Executives have been supportive, along with selected sectoral associations like the Canadian Cattlemen's

Association, there have been few examples of Canadian CEOs articulating exactly what benefits they expect to derive from any of these negotiations in terms of growth, employment, and investment. With the best will in the world, government negotiators cannot get too far in front of those whose interests they are trying to serve. Since any successful negotiation will ultimately involve trade-offs, the government will need credible voices other than their own to explain the benefits to Canadians, credibility that was integral to acceptance of the Canada-US FTA and NAFTA. If, however, business leaders choose to sit on their hands, the predictable critics of any trade liberalization initiative will have an open field to run on.

Missing from the various trade negotiating initiatives by the government is a systematic structure for consultations with stakeholders along the lines of the International Trade Advisory Council and Sectoral Advisory Groups of International Trade which provided valuable insights and credible support for the FTA, NAFTA, and the Uruguay multilateral round of trade negotiations. Something similar is needed to stimulate both private-sector interest and public awareness of negotiations in process.

SUPPORTING OUR BUSINESS CHAMPIONS

Federal and provincial governments also need to support our champions better at home, especially on procurement, and also abroad, given the competition from state-directed emerging economies. There is also the need for foreign investment decisions and agreements that provide "balanced" access for Canadian investors in foreign markets. Namely, code words for reciprocity, the real issue in the recent telco dispute where the "big three" – Rogers, Bell, and Telus – have fought bitterly against government plans to open up the Canadian wireless market to US firms on terms of access that no Canadian firm would get in the US.

Enhancing and safeguarding the national interest provides an umbrella for both points and engagement is the manner in which appropriate policies can be determined. But a government that does not consult and is mesmerized by the populist appeal of SMEs will not get us there.

When it comes to seizing trade opportunities, the chronic problem is not really a lack of funding or insufficient trade promotion efforts but the hard reality that Canada has too few global champions. And some we do develop either falter under the weight of global success, like Nortel and BlackBerry, or because they cannot cope with unexpected global demand.

Canada Goose is a recent example of a hugely successful Canadian manufacturer that, ultimately, could not manage its stunning global success. The unique made-in-Canada product and the Canada Goose brand became an overnight, global phenomenon, treasured by world leaders and Hollywood starlets alike, to the point where demand badly out-stripped supply, most notably in the pre-Christmas, major sales season. In 2013, while comparable parka products languished unsold on store shelves, Canada Goose supplies were virtually exhausted by mid-November. The owner–managers could not revamp production capacity to meet the burgeoning demand. In December, Bain Capital swooped in to relieve the miracle company of its operational burden, taking over what might otherwise have been sustained as a world-beating Canadian brand. The story of Canada Goose is a sobering symptom of a chronic Canadian problem – deficient managerial vision and capability.

If we really want a "Brave New Canada," our private sector must be systematically engaged by government as players, not bystanders, in pursuit of a bold global strategy for growth. Instead of accepting baseball's third-base analogy to guide our future, we should adapt a Wayne Gretzky approach. Gretzky had a knack for going to where the puck would be and not where it was. In 1983, in response to Bob MacKenzie's question about why he had taken so many shots that season, Gretzky replied, "You miss one hundred per cent of the shots you don't take, even if there is only a 1 to 5 per cent chance of scoring."[55] Persistence and grit matter. Our business leaders need to show similar ingenuity and dexterity to go where market opportunities beckon. Otherwise, Canada will fall farther behind.

9

A Third Option with Legs

On Canada Day, 1 July 2013, Prime Minister Harper described Canada as a "land of hope in a sea of uncertainty."[1] A combination of frustration, fear, and fatigue is more evident than hope or optimism. It is a time of global uncertainty. There is much in the world that prompts deep concern: a sluggish jobless recovery following the fiscal crisis that paralyzed many western economies; the Arab Spring and unpredictable risks posed by Islamic extremists; the spectacular rise of China economically and potentially politically as well; the spectre of a nuclear Iran even as arms control talks continue; the unravelling of Afghanistan and Iraq after huge military engagements in each; and the daunting challenge of attacks on liberty from cyberspace. America's capacity and inclination for global leadership is waning. Sharp political divides on the home-front undermine consensus on domestic and foreign policy. US military prowess remains in a class of its own, but the twenty-first-century security threats – whether from terrorists on the ground or from cyberspace – cannot be tempered by massive military assaults.

As argued in chapter 4, global institutions are not responding effectively to the need for greater certainty and stability. It is a multipolar world at best, but increasingly a G-zero world, in which self-interest is the prime motivator. Noble concepts of multilateralism – the traditional lynchpin for middle powers like Canada – need to be recalibrated for this new world. The fundamental reform of global multilateral institutions is long overdue and Canada must not shy away from taking a tough stance on the restructuring on the United Nations Security Council. But we can't stop there. We also have to broaden the bandwidth of our global economic and security engagements to regions and corners of the globe, especially in the Asia-Pacific, that are fast becoming the drivers of global economic growth and prosperity, and sources of insecurity.

Canada is one of the few countries for which the opportunities are more apparent than the risks and we cannot afford to lag behind. We need to adapt nimbly to reap the benefits of the global transformation, using our comparative advantages as leverage to enhance a broader network of global relationships. We need to move beyond craving a "special relationship" with the US – an objective with a long queue of aspirants – and adjust our diplomatic priorities on a more balanced and selective basis. Most of all, as we confront the major challenges of this new world we cannot afford as a nation to be timid or meek. We must yank ourselves out of our complacent cocoon and be brave. To quote Iachimo in Shakespeare's *Cymbeline*, "Boldness be my friend! Arm me, audacity, from head to foot!"

REDUCING OUR RELIANCE ON THE UNITED STATES

Canada's greatest trade advantage is our proximity to the US market. A robust recovery of the American economy would do more in the short term for economic growth in Canada than virtually any new trade agreement. But excessive reliance on the US has bred complacency in Canada. Because of changes occurring in Canada's economy, the boost from the US economic recovery will not be as strong in the future as it customarily has been. For one thing, as other competitors capture sales in the US, Canada's share of the US market is shrinking, obliging Canadian exporters to pursue opportunities farther afield. We are losing ground in the US market but we are not making much headway elsewhere. If ever there was a wake-up call, this is it.

A THIRD OPTION WITH LEGS

The time has come for a "Third Option with Legs," counterbalancing our vital relationship with the United States with a strategic focus on Europe but especially the dynamic emerging markets that are capturing an increasing share of global growth. A Third Option with Legs represents a mature response by Canada to an increasingly turbulent world. Having weathered the economic recession better than most, Canadians have a more confident sense of self.

The irony is that this is not the first time that Canada has attempted to diversify its trade and investment linkages. More than forty years ago, in 1971, in response to a balance of payments crisis, President Nixon surprised the world with a 10 per cent levy on all US imports. That hit Canada harder than most at the time, even though Nixon was somewhat oblivious. He and many Americans thought, incorrectly, that Japan, not Canada, was America's largest trading partner and Japan had certainly been the prime target for the sudden tariff. But Nixon's action prompted our prime minister, Pierre Trudeau, to seek to recalibrate relations with the US.

Trudeau advocated a Third Option, one that would see Canada reduce its vulnerability to US "shocks" by diversifying and developing complementary, political, and economic links with Europe and Asia. The idea became the topic for many press releases, visits, and consultations about frameworks for cooperation, etc., but yielded little in terms of substance because the trade winds were blowing the other way – toward deeper economic integration with the US, especially after its economy recovered from the recession brought on by the Arab oil embargo of 1973. As Stephen Clarkson and Abdi Aidid also note, "there were many slips between cup and lip. The private sector was not interested in coping with the linguistic, political, and cultural challenges presented by overseas markets given that businesses could so easily deal with customers and suppliers in the United States to whose market they had geographically privileged access."[2]

Two decades earlier, Prime Minister John Diefenbaker had also tried his own version of reducing ties to the US, when he announced that Canada would divert 15 per cent of its exports to the UK. He learned abruptly that governments cannot dictate flows of trade. Patterns of commerce follow their own path.

In the late 1980s, Prime Minister Mulroney reverted to the First Option – closer relations with the US – negotiating the FTA, NAFTA, an extension of NORAD, environmental agreements on acid rain and the Great Lakes, and an understanding on the Northwest Passage, all of which produced real dividends for Canada and also gave us a unique voice and status in Washington at a time of dramatic change in the world: the collapse of the Soviet Union, the end of apartheid, the unification of Germany, the first Gulf War and the creation of the WTO. Prime Minister Mulroney put a premium on good relations with the US. Despite the customary wariness of many Canadians about getting too close, he chose more often than not to give the Americans the benefit of the doubt. As a Quebecer, Mulroney did not share much of the angst about excessive American influence on Canada – the frequent topic for debate among the cultural literati, notably in Toronto.

The Chrétien–Martin decade that followed had spasmodic moments of the Second Option – moving away from the US relationship and adopting positions of differentiation, notably on Iraq and ballistic missile defence. These commanded instinctive popular support in Canada, but the fundamental character of our economic dependence on the United States remained constant.

What did, of course, change at the beginning of this century was the "thickening" of the Canada-US border in the decade that followed the 9/11 terrorist attacks as the US imposed a whole new series of measures to control the movement of peoples and goods across its borders. Growing protectionism in the US as recessionary pressures followed the financial crisis of 2008–09, which took a huge bite out of US jobs and growth, have not helped matters. With President Obama's election in 2008, the moment seemed propitious for another attempt to revive the First Option. However, despite a flurry of initiatives, very little of real substance has materialized on the bilateral agenda, as discussed in chapter 2. Moreover, as the personal commitment at the top to remove barriers has faded, the institutions involved in managing relations have become even more noticeably deficient. The prolonged wrangling over the Keystone pipeline is also a harsh reminder of just how vulnerable Canada is to excessive reliance on the US market, even for a vital commodity such as oil.

Much of the initial euphoria from President Obama's election victory in 2008 is wearing off on both sides of the border. As Jack Mintz observed late last year in the *National Post*, "Canada, fed up with Obama shifts over Keystone, is looking at 'market diversification,' not only for energy but also for other products and services. With Buy-American policies, beef restrictions and other irritants, the United States is not a reliable friend these days."[3]

BREAKING OUT OF THE NORTH AMERICAN COCOON

Geography may well determine much of our destiny, but geography and sentiment should not limit our outlook or our ambition. One way or other, we need to break out of the North American cocoon, replace sentiment with substance, set priorities and goals in terms of what we want and from whom, and what we are prepared to pay to secure new trade agreements, and apply political will and negotiating expertise to the task. Without a doubt, we are going to have to work a lot harder to attract similar interest from markets that have other choices, but that is no reason to let matters languish.

Two-thirds of the global economic growth in the past five years has been in emerging markets, mostly in Asia and notably in China (as discussed in chapter 3). By 2020, emerging markets' share of global growth is expected to rise to 75 per cent as more than 1 billion new middle-class consumers enter the global market. Many of these markets, and especially several in Asia, need not just energy, mineral, and agricultural commodities, but also education facilities, banking, insurance, and IT services, all of which are Canadian strengths.

At a time when countries like China, India, Indonesia, and Brazil are in the ascendant, Canada has many of the resources and skills that these markets want and need. While our economy remains prominently linked to the US and management of relations with the US will continue to be the overriding priority for any government in Ottawa, it is time to recalibrate and seek complementary ties beyond North America. It is a matter of enlightened self-interest.

The Harper government has tried to compensate by broadening its economic reach to Europe and Asia. But, even with these initiatives, the integrated nature of our economy with the US has proved to be an inhibiting factor and negotiations to diversify our trade relations have not been easy. The CETA negotiations with the EU took twice as long as the FTA with the US. Nonetheless, its success adds real substance to the Third Option approach. Better still, Canada can now concentrate its trade-negotiating energy and resources on markets in Asia with, potentially, even larger dividends.

Paradoxically, as our global profile and engagement grows, so too will our influence with Washington, as the bonds of dependence weaken. It was the late Nelson Mandela who said, "I like friends who have independent minds because they tend to make you see problems from all angles." Well, that is also true of Americans and their leaders. While we must always be attentive to bilateral issues, we are far more credible when we are deeply engaged with the world, and not, as some would prefer, acting as a detached unbiased "honest broker" or "peacekeeper" with no real interests of our own. When we respond in concrete ways to the broader economic and security challenges that preoccupy US policymakers, we will be taken seriously.

THE BUSINESS CHALLENGE

In anticipating the 1989 FTA with the US, many Canadian firms adjusted to become more competitive and better serve a more integrated North American market. With a comprehensive economic agreement with the EU and the prospect of similar agreements with major Asian countries, there is a similar incentive now for bold restructuring of Canadian firms, for coherent investments by government in infrastructure that will support broader global growth, and for policy changes that will safeguard and enhance Canada's comparative advantages.

Two challenges stand out:

(a) Excessive reliance on the US is the prime cause of complacency in Canada. It is not the answer to our economic future. While the US market will always be vital to growth, Canada needs to harness the potential in markets that are growing at a much faster rate.

(b) It is apparent that many of the emerging market governments play a substantial role in directing economic growth. Conventional, market-based rules for trade and investment will therefore not be sufficient. Instead of urging these countries to adapt to the rules of the twentieth century, Canada should adapt its own policies and tactics to tackle this twenty-first-century trend. Governments – both federal and provincial – need to work out rules and arrangements that reflect this new reality and support Canadian firms accordingly.

Some element of reciprocity in terms of market access for exporters and investors alike should also be part of our negotiating tool kit, especially vis-à-vis countries, such as China and Korea, that enjoy a lopsided trade relationship with Canada today. It is time to turn our comparative advantages, including market access to Canada and opportunities to invest in our natural resource sectors, to our advantage. We should not hesitate to advocate tactics that serve the national interest, particularly at a time when self-interest is on the rise globally and when the liberal order that underpinned much of trade policy in the last half of the twentieth century is no longer sacrosanct.

Australia does not have the advantage of living cheek by jowl beside the world's largest economy. That is undoubtedly why

Australia has instituted a coherent trade and investment strategy for growth, with particular emphasis on Asian partners. While Canada's circumstance is not the same, there are elements of Australia's plan that should be studied carefully. A good start would be taking steps to emulate Australia's dismantling of supply-managed agriculture sectors like dairy and poultry.

IT'S NOT JUST ABOUT OIL

Energy is a classic example of a natural fit between Canada and Asia, one that the Keystone XL pipeline controversy puts in stark relief. As long as Canadian oil exports are captive to a single market, we not only sell at a sharply discounted price – as much as $30 to $40 per barrel – we are also subject to the whim of an administration preoccupied with domestic politics.

When it comes to energy, it is not just about oil. Investments today in Canadian LNG (liquified natural gas) are, significantly, coming from Asia – from China, Japan, Korea, and Malaysia – because that is precisely where market demand for LNG is growing. Those investments are generally welcome. We need foreign investment to develop our substantial gas resources. Some will involve infrastructure as well, because we will need to upgrade our pipelines, port, and refinery capabilities in order to serve markets beyond North America. But we should turn the needs of these markets to our advantage and seek comparable access from them.

Canada also has prodigious uranium resources and produces, primarily in Saskatchewan, between 14 and 25 per cent of the world's supply in any given year. The federal government has already concluded Nuclear Cooperation Agreements with China and India in order to secure long-term shipments. The Chinese market alone is expected to generate up to $3 billion in sales for Canadian producers in the coming decade.

The more diverse our markets for energy and other commodities, the more globally competitive we will be and the better we should also be in managing our extensive relations with the US. That is a major reason why a Third Option with Legs makes eminent sense for Canada.

However, energy is simply one of many sectors where there is scope for growth. Aerospace, financial services, and IT are among others. Bombardier, CAE, Power Corp, Manulife, Air Canada, and

Linamar are other examples of major Canadian firms with global reach that recognize the value and the potential of the Asia-Pacific markets and are actively pursuing expanded opportunities.

DEVELOPING A COHERENT GLOBAL TRADE AND INVESTMENT STRATEGY

As former trade minister David Emerson warned, "We are in a world of rapid and massive geopolitical and economic change, where a moment of lassitude, complacency or lapse of judgement can be crippling."[4] It is very much in our own self-interest to engage in more strategic negotiations with our Asian partners. This would complement and balance but not displace relations with the US.

However, it is one thing to talk about diversifying our trade to Asian markets, and quite another to conclude agreements that will secure and stimulate our access to these markets. Since the turn of the new century, the government has had an ambitious but, until the recent success with the EU and South Korea, a quiet trade agenda.

Canada needs a coherent negotiating strategy with clear priorities on what we want from whom and what we are prepared to give in order to achieve our objectives. Because it does indeed "take two to tango," we also need clearer signals of engagement from our Asian dance partners, some of whom often seem more preoccupied with Washington than even we Canadians are. Japan, India, and China, in some rational sequence, are obvious priorities. Instead of a flurry of more than fifty separate trade initiatives we need to focus on those that will reap significant dividends for Canada.

Canada has what emerging markets need. We must negotiate customized trade and investment arrangements with this in mind and use our comparative advantage as leverage to gain better access for Canadian exporters. When Canada engages with emerging markets on trade and investment, it should only give equivalent value for what it can gain in terms of access.

After almost grovelling for acceptance, Canada did manage to force its way into the TPP negotiations. Some see the TPP as "NAFTA on steroids" whereas others view it as a cornerstone of America's pivot to Asia, intended strategically to counter the rise of China. While TPP is the centrepiece of US trade policy initiatives, it also has hub-and-spoke features that should be of concern to other participants. Some new rules will be generally applicable but the hard bargaining will focus on a rolling series of bilateral "divide and con-quer" agreements in which the US wields the lopsided power of its own market to its own advantage. Many participants are involved more because they fear exclusion than for potential economic benefits.

The TPP is obviously part of the equation, especially because this is the almost exclusive priority at the moment for US trade practi-tioners. But we need to be sure that Canada is not disadvantaged by any benefits the US negotiates in its bilateral agreements with others under the TPP umbrella. In any event, well-planned bilateral initia-tives can systematically complement a regional approach provided there are governments with the political courage and the stamina needed to produce results.

It remains to be seen if China will react to the US's Asian pivot with a counter-pivot of its own. China is involved in trade discus-sions with various, regional players, some of whom will not want to have to make a choice between the US and China as their preferred dance partner.

THE NEED FOR CONSISTENCY AND COHERENCE

Canada's economic relations with China have blown cold and hot and then cold again in recent years. Overtures from China to forge deeper economic links, including ones that could bolster other aspects of Canada's trade agenda, notably the TPP, have been inexplicably stymied. Some suggest that the reasons are ideological – deep aver-sions among Reform elements of the government in particular to all things Chinese. Others contend that it is simply prudence about deal-ing with an economy as large, and as largely directed by the heavy hand of government, as that of China. Either way, Canada is left on the outside looking in, running on idle while others pass us by.

Canada needs a more determined and consistent course of action with China and other countries in the region. Our relationship may never be a priority for Beijing so the initiative will have to come from Ottawa. (That is also true, incidentally, as we cultivate deeper relations with New Delhi, Hanoi, and Jakarta.) We can choose a pragmatic path with China without abandoning our fundamen-tal concerns about human rights and democratic pluralism, but we should not allow differences over values obscure opportunities for mutual benefit. The more engagement China has with countries like Canada, the more likely it is that some of our values may actually take root there.

Perhaps the most promising initiative with Northeast Asia involves Canada's negotiations with Japan. The complementary nature of the two economies offers a promising foundation for deeper cooperation, one that would also reinforce shared objectives for the TPP. But the level of interest in Tokyo waxes and wanes. For understandable reasons, the Japanese are preoccupied with their relations with the US and the hub-and-spoke character of the TPP, often even more so than Canadians.

The Joint Study concluded by the government of Canada with its Japanese counterpart in 2007 as a basis for negotiation suggested that a comprehensive agreement could add between USD$3.8 billion and USD$9 billion to Canada's GDP. The biggest challenge is to secure Japan's political commitment to the negotiation. The TPP and relations with the US more generally attract much more consistent attention. But Japan is an attractive partner for Canada on many fronts. Despite its recent economic decline, Japan remains a major source of technological innovation and a world leader in commercializing new technologies into market products. Equally, and particularly with its move away from nuclear power following the Fukushima disaster, Japan can be a major and reliable partner for Canada on energy. Several Japanese investments have already been made in Canadian projects aimed at LNG exports. We could, for instance, offer Japan a secure supply of energy and agriculture commodities that Japan needs as a catalyst for expanded bilateral commerce. The potential is there, provided there is the political will to engage and provided that Japan is not mesmerized by relations with the US to the exclusion of other opportunities.

And we should not lose sight of the major trade and investment opportunities that exist with India, Indonesia, and Vietnam, as discussed in chapter 3. These are the new tigers of Asia, whose growth rates in some cases now match or exceed those of China. If we move quickly in these newer emerging markets we will not have to play the kind of catch-up game we have been playing in China. A beachhead in these markets, which are also increasingly integrated with each other and the Chinese economy, also gives us access to other markets in Asia.

A COMPLEMENTARY SECURITY AGENDA

The Asia-Pacific is undergoing a cosmic shift in security relations and the regional balance of power. China is in the process of determining how best to translate its burgeoning economic strength into a more strategic regional and global role. New tensions over security are complicating attempts at deeper economic integration. China is obviously aware of the fact that America's capacity for leadership is in decline, but it is not rushing just yet to fill the vacuum. There is some sign that China's new leadership, for now, will concentrate primarily on domestic priorities – problems associated with income and regional inequities and corruption – on regional relations (e.g., with Japan, Korea, Vietnam, and Indonesia), and, very gingerly, relations with the US. How China and the US relate to one another is probably the most critical issue affecting the region's future and stability if not the globe's.

As argued in chapter 5, deeper diplomatic and security engagement in the Asia-Pacific region must accompany our efforts to forge stronger trade and investment linkages. Our new economic partners in the region expect us to be not just "present," but also visibly engaged. Canada poses a threat to no one. We can stickhandle nimbly around territorial disputes and conflicts over threats from cyberspace. But if we want to be taken seriously and earn the respect of those countries with which we seek to do business, we are going to have to do a lot more than show up for the occasional security meeting or port visit. In addition to stationing military attachés in key countries, such as Indonesia, we need to explore opportunities to undertake joint military exercises and training, as well as enhancing law enforcement collaboration and information sharing.

We also have an important role to play in addressing new security challenges, such as food, energy, environment, and cyber security, which are increasingly issues of friction among states in the region. In addition, we should support regional architecture initiatives that include all players, but especially China. For Canada, it is not a matter of a pivot to Asia. Rather, our values and our interests oblige a deeper commitment to promoting regional stability and the basic ingredients of proper governance – the rule of law versus the law of the jungle.

The same general principles of commitment and engagement apply to security relations in other parts of the world. We need to continue to be attentive to addressing deficiencies in governance and the rule of law in our development assistance programming, recognizing that poverty alleviation and economic growth depend on strong, effective, and stable public institutions. If there is a broader lesson from the military interventions of the past decade, it is that the military is also a blunt and unwieldy instrument for promoting nation-building. There is also little support for it in a public that has grown weary of military intervention and the uncertain achievements of Afghanistan, Libya, and beyond. As argued in chapters 5 and 6, we need better systems and tools of conflict prevention to address the problems of failed (or failing) states before violence erupts and the game is lost. Promoting greater religious tolerance and freedom in societies in transition is one potential means of averting conflict. So too is the development of a strong and engaged civil society, which is critical to the formation of a healthy and viable democracy.

One of the biggest lessons of recent years in the lacklustre and disarrayed response of western democracies to the Arab Spring. Its sorry aftermath is that democratic countries need to work much more closely together. As discussed in chapter 6, we find much merit in the idea of a D10 that brings western democracies together in an informal grouping to coordinate responses and actions to the great political awakening that is sweeping the world. Not only is there strength in numbers, but the United States, as the world's most powerful nation, cannot stand alone as the sole champion of democratic values and principles. Canada, as a nation that has made a virtue of promoting tolerance and accommodation in its own federal system of governance, is especially well-positioned to play a leadership role in such an initiative.

The seeds of pluralism and democracy take a long time to grow. As we know all too well, progress will be uneven and marred by frequent setbacks. That is all the more reason to share the burdens of failure and success by working closely with those who share our values and commitment to creating a more democratic and peaceful world.

SELECTIVE VERSUS AIMLESS MULTILATERALISM

Multilateralism is not an end in itself. Canada needs to select multilateral institutions prudently where its voice and commitments have potential for influence, advocating reforms where necessary, and disassociating itself from institutions that are bound in gridlock or consistently proven not to be up to the task. We should champion UN reform, not shy away from it. And we need to ensure that our major financial commitments to multilateral institutions, such as the World Bank and the World Food Programme, are matched by efforts to direct the operations of these institutions. The old saw "no taxation without representation" should determine the quantity as well as the quality of our engagement.

CONCLUSION

A reinvigorated Canadian response to twenty-first-century geopolitical and economic changes must therefore concentrate on the following:

1 Implement a Third Option with Legs strategy by moving beyond excessive reliance on the US market and concluding trade and investment agreements with Europe and key players in Asia and Latin America to complement, balance, and simultaneously strengthen our capacity to manage relations with the US. Canada should use its comparative advantages assertively (and demand some degree of reciprocity from others) to safeguard and enhance our national interests.

2 Recalibrate foreign policy priorities to reinforce a broader global reach by Canada with a better balance between the advancement of Canadian interests and the nurturing of Canadian values, including, specifically, efforts to refresh multilateral institutions and streamlining and replacing commitments where appropriate, while investing in new approaches to meet twenty-first-century challenges (such as transnational terrorism, competition in cyberspace, and environmental degradation).

3 Institute domestic policies, commitments, and governmental structures to ensure that we have the right infrastructure, the skills, and the decision-making capacities to seize new opportunities, including, notably, educational and training reforms geared to employment needs.

4 Directly engage both business and labour to ensure cohesive implementation of an enlightened coherent global strategy.

5 Assume and assert a role in world affairs commensurate with our capabilities and our potential by being selective and opportunistic.

Canadians want their country to do constructive things in the world. We clearly have the capacity and inclination. What is needed now is the political will to deliver.

It is not a question of the world needing "more Canada." It is a matter of "more from Canada to the world." The key to a more mature global outlook for Canada is recognizing our limitations as a country of 35 million in a world of more than 6 billion people. We should not aspire to be all things to all people. Rather, we should muster and focus everything we've got: our economic strengths and our diplomatic skills into avenues where there are real prospects for influence and success in a world that cries out for us to be bold and brave.

Notes

CHAPTER ONE

1 Francis Fukuyama, *The End of History and the Last Man* (New York: Free Press, 1992).

2 Aaron L. Friedberg, *The Weary Titan: Britain and the Experience of Relative Decline, 1895–1905* (Princeton: Princeton University Press, 1988).

3 Samuel P. Huntington, *The Clash of Civilizations and the Remaking of World Order* (New York: Simon & Schuster, 1996).

4 "The World Needs More Canada: But How Much Is Enough?" *Maclean's*, 2 July 2012, 4.

5 Ibid.

6 Two such examples are Andrew Cohen, *While Canada Slept: How We Lost Our Place in the World* (Toronto: McClelland & Stewart Ltd., 2003); Jennifer Welsh, *At Home in the World: Canada's Global Vision for the 21st Century* (Toronto: HarperCollins, 2004).

7 John Godfrey Saxe, *The Poems of John Godfrey Saxe: Complete in One Volume* (Boston: Ticknor and Fields, 1868), 259–60.

8 Richard N. Haass, *Foreign Policy Begins at Home: The Case for Putting America's House in Order* (New York: Basic Books, 2013).

9 See, for example, *The Tonight Show with Jay Leno*, 6 August 2013.

10 "Emerging World Loses Economic Growth Lead," *Wall Street Journal*, 11 August 2013.

11 Paul Krugman, "How the Case for Austerity Has Crumbled," *The New York Review of Books*, 6 June 2013; Jeanna Smialek, "Stiglitz Says More Fiscal Stimulus Needed in U.S.: Tom Keene," *Bloomberg*, 9 April 2013.

12 Leslie H. Gelb and Dimitri K. Simes, "A New Anti-American Axis?," *New York Times*, 7 July 2013, 5.

13 Chester A. Crocker, Fen Osler Hampson, and Pamela Aall, "Introduction," in *Conflict Management and Global Governance in an Age of Awakening,* Corcker, Hampson, and Aall, eds. (Washington and Waterloo: United States Institute of Peace Press and Centre for International Governance Innovation, forthcoming 2014).

14 Ian Bremmer, *Every Nation for Itself: Winners and Losers in a G-Zero World* (New York: Penguin Group, 2012).

15 Henry Blodget and Paul Szoldra, "Bremmer: The Japan-China Crisis is the Most Significant Geopolitical Tension in the World," *Business Insider,* 24 January 2013, http://www.businessinsider.com/japan-china-crisis-is-a-huge-geopolitical-problem-2013-1.

16 Yuka Hayashi, "As Tensions Rise, Pacifist Japan Marches Into a Military Revival," *Wall Street Journal,* 18 July 2013, A1.

17 Raissa Robles, "Abe Pushes Peacemaker Role in Manila," *South China Morning Post,* 28 July 2013, 3.

18 Odd Arne Westad, *Restless Empire: China and the World Since 1750* (New York: Basic Books, 2012), 413.

19 Stockholm International Peace Research Institute, *SIPRI Military Expenditure Database.* http://www.sipri.org/research/armaments/milex/milex_database.

20 Reuters, "Malacca Strait is a Strategic 'Chokepoint'," *Reuters,* 4 March 2010, http://in.reuters.com/article/2010/03/04/idINIndia-46652220100304.

21 United States Energy Information Administration, "The South China Sea is an Important World Energy Trade Route," *Today in Energy,* 4 April 2013, http://www.eia.gov/todayinenergy/detail.cfm?id=10671.

22 Bill Tarrant, "Balancing Powers in the Malacca Strait," *Reuters Global News Journal,* 7 March 2010, http://blogs.reuters.com/global/2010/03/07/balancing-powers-in-the-malacca-strait/.

23 Zbigniew Brzezinski, "The Global Political Awakening," *International Herald Tribune,* 17 December 2008, 26.

24 This maxim is attributed to Winston Churchill, who said, in the British House of Commons, "No one pretends that democracy is perfect or all-wise. Indeed, it has been said that democracy is the worst form of Government except all those other forms that have been tried from time to time," *Hansard,* Official Report, House of Commons, 11 November 1947, vol. 444, cc. 206–7.

25 Ian Bremmer, *Every Nation for Itself: Winners and Losers in a G-Zero World* (New York: Portfolio/Penguin, 2012).

26　Derek H. Burney, "A Third Option with Legs," Asia Pacific Heads of Missions' Luncheon, Residence of the Ambassador of Korea, Ottawa, Canada, 9 April 2013.

27　David Gordon and Ash Jain, "Forget the G-8. It's Time for the D-10," *Wall Street Journal*, 17 June 2013, A15.

CHAPTER TWO

1　Dean Acheson, "Canada: 'Stern Daughter of the Voice of God,'" in Livingston Merchant, ed., *Neighbors Taken for Granted: Canada and the United States* (Toronto: Burns & MacEachern, 1966), 139–47.

2　John F. Kennedy, "Address Before the Parliament of Canada," Ottawa, 17 May 1961.

3　Pierre Elliott Trudeau, "Pearson ou l'abdication de l'esprit," *Cité Libre* 56 (1963): 7.

4　While Prime Minister Trudeau got rid of Canada's Bomarcs, Canadian air defence plans continued to rely in part on American nuclear weapons. From 1965 to 1984, Canada stored AIR-2 Genie air-to-air rockets armed with nuclear warheads at several Canadian airbases. The weapons, though owned by the United States, would be used by Canada's CF-101B VooDoo interceptors in the event of a major military confrontation with the Soviet Union. For more details, see John Clearwater, *Canadian Nuclear Weapons: The Untold Story of Canada's Cold War Arsenal* (Toronto: Dundurn Press, 1998).

5　Ronald Reagan, "Speech at the Brandenburg Gate," Berlin, 12 June 1987.

6　Derek H. Burney, *Getting It Done: A Memoir* (Montreal: McGill-Queen's University Press, 2005), 105.

7　Bob Plamondon, *The Truth About Trudeau* (Ottawa: Great River Media, 2013).

8　Carleton University, *From Correct to Inspired: A Blueprint for Canada-US Engagement* (Ottawa: Centre for Trade Policy and Law, 2008), vi.

9　Ibid., vii.

10　Genevieve Walker, *Draft Supplemental Environmental Impact Statement for the Keystone XL Project Executive Summary* (Washington, DC: United States Department of State, 2013), ES-13-ES-14.

11　Barack Obama, "Speech at Georgetown University," Washington, DC, 25 June 2013.

12　See, for example, Environment Canada, *Canada's Emissions Trends 2012* (Ottawa: Her Majesty the Queen in Right of Canada, 2012), 1.

13   Environment Canada, *National Inventory Report 1990–2011: Green-house Gas Sources and Sinks in Canada*, Part 1 (Ottawa: Environment Canada Pollutant Inventories and Reporting Division, 2013), 53.
14   Scott Barlow, "Ottawa's GM Share Sale Highlights Bailout's Mixed Blessings," *Globe and Mail*, 7 August 2013, B2; Greg Keenan, "Foggy Future," *Globe and Mail*, 22 June 2013, p. B6.
15   Konrad Yakabuski, "Harper and Co.'s Auto Policy Running on Fumes," *Globe and Mail*, 19 September 2013, A17.
16   William Galston, "A Decade of Decline in the American Dream: Today's Volatile Mood is a Reminder of the Early Post-Vietnam Years," *Wall Street Journal*, 18 December 2013, http://online.wsj.com/news/articles/SB10001424052702304858104579264271656203200.

CHAPTER THREE

1   Mark Carney, "Exporting in a Post-Crisis World," Remarks to the Greater Kitchener-Waterloo Chamber of Commerce, 2 April 2012.
2   Ibid.
3   Bank of Canada, "Monetary Policy Report Summary," July 2013, 1.
4   Statistics Canada, "Imports, exports and trade balance of goods on a balance-of-payments basis, by country or country grouping," 2013, http://www.statcan.gc.ca/tables-tableaux/sum-som/l01/cst01/gblec02a-eng.htm.
5   Tiff Macklem, "Regearing Our Economic Growth," W. Edmund Clark Distinguished Lecture, Queen's University, Kingston, ON, 10 January 2013.
6   Derek Burney, Leonard J. Edwards, Thomas d'Aquino, and Fen Osler Hampson, *Winning in a Changing World: Canada and Emerging Markets* (Ottawa: iPolitics, 2012), 5.
7   Ibid., 1.
8   Ibid.
9   Pricewaterhousecoopers, *World in 2050 – The BRICs and Beyond: Prospects, Challenges and Opportunities*, 2013, 8.
10   Pricewaterhousecoopers, 2.
11   Burney et al., 1.
12   Ibid.
13   Export Development Canada, *Global Export Forecast Spring 2013*. http://www.edc.ca/EN/Knowledge-Centre/Economic-Analysis-and-Research/Documents/gef-spring-2013-summary.pdf.
14   World Bank, *World Development Indicators*, 2013.
15   http://www.bankofcanada.ca/2013/01/publications/speeches/regearing-our-economic-growth/.

16 Ibid.
17 Mykyta Vesselovsky, "Canadian Market Share in the U.S. and the Roles of Product Mix and Competitiveness," *Office of the Chief Economist Issue Brief*, Foreign Affairs and International Trade Canada, 2010.
18 Statistics Canada, CANSIM Table 228-0058.
19 United States Department of Commerce International Trade Administration, TradeStats Express – National Trade Data, 2013.
20 Derek Burleton and Diana Petramala, "Canada's Declining Reliance on the U.S. – Where to Grow from Here?," *TD Economics Observation*, 2012, http://www.td.com/document/PDF/economics/special/dp0212_trade.pdf.
21 World Trade Organization, *International Trade Statistics 2001* (Geneva: WTO Publications, 2001), 21; World Trade Organization, *International Trade Statistics 2011* (2011), 24.
22 Burney et al., *Winning in a Changing World*, 6.
23 Organisation for Economic Co-operation and Development, *Strategic Transport Infrastructure Needs to 2030* (OECD Publishing, 2012).
24 Asian Development Bank, *Asia 2050: Realizing the Asian Century* (Manila: Asian Development Bank, 2011).
25 World Trade Organization, 2001 and 2011.
26 International Monetary Fund, *World Economic Outlook Database*, April 2013.
27 Valentin Pekantchin, "Reforming Dairy Supply Management in Canada: The Australian Example," *Montreal Economic Institute Economic Note*, 2006.
28 Burney et al., *Winning in a Changing World*, 8.
29 For example, after the US and UK, Australia is the third most popular destination in the world for foreign university students, and in 2010–11, international education activity contributed over $16 billion to the Australian economy. See Australian Bureau of Statistics, *Australian Social Trends December 2011: International Students* (ABS Catalogue no. 4102.0) (Commonwealth of Australia, 2011), 5; Australian Education International, "Export Income to Australia from Education Services in 2010–2011," *Research Snapshot*, November 2011, https://www.aei.gov.au/research/Research-Snapshots/Documents/Export%20Income%202010-11.pdf.
30 Australia Department of Foreign Affairs and Trade, *Australia's Trade with East Asia 2012* (Commonwealth of Australia, 2013), 1, 7.
31 Australian Government, *Australia in the Asian Century* (Canberra: Commonwealth of Australia, 2012).
32 Ibid., 195.

33   Ibid., 170, 251.

34   Ibid., 198.

35   Ibid., 179.

36   Kathryn McMullen and Angelo Elias, "A Changing Portrait of International Students in Canadian Universities," Statistics Canada, 2011 http://www.statcan.gc.ca/pub/81-004-x/2010006/article/11405-eng. htm#d; Statistics Canada, "Public Postsecondary Enrolments, by Registration Status, Pan-Canadian Standard Classification of Education (PCSCE), Classification of Instructional Programs, Primary Grouping (CIP_PG), Sex and Immigration Status," CANSIM Table 477-0019, 2013, http://www5. statcan.gc.ca/cansim/a26?lang=eng&retrLang=eng&id=4770019& tabMode=dataTable&srchLan=-1&p1=-1&p2=9.

37   For example, Canada's foreign investment position grew from about one-third of annual GDP in 2000 to 39 per cent of annual GDP in 2011; the rest of the world's direct investment position in Canada grew from around 29 per cent of GDP to 35 per cent over the same period, according to calculations made using Statistics Canada data. See Statistics Canada, CANSIM Tables 376-0051 and 380-0016.

38   Burney et al., *Winning in a Changing World*, 8.

39   Knight Frank Research, *The Wealth Report 2012: A Global Perspective on Prime Property and Wealth*. New York: CITI Private Bank. http://www. thewealthreport.net/The-Wealth-Report-2012.pdf.

40   World Trade Organization, *World Trade Statistics 2012*, 26.

41   Pricewaterhousecoopers, *World in 2050*, 8.

42   Przemyslaw Kowalski, Max Büge, Monika Sztajerowska, Matias Egeland, "State-Owned Enterprises: Trade Effects and Policy Implications," Organisation for Economic Co-operation and Development, OECD Trade Policy Paper No. 147, 2013, 6.

43   Ibid., 20.

44   Ibid., 6

45   "China's Economy Perverse Advantages," *The Economist*, http://www. economist.com/news/finance-and-economics/21576680-new-Book-lays-out-scale-chinas-industrial-subsidies-perverse-advantage.

46   Kowalski et al. "State-owned Enterprises."

47   HSBC Global Connections, February 2013. https://globalconnections. hsbc.com/downloads/hsbc-trade-forecast-ca-february-2013.pdf.

48   Perrin Beatty and Andrés Rozental, *Forging a New Strategic Partnership Between Canada and Mexico* (Waterloo, ON: Centre for International Governance Innovation, 2012), 5.

49 Ibid., 5.

50 Ibid.

51 Foreign Affairs, Trade and Development Canada, "Indonesia," http://www.acdi-cida.gc.ca/acdi-cida/ACDI-CIDA.nsf/En/JUD-129154747-SDY.

52 Ibid.

53 Statistics Canada, "International Investment Position, Canadian Direct Investment Abroad and Foreign Direct Investment in Canada, by Country," CANSIM Table 376-0051.

54 International Monetary Fund, Direction of Trade Statistics (DOTS) Database.

55 Canadian International Development Agency, *Indonesia Country Strategy* (Gatineau, QC: Canadian International Development Agency, 2009), 2–4.

56 Government of Canada, "Canada – Indonesia Relations," 2012, http://www.canadainternational.gc.ca/indonesia-indonesie/bilateral_relations_bilaterales/canada-indonesia-indonesie.aspx.

57 World Bank, *World Development Indicators*, 2013.

58 Deepak Mishra and Viet Tuan Dinh, *Taking Stock: An Update on Vietnam's Recent Economic Developments* (Hanoi: The World Bank, 2013), 22.

59 Central Intelligence Agency, *The World Factbook 2013–14* (Washington: Central Intelligence Agency, 2013).

60 World Bank, *Vietnam Urbanization Review Technical Assistance Report* (World Bank, 2011), 71–2, 191–9.

61 KPMG, *Investing in Vietnam* (KPMG Vietnam Ltd., 2011), 10.

62 Ibid., 12.

63 David Bloom, "Population Dynamics in India and Implications for Population Growth," in *The Oxford Handbook of the Indian Economy*, ed. Chetan Ghate (New York: Oxford University Press, 2012), 484.

64 Jamil Anderlini and Ed Crooks, "Chinese Labour Pool Begins to Drain," *Financial Times*, 18 January 2013, http://www.ft.com/intl/cms/s/0/ad1e00e6-6149-11e2-957e-00144feab49a.html?siteedition=intl#axzz2e8sVYM5i.

65 Allen T. Cheng, "India Risks Falling Further Behind China in the BRICS Growth Race," *Institutional Investor* (American Edition), July 2013.

66 Jason Overdorf, "When More Is Worse," *Newsweek* 152, no. 8, 25 August 2008.

67 Robin Pagnamenta, "Doubts Grow Over Quality of India's Graduates," *The Times* (London), 14 November 2011, 46.

68 Seung-Hun Chun, *Strategy for Industrial Development and Growth of Major Industries in Korea* (Seoul: Korea Institute for Development Strategy, 2010), 4, 11.

69 Sang M. Lee, "South Korea: From the Land of Morning Calm to ICT Hotbed," *Academy of Management Executive* 17, no. 2 (2003): 7–18.

70 Dong Cheol Kim, *Korean Experience of Overcoming Economic Crisis through ICT Development* (Bangkok: United Nations Economic and Social Commission for Asia and the Pacific, 2009), 2, 6.

71 GlobeScan/PIPA, "BBC World Service 2013 Country Ratings Poll," May 2013, 21, 33.

72 Richard G. Anderson, "Japan as a Role Model?" *Federal Reserve Bank of St. Louis Economic Synopses* 19 (2013): 3.

73 World Intellectual Property Organization, WIPO *Facts and Figures 2012* 19.

74 In 2010 Japan slipped to second place in terms of patent filings. See Word Intellectual Property Organization, "Statistical Country Profiles: Japan," 2013, http://www.wipo.int/ipstats/en/statistics/country_profile/countries/jp.html.

75 Organisation for Economic Co-operation and Development, OECD *Science, Technology and Industry Outlook 2012* (OECD: 2012), 332.

76 "R&D Outlays Surge with Focus on Energy," *The Nikkei Weekly*, 12 August 2013.

77 Japan Automobile Manufacturers Association of Canada, *The Japanese Auto Industry in Canada 2013 Edition: Facts & Figures* (Toronto: JAMA Canada, 2013), 1, 4, 6.

78 World Bank, *World Development Indicators*.

CHAPTER FOUR

1 Fen Osler Hampson and Paul Heinbecker, *Leadership in a Turbulent Age* (Waterloo: The Centre for International Governance Innovation, 2013), 5–6.

2 Li Mingjiang, "Rising from Within: China's Search for a Multilateral World and its Implications for Sino-US Relations," *Global Governance* 17, no. 3 (2011): 331.

3 Robert B. Zoellick, "American Exceptionalism: Time for New Thinking on Economics and Security," Alastair Buchan Memorial Lecture, Arundel House, London, 25 July 2012.

4 Richard Haass, "The Case for Messy Multilateralism," *Financial Times*, 5 January 2010, http://www.ft.com/intl/cms/s/0/18d8f8b6-fa2f-11de-beed-00144feab49a.html#axzz2byq1qL5R.

5 An international reserve asset used by the IMF to supplement countries' official loan reserve levels.

6   Henry Chu, Jim Puzzanghera, and Paul Richter, "G-20 Summit Surprises with a Show of Unity," *Los Angeles Times*, 3 April 2009.

7   United Nations Framework Convention on Climate Change, "Copenhagen Climate Change Conference – December 2009," http://unfccc.int/meetings/copenhagen_dec_2009/meeting/6295.php.

8   Mark Lynas, "How Do I Know China Wrecked the Copenhagen Deal? I Was in the Room," *The Guardian*, 23 December 2009, 10.

9   John M. Broder, "What's Rotten for Obama in Denmark," *New York Times*, 13 December 2009, 1.

10   "Copenhagen Aftermath – With No Climate Deal Sealed, Where To Now?" ENDS *Report no. 420* (31 January 2010), 32–6.

11   Radoslav S. Dimitrov, "Inside UN Climate Change Negotiations: The Copenhagen Conference," *Review of Policy Research* 27.6 (2010): 795–821.

12   Louise Gray. "Copenhagen Summit 2009: US Warns Satellites Can Check China's Emissions Honesty," *Daily Telegraph* (London), 19 December 2009, 14.

13   Bernard Norwood, "The Kennedy Round: A Try at Linear Trade Negotiations," *Journal of Law and Economics* 12, no. 2 (1969): 297–319.

14   CUTS International, "'Multilateral Trading System is Dead': Professor Jagdish Bhagwati," Press Release, 27 September 2013.

15   Internet Society, "World Conference on International Telecommunications (WCIT)," http://www.internetsociety.org/wcit.

16   International Commission on Intervention and State Sovereignty, *The Responsibility to Protect* (Ottawa: International Development Research Centre, 2001).

17   United Nations Security Council, *Resolution 1973 (2011)*, S/RES/1973 (2011), 17 March 2011.

18   "Russia and China Veto Draft Security Council Resolution on Syria," *UN News Centre*, 4 October 2011, http://www.un.org/apps/news/story.asp?NewsID=39935#.UgoSmpKccXE.

19   Julie Tate, "White House's Arguments for Military Action," *Washington Post*, 10 September 2013, A06.

20   Dean Acheson, *Present at the Creation: My Years in the State Department* (New York: Norton, 1969).

21   Paul Heinbecker, "It's Not Just the Drought Treaty: Canada is Vanishing from the United Nations," *Globe and Mail*, 1 April 2013, http://www.theglobeandmail.com/commentary/its-not-just-the-drought-treaty-canada-is-vanishing-from-the-united-nations/article10600939/#dashboard/follows/.

CHAPTER FIVE

1 George Will, as quoted in Kevin Libin, "The Shadow of 9/11," *National Post*, 6 September 2011, A1.

2 Bernard-Henri Lévy, "The Syria Deal has a Hint of Munich," *Wall Street Journal*, 17 September 2013, A17.

3 J. Joseph Hewitt, Jonathan Wilkenfeld, and Ted Robert Gurr, with Birger Heldt, *Peace and Conflict 2012 Executive Summary* (College Park, MD: University of Maryland, 2012), 18.

4 Human Security Centre, *Human Security Report 2005: War and Peace in the 21st Century* (New York: Oxford University Press, 2005), 43.

5 Hewitt et al., *Peace and Conflict*, 20.

6 Prime Minister Brian Mulroney's initiative was known as the North Pacific Cooperative Security Dialogue.

7 William G. Stormont, "Managing Potential Conflicts in the South China Sea," *Marine Journal* 18, no. 4 (1994): 353–6.

8 Graham Allison, "Thucydides's Trap Has Been Sprung in the Pacific,: *Financial Times*, 21 August 2012. Available at: http://www.ft.com/cms/s/0/5d695b5a-ead3-11e1-984b-00144feab49a.html#axzz2omHC66Ow.

9 Pew Research Center, *U.S. Public, Experts Differ on China Policies* (Pew Research Center, 2012), 3.

10 U.S. Energy Information Administration, *World Oil Transit Chokepoints* (USEIA, 2012), 3.

11 Campbell Clark, "Canada Denied Seat at East Asia Summit," *The Globe and Mail*, 20 September 2012, A3.

12 Mike Blanchfield, "ASEAN Chief Wants Canada to Play Greater Role as Peacemaker in Asia," *The Canadian Press*, 20 September 2012, http://www.ipolitics.ca/2012/09/20/asean-chief-wants-canada-to-play-greater-role-as-peacemaker-in-asia/.

13 John Blaxland, *Closer Australia-Canada Defence Cooperation?* (Waterloo, ON: Australian Strategic Policy Institute Limited and the Centre for International Governance Innovation, 2013), 5.

14 Ibid., 8–10.

15 Ronald Reagan, "Address to the Nation on Defense and National Security," Washington, 23 March 1983.

16 George N. Lewis and Theodore A. Postol, "Technical Debate over Patriot Performance in the Gulf War: American Physical Society Panel Correctly Rejects Criticisms of Analysis Showing Patriot Failed to Destroy Scud Warheads," *Science and Global Security* 8, no. 3 (2000): 357–98.

17 Henry Kissinger, "Should We Try to Defend Against Russia's Missiles?" *Washington Post*, 23 September 1984, C8.

18 United States Department of Defense, *Ballistic Missile Defense Review Report* (United States Department of Defense, 2010).

19 North Korea also faces the very significant technical challenge of designing and building a reliable nuclear weapon that is small and light enough to fit on a missile that could reach North America. Building a miniaturized weapon of this type is an order of magnitude more difficult that building a run-of-the-mill nuclear bomb.

20 For an additional argument in favour of Canadian participation in BMD, see Frank Harvey, *North Korea, Ballistic Missile Defence and Canada-US Defence Cooperation* (Calgary: Canadian Defence & Foreign Affairs Institute, 2013).

21 Nicholas Eberstadt, "A Route to Reigning in North Korea," *Wall Street Journal*, 6 May 2013, A15.

22 Hillary Rodham Clinton, "Transcript of Clinton's Confirmation Hearing," *National Public Radio*, 13 January 2009, http://www.npr.org/templates/story/story.php?storyId=99290981.

23 Henry A. Kissinger and George P. Shultz, "What a Final Iran Deal Must Do: A Credible Agreement Must Dismantle or Mothball the Key Parts of Tehran's Nuclear Infrastructure." *Wall Street Journal*, 2 December 2013, http://online.wsj.com/news/articles/SB10001424052702304747004579 228110944819396.

24 International Atomic Energy Agency, *Nuclear Technology Review 2012* (Vienna: IAEA, 2012), 14–15.

25 Eric Schmitt, Michael S. Schmidt, and Ellen Barry, "Bombing Inquiry Turns to Motive and Russia Trip," *New York Times*, 21 April 2013, A1.

26 Kathryn Blaze Carlson, Ann Hui, and Tu Thanh Ha, "Ali Medlej, Xristos Katsiroubas, and Aaron Yoon Were Once Just Three Average Teenagers in London, Ont. – All High-School Friends," *Globe and Mail*, 6 April 2013, A10.

27 Patrick Martin, "Looking for Trouble," *Globe and Mail*, 27 April 2013, F5.

28 For a further discussion of the Dubai Process (as it is commonly known) on which this discussion is adapted, see Fen Osler Hampson, *Evaluating the Dubai Process and Its Applicability to Other Regions* (Ottawa: Norman Paterson School of International Affairs, 2011); and John B. Hay, *The Dubai Process: Lessons Learned and Implications for Third-party Engagement in Managing Cross-border Challenges in other Regions* (Ottawa: Norman Paterson School of International Affairs, 2011).

29 Robert Sibley, "An Independent Canada," *Ottawa Citizen*, 7 August 2013, A13.

30 Charles Ritchie, *The Siren Years: A Canadian Diplomat Abroad 1937–
    1945* (Toronto: Macmillan, 1974).

CHAPTER SIX

1   Ambrose Evans-Pritchard, "Fight for Control Over Libya's Oil Output
    Adds to Market Tensions," *Daily Telegraph* (London), 30 August 2013, 4.
2   Tim Arango, "Sectarian Attacks Return With a Roar to Iraq, Rattling a
    Capital Already on Edge," *New York Times*, 18 August 2013, 6.
3   Immanuel Kant, *Perpetual Peace: A Philosophical Essay*, trans. M.
    Campbell Smith (London: George Allen & Unwin, Ltd., 1903).
4   For a summary of the democratic peace literature, see John M. Owen,
    "Democratic Peace Research: Whence and Whither?" *International Pol-
    itics* 41 (2004): 605–17.
5   Arch Puddington, *Freedom in the World 2013: Democratic Breakthroughs
    in the Balance* (Freedom House, 2013), 27.
6   Ibid., 24.
7   Freedom House, "Freedom in the World 2013," http://www.freedomhouse.
    org/report/freedom-world/freedom-world-2013.
8   Ibid.
9   Charles A. Kupchan, "Democracy in Egypt Can Wait," *New York Times*,
    17 August 2013, 19.
10 Sarah Chayes, "Afghanistan Isn't Ready to Vote.," Bloomberg News,
    23 October 2013, http://www.thejakartapost.com/news/2013/10/23/
    afghanistan-isn-t-ready-vote.html.
11 John Locke, *The Second Treatise of Government* (Indianapolis: Bobbs-
    Merrill, 1952), 5.
12 Osgoode, Robert Endicott, *Ideals and Self-Interest in America's Foreign
    Relations* (Chicago: University of Chicago Press, 1974); Roland Paris,
    "Wilson's Ghost: The Faulty Assumptions of Postconflict Peacebuild-
    ing," in Chester A. Crocker and Fen Osler Hampson with Pamela R. Aall,
    eds., *Turbulent Peace: The Challenges of Managing International Conflict*
    (Washington: United States Institute of Peace Press, 2001), 765–81.
13 John Stuart Mill, "On Liberty," in Edwin A. Burt, ed., *The English Philoso-
    phers from Bacon to Mill* (New York: The Modern Library, 1939), 952.
14 Alexander Hamilton, James Madison and John Jay, *The Federalist Papers*
    (New York: Times Mirror, 1961).
15 Fareed Zakaria, *The Future of Freedom: Illiberal Democracy at Home and
    Abroad* (New York: W.W. Norton, 2003).
16 Larry Diamond, "What Went Wrong and Right in Iraq," in Francis Fuku-
    yama, ed., *Nation-Building: Beyond Afghanistan and Iraq* (Baltimore:

The Johns Hopkins University Press, 2006), 173–95; Johanna Mendelson Forman, "Striking Out in Baghdad: How Postconflict Reconstruction Went Awry," in Fukuyama, ed., 196–217.

17 Fen Osler Hampson and David Mendeloff, "Intervention and the Nation-Building Debate," in Chester A. Crocker, Fen Osler Hampson, and Pamela R. Aall, eds., *Leashing the Dogs of War: Conflict Management in a Divided World* (Washington: United States Institute of Peace Press, 2007), 684.

18 Chaim D. Kaufmann, "Possible and Impossible Solutions to Ethnic Civil War," *International Security* 20.4. (1996): 136–75; Alexander B. Downes, "The Problem with Negotiated Settlements to Ethnic Civil Wars," *Security Studies* 13, no. 4 (2004): 230–79.

19 I. William Zartman, "Negotiations in Transitions: A Conceptual Framework," working paper, 2013.

20 Larry Diamond, "What Went Wrong in Iraq," *Foreign Affairs* 85, no. 3 (2004): 38.

21 Kupchan, "Democracy in Egypt Can Wait."

22 Jeremy Kinsman and Kurt Bassuener, *A Diplomat's Handbook for Democracy Development Support*, 3rd ed. (Waterloo: The Centre for International Governance Innovation, 2013), 49

23 "Toward Better, Smarter Foreign Aid," *The Globe and Mail*, 30 March 2013, F9.

24 Peter Koven, "Man Dies in Protests at HudBay Project," *National Post*, 30 September 2009, FP2; "Lawsuits Over Alleged Gang Rapes Will Proceed," *Toronto Star*, 24 July 2013, B2.

25 Duncan and John Gray Memorial Lecture by The Right Honourable Louis St Laurent, Secretary of State for External Affairs, 13 January 1947, http://www.russilwvong.com/future/stlaurent.html.

26 Foreign Affairs, Trade, and Development Canada, "Canada's Office of Religious Freedom," 2013, http://www.international.gc.ca/religious_freedom-liberte_de_religion/index.aspx.

27 Ibid.

28 Global Centre for Pluralism, "About Us," 2013, http://www.pluralism.ca/index.php?option=com_content&view=category&layout=blog&id=90&Itemid=612.

29 Ibid.

30 David Gordon and Ash Jain, "Forget the G-8. It's Time for the D-10," *The Wall Street Journal*, 17 June 2013, A15.

31 Ash Jain, *Like-Minded and Capable Democracies: A New Framework for Advancing a Liberal World Order* (New York: Council on Foreign Relations, 2013), 8.

32 Ibid., 11.

33 Ibid.

34 Ibid.

CHAPTER SEVEN

1   Thomas R. Berger, *Northern Frontier, Northern Homeland: The Report of the Mackenzie Valley Pipeline Inquiry, Volume 2: Terms and Conditions* (Ottawa: Minister of Supply and Services Canada, 1977), 230.

2   "Mackenzie Valley Pipeline Inquiry," *Wikipedia*, 2013, http://en.wikipedia.org/wiki/Mackenzie_Valley_Pipeline_Inquiry.

3   Shaun Polczer, "TransCanada Shifts Focus off Mackenzie Valley," *The Calgary Herald*, 28 April 2007, D4.

4   Canadian Broadcasting Corporation, "Mackenzie Valley Pipeline: 37 years of Negotiation," 2013, http://www.cbc.ca/news/business/story/010/12/16/f-mackenzie-valley-pipeline-history.html.

5   Correspondence with Canada's National Energy Board, 2013.

6   Barbara Baker, Ioulia Sklokin, Len Coad, and Todd Crawford, *Canada's Electricity Infrastructure: Building a Case for Investment* (Ottawa: The Conference Board of Canada, 2011).

7   Stephen Blank, "China's Arctic Strategy," 2013, http://thediplomat.com/2013/06/20/chinas-arctic-strategy/.

8   John Higginbotham, *Nunavut and the New Arctic* (Waterloo: The Centre for International Governance Innovation, 2013), 5, 10.

9   Human Resources and Skills Development Canada, "Canadians in Context – Aboriginal Population," 2013, http://www4.hrsdc.gc.ca/.3ndic.1t.4r@-eng.jsp?iid=36.

10 Citizenship and Immigration Canada, *Canada Facts and Figures: Immigration Overview Permanent and Temporary Residents 2012* (Ottawa: Her Majesty the Queen in Right of Canada, 2012), 5.

11 Randall Monger and James Yankay, *Annual Flow Report: U.S. Legal Permanent Residents: 2012* (United States Department of Homeland Security, 2013), 2.

12 Daniel Stoffman, "Too Much of a Good Thing," *Report on Business Magazine*, 27 September 2002, 70.

13 Joe Friesen, "Why Canada Needs a Flood of Immigrants," *The Globe and Mail*, 4 May 2012, http://www.theglobeandmail.com/news/national/time-to-lead/why-canada-needs-a-flood-of-immigrants/article4105032/?page=8#dashboard/follows/.

14 Alexander Norris, "Ethnics Putting Their Trust in Liberals," *Gazette* (Montreal), 12 October 1993, A1; Marina Jiménez, "Is the Current Model

of Immigration the Best One for Canada?" *Globe and Mail*, 12 December 2005, A7; Dakshana Bascaramurty, "Politics and Prayer Go Hand in Hand Here," *Globe and Mail*, 20 June 2013, A9.

15 Employment and Social Development Canada, "Labour Market Opinion (LMO) Statistics – Annual Statistics 2012," 2013, http://www.hrsdc.gc.ca/eng/jobs/foreign_workers/lmo_statistics/annual2012.shtml.

16 Ken Coates and Bill Morrison, "The Uses and Abuses of University," *The Walrus* 9, no. 8 (2012), http://thewalrus.ca/the-uses-and-abuses-of-university/.

17 Matt Gurney, "EI Strategy All in a Hard Day's Work," *National Post*, 20 April 2012, A4.

18 Coates and Morrison, "The Uses and Abuses."

19 Simona Chiose, "Oh, the Humanities," *Globe and Mail*, 7 September 2013, R17.

20 William J. Bennett with David Wilezol, *Is College Worth It?* (Nashville, TN: Thomas Nelson, Inc., 2013).

21 Graham Opwood, Bonnie Schmidt, and Hu Jun, *Competing in the 21st Century Skills Race* (Canadian Council of Chief Executives, 2012), 10.

22 Statistics Canada, "Public postsecondary graduates, by Pan-Canadian Standard Classification of Education (PCSCE), Classification of Instructional Programs, Primary Grouping (CIP_PG), sex and immigration status," CANSIM Table 477-0020, 2013.

23 Tiger Leap Foundation, "Programming at Schools and Hobby Clubs," http://www.tiigrihype.ee/en/programming-schools-and-hobby-clubs.

24 Amanda Ripley as quoted in Ellen Gamerman, "What Makes Finnish Kids So Smart? Finland's teens score extraordinarily high on an international test. American educators are trying to figure out why." *Wall Street Journal*, December 17, 2013. http://online.wsj.com/news/articles/SB120425355065601997.

25 Paul Cappon, "Canada Must Stop Being 'a School that Never Issues Report Cards,'" *Globe and Mail*, 4 December 2013, http://www.theglobeandmail.com/globe-debate/why-is-canada-a-school-that-never-issues-report-cards/article15758230.

26 Geoffrey York, "Banned Aid," *Globe and Mail*, 30 May 2009, F1; "Ottawa Mulls African Embassy Closings," *Globe and Mail*, 10 November 2010, A17.

27 When he resigned somewhat ingloriously as premier of Ontario, Dalton McGuinty was appointed to Harvard University as an "expert on international affairs," based presumably on several such missions!

28 Government of Alberta, "Benefits of the Agreement on Internal Trade," 2013, http://www.international.alberta.ca/662.cfm.

29   Fortunately, the Hupacasath First Nation of British Columbia challenge through the Courts of the Foreign Investment Protection Agreement with China on the grounds that it violated the "duty to consult" provisions of Section 35 of the Constitution Act of 1982 was rejected. If the courts had ruled against the government, this would have complicated virtually all trade and investment agreements.

30   Shawn McCarthy, "Ottawa Risks Resource Slowdown," *Globe and Mail*, 10 December 2012, B1.

31   Shawn McCarthy and Bill Curry, "Looming Nexen Deal Reveals Fault Lines," *Globe and Mail*, 15 September 2012, A7.

32   Energy Politics: China, Nexen, and CNOOC, Abacus Data Poll, 1,208 Canadians, 18 years of age or older, 14–18 September 2012.

33   Stephen Harper quoted in transcript, "Government Approves CNOO–Nexen Deal," *Power Play with Don Martin*, 7 December 2012.

34   L. Ian Macdonald, "Harper's Sensible Decision," *Gazette* (Montreal), 12 December 2012, A23.

35   Preston Manning, "Use Principles, Not Mere Pragmatism," *Globe and Mail*, 22 November 2012, A21.

36   Macdonald, "Harper's Sensible Decision."

37   Mark MacKinnon, "Ottawa, China Deal to Protect Investors: Harper," *Globe and Mail*, 10 September 2012, B7.

38   Government of Saskatchewan, *Saskatchewan Plan for Growth: Vision 2020 and Beyond* (Government of Saskatchewan, 2012), 4–5.

39   Ibid.

40   Ibid.

CHAPTER EIGHT

1   Joseph A. Day, Larry Smith, Richard Neufeld, and Irving R. Gerstein, *The Canada-US Price Gap: Report of the Standing Senate Committee on National Finance* (Ottawa: Senate of Canada, 2012), 30.

2   Alberta Motor Association, "Canada-U.S. Vehicle Price Differences," 2013, http://www.ama.ab.ca/automotive/canadaus-vehicle-price-differences.

3   John Manley, "Hunting for Gazelles: Why Canada Needs More High-Growth Firms – Notes for an Address by the Honourable John Manley to the Economic Club, Ottawa, September 16, 2013" (Canadian Council of Chief Executives, 2013), 16.

4   Manley, "Hunting for Gazelles," 17.

5   Eric Reguly, "Strike BlackBerry from the Shrinking List of Canada's Global Corporate Superstars," *Globe and Mail*, 17 August 2013, B1.

6   Ibid.

7   Ibid.

8   Interview by the authors with Marc Parent, 2012.

9   "CAE Expected to Remain Leader in Industry," *Gazette* (Montreal), 22 August 2013, A19.

10 CAE, "Who We Are," 2013, http://www.cae.com/about-cae/corporate-information/who-we-are/.

11 Bombardier Inc., *Stepping Into the Future: Annual Report Fiscal Year Ended December 31, 2012* (Bombarider Inc., 2013), 3.

12 Bombardier Inc., *Bombardier Aeropsace: Profile, Strategy, and Market* (Bombardier Inc., 2013), 4; Bombardier Inc., *Bombardier Transportation: Profile, Strategy, and Market* (Bombardier Inc., 2013), 4.

13 Quoted in Robert Gibbons, "Bombardier's ambassador: Laurent Beaudoin says he want to be remembered for creating an industrial base out of a small Quebec snowmobile firm," *Gazette* (Montreal), 19 June 2008, B1.

14 Mehrdad A. Baghai, Stephen C. Coley, Ronald H. Farmer, and Hugo Sarrazin, "The Growth Philosophy of Bombardier: An Interview with Laurent Beaudoin, Chairman and CEO of Bombardier Inc.," *McKinsey Quarterly* (Spring 1997): 4–29.

15 Bertrand Marotte, "Bombardier Learns to Balance ... and Fly Right," *Globe and Mail*, 1 April 2006, B3; Miville Tremblay, *Le Sang Jaune de Bombardier: La Gestion de Laurent Beaudoin* (Quebec, QC: Les Presses de l'Université du Québec, 1994), 15.

16 Baghai et al., "The Growth Philosophy of Bombardier."

17 Francois Shalom, "CSeries Customers Stand Up and Cheer," *Gazette* (Montreal), 17 September 2013, B1.

18 Linamar Corporation, *Managements' Discussion and Analysis for the Year Ended December 31, 2007*, 53; Linamar Corporation, *Annual Report 2012*, 75.

19 Gordon Pitts, "Message for Manufacturers: Go Big, Don't Stay at Home," *Globe and Mail*, 6 December 2005, B1.

20 Christopher Trump, "Linamar's Training Example Right on the Mark," *Financial Post*, 24 December 1992, 9.

21 Boyd Erman, "Winning? Frank Hasenfratz Has a Chart for That," *Globe and Mail*, 18 December 2012, B2.

22 Ibid.

23 GardaWorld, "Our History," 2013, http://www.gardaglobal.com/about-us/our-history/; "Fast Facts," 2013, <http://www.gardaglobal.com/about-us/garda-fast-facts/.

24 In conversation: Stephan Crétier of Garda, http://www2.macleans.ca/2012/03/21/on-becoming-the-wal-mart-of-security-and-what-exactly-garda-is-doing-in-the-middle-east.

25 In conversation: Stephan Crétier of Garda.
26 Interview with Profit Guide, http://www.profitguide.com/manage-grow/success-stories/ask-the-legends-stephan-cretier-30117.
27 Rod McQueen, *Manulife* (Toronto: Viking Canada, 2009), 35–6.
28 Ibid., 108; Rod Mickelburgh, "Manulife Approved for Sales in China," *Globe and Mail*, 13 December 1995, B1.
29 Michael Bociurkiw, "Manulife Braces for Push into China," *Globe and Mail*, 10 March 1994, B3.
30 Susan Helwig, "Companies Get Access to China," *Globe and Mail*, 6 October 1992, B25.
31 Rod Mickelburgh, "Manulife Open for Business in Shanghai," *Globe and Mail*, 27 November 1996, B9.
32 Mickelburgh, "Manulife Approved for Sales in China."
33 McQueen, *Manulife*, 110.
34 Manulife Financial Corporation, *Annual Report 2012: Growth with Discipline*, 2013.
35 Elizabeth Church, "Bombardier Ranked First by 300 CEOs," *Globe and Mail*, 27 October 2001, B1.
36 OECD, *OECD Science, Technology and Industry Outlook 2012* (OECD Publishing, 2012), 256.
37 Science, Technology, and Innovation Council, *State of the Nation 2012 – Canada's Science, Technology, and Innovation System: Aspiring to Global Leadership* (Ottawa: Science, Technology, and Innovation Council, 2013), 2.
38 Organisation for Economic Co-operation and Development, "Labour Productivity Growth in the Total Economy," OECDStat.Extracts, 2013, http://stats.oecd.org/.
39 Konrad Yakabuski, "Burned Out: The Search for a New Innovation Identity," *Globe and Mail*, 17 August 2013, B7.
40 Alexandra Bibbee, "Unleashing Business Innovation in Canada," OECD *Economics Department Working Papers* No. 997 (2012), 6.
41 Jack Mintz, "Small-Minded R&D," *National Post*, 3 April 2012, FP11.
42 October 2013, *Report on Business*, 30.
43 Organisation for Economic Co-operation and Development, *Entrepreneurship at a Glance 2013*; OECD (2011), *Entrepreneurship at a Glance 2011*, based on OECD Entrepreneurship Financing Database, June 2011.
44 James Brander, Thomas Hellmann, and Tyler Meredith, "Start Me Up: Will Canada Ever Get Venture Capital on Track?" *Policy Options*, November 2012: 35–44.

45 Ibid.

46 Manley, "Hunting for Gazelles," 4.

47 John R. Baldwin, Danny Leung and Luke Rispoli, *Canadian Labour Pro-ductivity Differences Across Firm Size Classes, 2002 to 2008* (Ottawa: Minister of Industry, 2013, 6, http://www5.statcan.gc.ca/bsolc/olc-cel/olc-cel?catno=15-206-XIE2013032&lang=eng#formatdisp.

48 William Watson, "Small Beautiful but Big Works," *Financial Post*, August 28, 2013: FP9.

49 Global Economics Limited, *Mining Innovation: An overview of Canada's dynamic, technologically advanced mining industry.* Paper prepared for the Mining Association of Canada, November 2001, http://global-economics.ca/mining_innovation.pdf.

50 For examples, see James Stuckey and Daniel Munro, *The Need to Make Skills Work: The Cost of Ontario's Skills Gap* (The Conference Board of Canada, 2013); Dan Pontefract, *Canada Should Unlearn to Relearn* (TELUS Transformation Office, 2013); Douglas Watt and Jessica Edge, *Business Leaders' Perspectives: Canada's Competitiveness and Innovation Doldrums* (The Conference Board of Canada, 2013), and; Rick Miner, *People Without Jobs, Jobs Without People* (Miner Management Consultants, 2010).

51 Stuckey and Munro, *The Need to Make Skills Work*, 9.

52 Watt and Edge, *Business Leaders' Perspectives Canada Should Unlearn*, 11; Pontefract, *People without Jobs*, 4.

53 Klaus Schwab, ed., *The Global Competitiveness Report 2013–2014* (Geneva: World Economic Forum, 2013), 467.

54 Miner, 16.

55 *The Hockey News*, 16 January 1983.

CHAPTER NINE

1 "A Love Note to Canadians on Our 146th," *Toronto Star*, 2 July 2013, A6.

2 Stephen Clarkson and Abdi Aidid, "Caught in the Middle: Canada in the Changing Configuration of Global Regions." CPSA Annual Conference, June 2012, http://www.cpsa-acsp.ca/papers-2012/Clarkson.

3 Jack Mintz, "Obama's Wrong-Headed Red Lines," *National Post*, 19 September 2013, FP13.

4 David L. Emerson, "Comfortable Canada: But for How Long?" *Policy Options* (July–August 2013), 60.

Index

5 Eyes, 95
9/11 terrorist attacks, 11, 21–2, 27, 30–1, 32, 67, 84, 101, 107, 157, 161, 177

Abe, Shinzo, 12
Aboriginal peoples of Canada, 129–30, 134–5, 146, 151, 204n29
Acheson, Dean, 77
Afghanistan, 4, 6–7, 9, 13, 17, 22, 85, 92, 103, 115–16; Canadian diplomacy in, 107–10; democracy building in; 117–18; failed state, 85
Aga Khan, 124
Aidid, Abdi, 176
Air Canada, 163, 180
Air Defence Identification Zone (ADIZ), 89
al-Assad, Bashar, 73, 75–6
Alberta, 25, 129, 133, 169; international representation of, 140–1
Alcan, 156
al-Ghanim, Mohamed. See Internet governance

al-Qaeda. See bin Laden, Osama
Allan, Elyse, 156
Angola, 85
Apotex, 52
Apps, Victor, 163
Arab League, 73–5
Arab Spring, 75, 92, 112–16, 125–6, 132, 185. See also Egypt; Libya; Syria
Arctic, 23, 129, 132–3
Argentina, 41
Argus, Don, 156
Asia-Pacific region, 13–16, 18, 36, 46, 85–96, 145, 184; US Pacific Pivot, 7, 16, 30, 89–90, 94, 181–2, 184. See also China; Indonesia; Japan; Korea (South); Korea (North); Trans-Pacific Partnership (TPP); Vietnam
Asian Development Bank, 43
Association of Southeast Asian Nations (ASEAN), 91, 94–5
ASEAN Defence Ministerial Meeting-Plus (ADMM-Plus), 94
Australia, 17, 41, 43–5, 48, 80, 90, 95, 127, 145, 148, 179–80, 193n29